How to Use a Discursive Approach to Study Organizations

How to Use a Discursive Approach to Study Organizations

Cynthia Hardy

Laureate Professor Emerita, Department of Management and Marketing, University of Melbourne, Australia

Edward Elgar
PUBLISHING

Cheltenham, UK • Northampton, MA, USA

Published by
Edward Elgar Publishing Limited
The Lypiatts
15 Lansdown Road
Cheltenham
Glos GL50 2JA
UK

Edward Elgar Publishing, Inc.
William Pratt House
9 Dewey Court
Northampton
Massachusetts 01060
USA

Paperback edition 2023

A catalogue record for this book
is available from the British Library

Library of Congress Control Number: 2022932196

This book is available electronically in the **Elgar**online
Business subject collection
http://dx.doi.org/10.4337/9781839106231

ISBN 978 1 83910 622 4 (cased)
ISBN 978 1 83910 623 1 (eBook)
ISBN 978 1 0353 1691 5 (paperback)

Printed and bound by CPI Group (UK) Ltd, Croydon, CR0 4YY

Contents

Preface

This book has been written for researchers interested in using a discursive approach to study organizations. For those who are new to the subject, it explains what this approach involves and provides practical examples of how it can be integrated into empirical studies of organizations. For management scholars who are familiar with discourse, the book displays the value and scope of using a discursive approach to learn about diverse aspects of organizations. For discourse scholars from other domains, the book shows how a discursive approach has been applied to wider, societal issues. The book consists of three parts. Part I provides an overview of theoretical assumptions associated with a discursive approach and introduces the reader to key concepts. Part II explains how an understanding of discourse can help researchers to examine organizations at different levels of analysis and gain insight into a wide range of issues. Part III identifies some of the current challenges facing researchers in conducting empirical studies, as well as considering how future research can continue to provide rich, nuanced understandings of organizational life.

The book emphasizes the importance of empirical work. It explains how theoretical ideas associated with a discursive approach can be incorporated into the design of empirical studies in ways that allow researchers to investigate important organizational and societal challenges. It shows how creativity and innovation in how discursive data are collected and analyzed can reveal additional insights into organizations. The rationale for this empirical emphasis is that, while there are many articles and books that theorize discourse, far fewer tackle the challenges associated with analyzing specific empirical settings. Nor do they demonstrate, first hand, how such studies contribute to a deeper understanding of organizations. Moreover, while there are many methods books on discourse analysis, they tend to be generic, whereas the aim here is to explain how theoretical ideas translated into a specific study, show how the study was carried out, and present the theoretical and practical insights that it produced.

The book revisits some of the studies that I have carried out over a 25-year period. They feature investigations of refugees, older workers, people living with HIV/AIDS, and a Palestinian non-governmental organization, as well as environmental regulation and chemical risk (see the Appendix). Collectively, they indicate that a discursive approach can be used to investigate a range of complex challenges. To me, this is an important 'selling point.' There is considerable value in using a discursive approach to study organizations because it can be used to investigate questions of value – matters that concern diverse organizations and impact on all sectors of society. The more we explore such questions, the greater the contribution we are likely to make. A discursive approach is particularly useful in this regard because, as the studies in this book demonstrate, it is flexible enough to be applied to different levels of analysis and a wide range of themes. It allows researchers to question things that are taken for granted, to 'see' and 'know' things differently, and to contribute to contemporary theoretical debates.

These studies have been published in a series of articles (see the Appendix). I have rewritten the original articles to suit the aims of the book. In some cases, I have combined multiple articles to provide a more holistic view of a complicated topic. In other cases, I have divided up articles to draw attention to specific nuances or to illuminate certain ways of conducting empirical research. In many cases, I have simplified the language used in the original article, as well as the descriptions of data collection and analysis, to make it easier for readers to understand. Sometimes, I have simply written more freely – without the demands of editors and reviewers. The chapters in this book are not intended to provide a clearly defined blueprint for a discursive approach. This methodology is far too 'messy' – it requires tailoring, revising, and honing to accommodate the needs of a particular study. Accordingly, the chapters provide tentative roadmaps that point to different routes whereby a discursive approach might be used to analyze a particular problem.

Readers can use the book in different ways. They can read the chapters in the order they appear in the book to obtain an overview of a discursive approach. They can concentrate on the theoretical concepts that most interest them. They can select chapters that present a particular method or analytic approach, or concentrate on the research settings or substantive matters that are of the greatest concern. To the extent that a chapter resonates, it can be considered an entry point to further reading insofar as readers can then consult the original article where they will find more information and additional references.

The articles covered in this book were written with many different co-authors. Accordingly, I would like to emphasize that, when I refer to 'my' work, I am referring to ongoing, collective endeavours involving multiple collaborators. The original articles would never have been published without these individuals (although they are absolved from any responsibility for the claims and conclusions mentioned here). I owe them all – Susan Ainsworth, Vikram Bhakoo, Leanne Cutcher, Tom Lawrence, Steve Maguire, Ian Palmer, Nelson Phillips, Kat Riach, Leisa Sargent, and Robyn Thomas – my deep gratitude for their professional and intellectual contributions to my work and for sharing their companionship and friendship with me. They have helped to make my career more fulfilling – and much more fun – than it otherwise would have been. In addition, there are others whom I would like to mention. David Grant, Cliff Oswick, and Tom Keenoy (who sadly died recently) whose early leadership in the arena of organizational discourse studies set the scene for subsequent research. My thanks also go to Sierk Ybema and Ida Sabelis who have taken over this mantle, and to Linda Putnam and Joanne Martin who inspired many ideas and thoughts over the years, as well as being a constant source of encouragement. My interest in 'alternative' ways of conceptualizing organizations was initially sparked by the *SAGE Handbook of Organizational Studies* in 1996, a project that owed much to Sue Jones, then an acquisitions editor at SAGE, who brought me together with Stewart Clegg and Walter Nord as co-editors. These individuals, together with the *Handbook*'s contributors, opened my eyes to new and stimulating ways of thinking about organizations. Finally, my thanks to many unnamed colleagues at the University of Melbourne and Cardiff University, who have provided much camaraderie and collegiality over the years.

Abbreviations

BPA	bisphenol A
CMP	Chemicals Management Plan
CTAC	Canadian Treatment Advocates Council
DDT	dichloro-diphenyl-trichloroethane
EU	European Union
ICCA	International Council of Chemical Associations
INC	intergovernmental negotiating committee
IPEN	International Pollutants Elimination Network
NGO	non-governmental organization
OMT	organization and management theory
POP	persistent organic pollutant
PWA	people living with AIDS
UK	United Kingdom
UN	United Nations
US	United States
VAM	vinyl acetate monomer
WHO	World Health Organization

PART I

Basics

The discursive study of organizations comprises a 'multidisciplinary domain that looks at the ways in which language and meaning shape organizational phenomena' (Robichaud, 2015: 1). It stems from an interest in the 'linguistic turn' that started to emerge in philosophy as early as the 1920s (see Hacker, 2013) and then permeated the humanities and social sciences, problematizing the role of language as it did so. The linguistic turn finally reached organization and management theory (OMT) in the late 1980s as scholars began to explore the constructionist nature of language and the relevance of postmodern writers, especially Foucault, for the study of organizations (Burrell, 1988; Cooper and Burrell, 1988; Knights, 1992). The number of articles and books on discourse and discourse analysis began to grow (Prichard, 2006), leading to collections and critiques of what was becoming a body of work (e.g., Putnam and Fairhurst, 2001; Grant et al., 2004; Hardy et al., 2004; Alvesson and Kärreman, 2011). Today, discourse has a firm foothold in OMT whose proponents – of which I am one – argue that it has made a significant contribution to the study of organizations, helping to inspire novel theory development, investigate interesting empirical settings, and promote innovative ways of collecting and analyzing data.

The aim of this book is to explore how a discursive approach can be used in empirical studies to enrich our understanding of organizations. Part I provides an overview of a discursive approach and explains key building blocks for designing and conducting empirical studies. Chapter 1 introduces the reader to important theoretical assumptions, while Chapter 2 explores dominant discourses, Chapter 3 discusses discursive struggle, and Chapter 4 explores discursive change.

1. Theoretical underpinnings of a discursive approach

In this chapter, I introduce some of the theoretical ideas that underpin a discursive approach by drawing on the work of Michel Foucault (1978, 1979, 1980, 1981) and Norman Fairclough (1992, 1995, 2003). These are not the only theorists who have contributed to an understanding of discourse, but they have been particularly influential in OMT. My aim is to distil theoretical ideas derived from their work so that I can show how they have been employed in specific empirical studies later in the book.

Fairclough and, particularly, Foucault and have produced complex oeuvres of intricate ideas that have led to stimulating discussions, innovative developments, and intractable disputes. It is beyond the remit of this book to engage in detail with this nuanced and, at times, hotly contested domain of scholarship. To this end, readers are encouraged to consult the original work and develop their own theoretical understanding of discourse. This chapter is very much a starting point – not the final word. Nonetheless, it does provide insights into two key concepts – discourses and texts – as well as explain theoretical assumptions associated with a discursive approach to the study of organizations.

WHAT IS A DISCOURSE?

Foucault defines discourses as collections of interrelated texts and practices that 'systematically form the object of which they speak' (Foucault, 1972: 49). Texts and practices cohere to 'produce both meanings and effects in the real world' (Carabine, 2001: 268) by providing 'a language for talking about a topic and … a particular kind of knowledge about a topic' (du Gay, 1996: 43). For example, the discourse of psychology has produced a particular understanding of madness, as well as its causes and treatment. In the 1980s and 1990s, the discourse around HIV/AIDS brought into being a new disease that made sense of a set of symptoms and diseases thought to be unconnected. Today, the discourse of climate change is shaping our understanding of the material world in which we live. Discourses do not simply describe the social world, they help to create it by categorizing material and ideational phenomena and conferring meaning on them (Parker, 1992). In this regard, a discursive approach is *constructionist* – rather than simply describe a pre-existing situation, language helps to bring 'reality' into being. Accordingly, discourse is far more than 'just' language – it is an ensemble of ideas, concepts, and categorizations emanating from a collection of texts that become 'produced, reproduced and transformed in a particular set of practices and through which meaning is given to physical and social realities' (Hajer, 1995: 44). Organizational discourse refers to texts and practices that bring organizationally related phenomena into being (Grant et al., 2004), including the identities that populate them, the knowledge that informs them, and the power relations that permeate them. Instead of identifying a pre-existing object that happens to be called an organization, a discursive approach explores the texts, practices, and meanings that allow us to talk about organizations (and related entities, ideas, and activities) *as if* they existed naturally.

A discursive approach does not only identify the meaning of a particular phenomenon, it also allows researchers to investigate how this meaning came about, how it is maintained, and what might ensue if alternative meanings were to arise. The idea that meaning is unequivocal, singular, and inherent – regardless of how matter of fact it may appear – is rejected and, instead, researchers explore how meanings emerge, stabilize, and change. A discursive approach is thus founded on a profound interrogation of the precarious status of *meaning* (Hardy, 2001; Phillips and Hardy, 2002). It allows researchers to explore how apparently solid organizations derive 'from the stabilizing effects of generic discursive processes rather than from the presence of independently existing concrete entities' (Chia, 2000: 514).

Discourse is bound up with *power*. Foucault (1980) argues that power circulates through discourse, laying down 'conditions of possibility' that influence who can speak within particular settings, the claims that can be made, and the social practices that can be invoked (Fairclough, 1992). As such, discourses are saturated with power relations that both constrain and enable what individuals think, say, and do by defining 'who and what is normal, standard and acceptable' (Meriläinen et al., 2004: 544).

> [Discourse] governs the way that a topic can be meaningfully talked about and reasoned about. It also influences how ideas are put into practice and used to regulate the conduct of others. Just as a discourse 'rules in' certain ways of talking about a topic, defining an acceptable and intelligible way to talk, write or conduct oneself, so also, by definition, it 'rules out,' limits and restricts other ways of talking, of conducting ourselves in relation to the topic or constructing knowledge about it. (Hall, 2001: 72)

Discourse thus 'acts as a powerful ordering force in organizations' (Alvesson and Kärreman, 2000: 1127) by constructing objects of knowledge, forms of self, categories of social relationships, and conceptual frameworks (Fairclough, 1992; Fairclough and Wodak, 1997).

One important way in which power relations circulate through discourse is by producing *bodies of knowledge*. As Foucault's conception of power/knowledge indicates, knowledge cannot exist independently of the network of power relations in which it is produced or the individual identities that produce it.

> Each society has its regime of truth ... the mechanisms and instances which enable one to distinguish true and false statements, the means by which each is sanctioned; and the techniques and procedures accorded value in the acquisition of truth; the status of those who are charged with saying what counts as true. (Foucault, 1980: 131)

The way in which a discourse brings together power and knowledge serves to create certain 'known' objects with particular meanings. Rather than a field of knowledge arranging itself around a pre-existing object of analysis, 'the objects in question are constituted by the relevant bodies of knowledge as components of their own conditions of possibility' (Hook, 2007: 148). These objects can be ideational or material. The former refers to the 'ideas, categories, relationships, and theories through which we understand the world and relate to one another.' The latter refers to aspects of 'an ambiguous material world; a world that has an ontological status and a physical existence apart from our experience of them' (Hardy and Phillips, 1999: 3).

Power also circulates through the way in which discourses 'discipline' subjects in terms of how individuals are known – and know themselves (Mumby, 2001). Discourses create *subject positions* – locations in the discourse from which only certain, delimited identities can act (Knights and Willmott, 1989). Some individuals 'by virtue of their position in the discourse, will warrant a louder voice than others, while others may warrant no voice at all' (Hardy and Phillips, 1999: 4). Additionally, the individual is rendered knowable through discourse as it weaves knowledge and power into 'a coercive structure ... [that] forces the individual back on himself and ties him to his own identity in a constraining way' (Foucault, quoted in Alcoff, 1988: 415). In this way, the human subject is 'produced historically, that is, constituted through correlative elements of power and knowledge' (Townley, 1993: 522).

This discursive conceptualization of power is quite different to mainstream views that emphasize the idea of autonomous agents possessing and wielding sovereign power by mobilizing a battery of scarce, finite resources to achieve certain outcomes (Hardy and Clegg, 1996; Hardy and Thomas, 2014). Power is not 'something that is acquired, seized, or shared, something that one holds on to or allows to slip away ... [Instead, it] is exercised from innumerable points, in the interplay of nonegalitarian relations' (Foucault, 1978: 94). Power is an indeterminate network of relations, rather than a finite resource that can be strategically deployed. Not even privileged actors can stand 'outside' discourse. All individuals are situated in complex webs of power relations – fields of possible actions from which the prospects of escape are limited for both dominant and subordinate groups (Deetz, 1992). At the same time, power does not only constrain – it is also productive insofar as it creates bodies of knowledge and transforms 'individuals into subjects who secure their sense of what it is to be worthy and competent human beings' (Knights and Morgan, 1991: 269).

In the same way that power relations are constituted through discourse so, too, is *resistance*. Discourse is not simply an instrument of power, it is also 'a hindrance, a stumbling block, a point of resistance and a starting point for an opposing strategy. Discourse transmits and produces power; it reinforces it, but also undermines it and exposes it, renders it fragile and makes it possible to thwart it' (Foucault, 1978: 100–101). Consequently, power and resistance are inextricably intertwined – where there is power there is also resistance, which also forms at myriad points in an irregular, localized fashion, rather than at a central focal point. Despite the inescapabilty of resistance, discourses cannot easily be dislodged. Prevailing discourses are experienced as 'real,' making it difficult to conceive of alternatives, let alone enact them (Ashley, 1990). Additionally, individuals cannot stand 'outside' the discourse to mount attacks on it – they are products of it and cannot easily estrange themselves from 'the tradition that has formed his or her subjectivity' (Alvesson and Willmott, 1992: 447). Consequently, the prospects for transformational emancipation are limited, and resistance often serves merely to reinforce existing power relations (Sawicki, 1991).

While it may not be easy to overthrow existing discourses, the entwinement of power and resistance means that even dominant discourses have to be continually fortified against potential points of resistance. Fairclough (1992) points out that discourses are never completely cohesive or devoid of internal tensions and are therefore never able to totally determine reality. They are always partial, crosscut by inconsistencies and ambiguities, and almost always contested to some degree. Moreover, actors are commonly embedded in multiple discourses which may contradict each other. The tensions within and among discourses creates a space in which actors can exercise some agency by playing one discourse off against another (Hardy and Phillips, 2004). While some struggles are visible, others are not; but even when a discourse appears to be fixed and its meaning locked in, some form of discursive work will be going on behind the scenes to reproduce and maintain it.

WHAT IS A TEXT?

A text is a manifestation of discourse – a discursive 'unit' (Chalaby, 1996) – that can be investigated for clues to a particular discourse (Parker, 1992). A text is 'any kind of symbolic expression requiring a physical medium and permitting of permanent storage' (Taylor and Van Every, 1993: 109). For a text to be generated, it must be inscribed – spoken, written, or depicted in some way – thereby 'taking on material form and becoming accessible to others' (Taylor et al., 1996: 7). Texts take diverse forms – interviews, naturally occurring speech, written texts, artifacts, practices, and forms of embodiment (Grant et al., 2004). The systematic analysis of such texts is known as *discourse analysis* (van Dijk, 1997a, 1997b).

Texts tend to be more consequential when they 'travel' from the local to the global (Hardy, 2004) and are taken up by other actors and reinscribed in subsequent texts and practices (Taylor et al., 1996; Iedema and Wodak, 1999). Discourse is thus 'built up progressively' (Taylor and Van Every, 2000: 96), with meanings stabilizing as the circumstances of individual, local conversations are 'linked to the organizing properties of the [larger] network in which they figure' (Cooren and Taylor, 1997: 223). Therefore, it is not enough simply to author a text – it must also be widely distributed and consumed if its meanings are to be reproduced (or changed) and for there to be some sort of discursive effect (Phillips et al., 2004). Accordingly, discourse analysis encompasses the study of how texts are *produced, distributed and consumed* (Fairclough, 1992, 1995; Phillips and Hardy, 2002).

Discourse analysis is not confined to individual texts – it incorporates the study of *structured collections of texts* as researchers examine multiple texts and the connections among them. This may include the investigation of *intertextuality* since any individual text is 'a link in a chain of texts, reacting to, drawing in and transforming other texts' (Fairclough and Wodak, 1997: 262). The more that texts draw on one another in well-established ways and the more they converge in their explanations of social reality, the more dominant the discourse (Phillips et al., 2004; Hardy and Maguire, 2016). Researchers also explore *interdiscursivity*, which refers to the way in which an individual text or collection of texts refers to and invokes diverse discourses. 'Discourses are always connected to other discourses which were produced earlier, as well as those which are produced synchronically and subsequently' (Fairclough and Wodak, 1997: 277).

Researchers have used a range of qualitative techniques to study the meaning of diverse forms of text, although discourse analysis is more than a set of methods. It is 'a perspective on the nature of language and its relationship to the central issues of the social sciences ... a related collection of approaches to discourse … that entail not only practices of data collection and analysis, but also a set of metatheoretical and theoretical assumptions' (Wood and Kroger, 2000: x). In other words, discourse analysis is a *methodology* where appropriate methods are deployed in alignment with a 'strong' form of social constructionism (Burman and Parker, 1993; Hacking, 2000).

Researchers using a discursive approach strive to be *reflexive*. If power/knowledge relations are created through discourse, its investigation does not constitute the neutral application of impartial methods of textual analysis but, rather, represents 'a theory-driven process of constructing objects of research' (Fairclough, 1995: 5). In using language and producing texts, researchers both exploit – and are subject to – the effects of discourse (Prichard et al., 2004). What researchers present as facts, interpretations, and informed opinion are constructions produced by authoritative identities conforming to accepted procedures (Ainsworth and Hardy, 2012). Reflexivity helps to remind the reader – and the researcher – of the precarious nature of such 'knowledge.'

WHY BOTHER?

Given that a discursive approach involves a complex set of slippery constructionist assumptions, the time-consuming study of multiple texts, and the practices of production, dissemination and consumption, as well as the need to be continually reflexive, one might ask: why would anyone bother with a discursive approach to the study of organizations?

One reason for using a discursive approach is that it is flexible and can accommodate diverse settings. As this book will show, it can be used to investigate different 'levels' of analysis – from exploring institutionalized systems of ideas (Greckhamer, 2010) to providing close readings of individual texts (Kwon et al., 2014) or, indeed, combining elements of both (Barry et al., 2006). Insofar as discourses weave continuous threads connecting institutions, texts, and practices, this approach helps to avoid the arbitrary division of the social world into distinct layers while providing more holistic understandings. In the same way, a discursive approach can be used to study different kinds of organizations in a range of circumstances, enabling researchers to investigate a wide array of complex societal issues. In both these cases, the form that analysis takes can be tailored and customized to ensure that it is both empirically 'fit for purpose' and theoretically robust.

A second reason is that a discursive approach invites researchers to go beyond the conventional wisdom to challenge what is taken for granted. Studies that interrogate dominant discourses help to disabuse readers of the idea that they are inevitable or natural (e.g., Lefsrud and Meyer, 2012), while those that scrutinize discursive struggles help to illuminate how different discourses produce, maintain, or resist particular configurations of power (e.g.,

Russell and McCabe, 2015). A discursive approach helps us see who and what has been rendered invisible. As Fairclough (1992: 40) reminds us, 'that which a discourse marginalizes, indeed excludes, is as, if not more, important, from both an explanatory and political viewpoint, as that which it includes as legitimate objects of knowledge.' In this regard, a discursive approach is often associated with 'critical management studies' (e.g., Alvesson et al., 2011), where it is employed as a means of interrogating existing power relations, questioning the authority of mainstream thinking, and proposing alternative ways of being.

Finally, a discursive approach is aligned with recent theoretical thinking about the nature of identity, the meaning of materiality, and the status of knowledge. Ideas which gain substance and nuance through empirical study enable researchers to engage with and contribute to contemporary debates about ontology and epistemology. Accordingly, a discursive approach helps researchers to follow Foucault's (1985: 8–9) exhortation to think differently. 'There are times in life when the question of knowing if one can think differently than one thinks, and perceive differently than one sees, is absolutely necessary if one is to go on looking and reflecting at all?'

CONCLUSION

In this chapter, I have explained the concepts of discourse and text to provide a basis for using a discursive approach to study organizations (Box 1.1). There is, of course, considerable variation among researchers in how they adopt a discursive approach. Researchers differ on how strongly they advocate for social constructionism, the degree to which they focus on individual texts compared to collections of texts, the extent to which they privilege the role of language, and how interested they are in the power effects of discourse. Theorists other than Fairclough and Foucault also feature. Laclau and Mouffe's approach to discourse (1987) has been used in a range of empirical studies (Contu et al., 2013; Walton and Boone, 2014). Other theoretical underpinnings include the communicative constitution of organizations (Brummans et al., 2014; Boivin et al., 2017; Schoeneborn et al., 2019), the 'Montreal School' (Taylor et al., 1996; Taylor and Van Every, 2000; Cooren, 2015), discursive psychology (Potter and Wetherell, 1987; Molder, 2015; Wiggins, 2018), as well as 'Faircloughian' applications of critical discourse analysis and the discourse-historical method (Wodak, 2015; Reisigl, 2018). It is ultimately up to individuals to develop their own theoretical orientation in using a discursive approach to study organizations – the one presented here features in my work and, hopefully, provides a starting point for others seeking to conduct their own empirical work.

BOX 1.1   RECAP OF KEY IDEAS

- Discourses are collections of interrelated texts and practices that 'systematically form the object of which they speak' (Foucault, 1972: 49).
- A discursive approach to the study of organizations is constructionist: rather than assume that language merely describes a pre-existing reality, researchers assume that language helps to bring a particular 'reality' into being.
- A discursive approach to the study of organizations is founded on a profound interrogation of the precarious status of meaning.
- Discourses involve complex, indeterminate webs of power relations, which create bodies of knowledge – what can be said – and subject positions – who can and cannot speak.
- Power is always bound up with resistance, which also operates in localized, transversal ways, making it necessary to continually fortify even dominant discourses in ways that might not be obvious.
- Tensions within and among discourses provide a space for discursive struggle, where different actors may seek to change or exploit particular discourses.
- A discursive approach to the study of organizations relies on discourse analysis, which is the systematic analysis of texts and/or practices, as well as collections of texts, and/or how texts are produced, disseminated, and consumed.
- Texts are forms of symbolic expression requiring a physical medium; they contain traces of and clues to discourse.
- Intertextuality involves the study of how different texts relate to each other.
- Interdiscursivity refers to the examination of how different discourses are positioned against each other within a text or across a collection of texts.
- Discourse analysis is a methodology that embodies not only a set of methods for textual analysis, but also a set of assumptions concerning the constructive effects of language.
- Reflexivity is an important component of a discursive approach in that it makes it clear that researchers are part of the discursive processes that they are investigating.

2.   Understanding dominant discourses

This chapter examines dominant discourses – sometimes referred to as hegemonic discourses – to show how discourse analysis can be used to explore their implications for organizations. The idea of dominant discourses has been a catalyst for researchers using a discursive approach – the aim of 'unmasking' discourses that have been unthinkingly taken for granted has fuelled many studies (Fairclough, 2003). In this chapter, I explain what dominant discourses are, consider how they can be investigated, and argue why they are important. I then encourage researchers to move beyond the idea of a dominant discourse as a stable, monolithic structure with predetermined effects to examine how disparities in the degree of dominance occur, how fissures in a discourse arise, and how dominant discourses are maintained. In this way, readers can learn about both the reach and the fragility of dominant discourses.

WHAT IS A DOMINANT DISCOURSE?

In Chapter 1, discourses were defined as collections of interrelated texts and practices 'that systematically form the objects of which they speak' (Foucault, 1979: 49). In the case of dominant discourses, texts and practices draw on one another to provide a highly consistent, coherent, and convergent way of representing individuals, entities, ideas, and events (Phillips et al., 2004). A good example of a dominant discourse is the discourse of risk (Box 2.1). The collection of texts that make up the discourse of risk is extensive. It includes articles in dedicated risk journals, as well as countless other scientific, engineering, medical, legal, and environmental journals, textbooks on risk assessment and risk management, risk compliance policies, emergency preparedness handbooks, accident reviews, inquiry reports, compliance reports, media stories, government legislation, annual reports, scientific and technical reports, and so forth. Despite their number and diversity, these texts typically draw on each other in ways that reproduce a shared meaning of risk – the probability that some harm, hazard, or adverse consequence will occur. The organizational practices used to identify risks typically enact the principles and methods articulated in the various texts. They also produce findings and conclusions that reinforce the corpus of texts which make up the discourse of risk, thus contributing to further convergence (see Hardy and Maguire, 2016).

BOX 2.1   THE DOMINANT DISCOURSE OF RISK

Discourse	The discourse of risk
A discourse is a collection of interrelated texts and practices 'that systematically form the object of which they speak'	The discourse of risk is constituted by the following texts and practices that systematically bring 'risk,' as an object of knowledge, into existence. • Examples of texts include scientific articles, textbooks on risk assessment and risk management, International Organization for Standardization risk principles and guidelines, emergency preparedness handbooks, emergency procedure manuals, emergency preparedness checklists, aggregated risk data reports, accident reviews, inquiry reports, submissions to public hearings, compliance reports, actuarial reports, media stories, government legislation, annual reports, scientific and technical reports. • Examples of practices include use of probability and statistical techniques, preparation of risk matrices, carrying out event tree/fault tree analysis, calculating risk-benefit ratios, preparing emergency preparedness plans, filling in emergency preparedness checklists, rehearsing accident protocols, conducting emergency simulations, monitoring for early warnings, auditing, completing accident or incident reports, holding hearings, calling witnesses, drafting inquiry reports, and processing data to update actuarial tables.

A *dominant* discourse has additional features

Texts and practices draw on each other in well-established ways to construct convergent, widely shared meanings	• Risk is widely understood to be the probability of an adverse effect or negative event of some magnitude – a harm, hazard, or danger of some kind that can be managed if the likelihood of its occurrence and nature of its effects can be accurately assessed. • Risk assessment is widely understood as 'science' (evidence- and fact-based, value-free). • Risk management is understood as 'policy' (values-based, involving trade-offs between multiple objectives).
Texts and practices produce an accepted, taken-for-granted body of knowledge that functions as if it were true	The body of risk knowledge assumes risk to be 'true' as it is accurately and objectively identifiable through: • The development of knowledge derived from the past through scientific measurement and analytical reasoning. • The application of knowledge in the form of specific, widely accepted, institutionalized risk analysis/measurement techniques.

Discourse	The discourse of risk
It offers a delimited set of categories of identity that are meaningful and legitimate, some of which are authorized over others, and all of which are constrained and/or enabled by the discourse in different ways	Key risk identities include: • Risk assessors who determine the nature, level, and probability of harm, damage, or loss. • Risk managers who are responsible for reducing risk to some level deemed acceptable. • Risk producers whose actions potentially generate hazards or cause harms, damage, or losses. • Risk bearers who are harmed or bear losses when hazards are realized. • Risk adjudicators, who review incidents where risks have (or have almost) materialized to determine, after the fact, who produced the risk and who bore it, as well as who should have assessed or managed it more effectively.

Source: Adapted from Hardy and Maguire (2016: 83).

A dominant discourse produces a clearly defined, convergent body of knowledge through the way in which texts and practices reinforce each other. In the case of risk, texts and practices come together to produce a widely accepted body of knowledge about how to calculate the likelihood that a risk will materialize, as well as how to assess the best way to manage it. This body of knowledge is predicated on various forms of scientific analysis, which constructs risk as an objective phenomenon – a harm, hazard, or danger of some kind that can be managed if the likelihood of its occurrence and nature of its effects are measured through the application of scientific knowledge and techniques (Lupton, 2013; Hardy and Maguire, 2016).

Dominant discourses also create well-defined subject positions from which individuals have delineated 'rights to speak.' In the case of risk, prominent subject positions include risk assessors, who determine the probability and level of harm, and risk managers who are responsible for reducing risks (or exposure to them) to some level deemed acceptable. Risk producers are individuals or organizations whose actions potentially generate hazards or cause harm. Risk bearers are those who are harmed when hazards materialize. Risk adjudicators review incidents to determine, after the fact, who produced the risk and what should be done about it. Some of these subject positions have greater rights to speak than others and others are reserved for specific identities – risk assessors are typically scientific experts of some kind, while risk adjudicators are expected to be independent (Hardy and Maguire, 2016). The consequences of occupying – or not occupying – a certain subject position can be significant. For example, those who cannot assume the mantle of expert are often excluded from discussions as to whether a risk exists or not, even if they are affected by it (Hardy et al., 2020b). As a result, lay people, especially marginalized groups, often disproportionally bear environmental and health risks, while being excluded from positions where they can address them (Curran, 2016).

The dominant discourse of risk is thus an instrument and an effect of power. It privileges expert risk knowledge over other forms of knowledge and author-izes certain risk identities over others. The discourse is hard to escape – it is difficult to argue against risk without resorting to the quantitative methods and institutionalized techniques that reproduce the discourse because of 'the role of professional languages (such as quantitative risk assessment) and analytic practices (such as cost-benefit analysis) in shaping public perceptions of risk. Authoritative knowledge is created in this framework by people or institutions that master the relevant formal discourses' (Jasanoff, 1998: 94). So, although experts may quibble over different methods, politicians may argue over cost-benefit weightings, and the public may point out that their interests have been overlooked, they nonetheless resort to the discourse of risk to make their point. In this way, 'riskification' occurs as governments and organizations are increasingly authorized to intervene in individuals' lives in the name of risk (Hardy and Maguire, 2016).

In sum, a discursive approach adopts a particular perspective on risk. It does not deny the importance of realist techniques in assessing and managing risks. On the contrary, it acknowledges that they permeate the dominant discourse of risk. However, whereas from a realist perspective, these techniques 'reveal' whether features of reality constitute an objective risk; from a discursive per-spective, they constitute the rhetorical means by which a 'risk' is constructed (see Hardy et al., 2020b). In other words, because of its authoritative status, the application of the existing body of risk knowledge makes it possible to name an object and link it to a harm, thereby constructing a 'risk object' (Hilgartner, 1992). The discourse produces 'truths' about risk that then become the basis for action (Lupton, 2013).

CRACKING THE DISCURSIVE MONOLITH

In the remainder of this chapter, I discuss why, despite dominant discourses appearing to be totalizing and deterministic, there are always cracks in the monolith. I first compare the discourses of lean production and sustainability to show how different degrees of dominance arise in different settings. I then reveal some of the fissures that appear when the dominant discourse of strategy plays out in local circumstances. Finally, I return to the dominant discourse of risk to explore the work that goes into maintaining and repairing it.

Degrees of Dominance

In this section, I show the contingency rather than the inevitability of discourses. I first explore the dominance of the discourse of lean production in supply chain management to show how it conforms to many of the features associated with risk. Building on earlier work (Hardy et al., 2020a), I compare it to the discourse of sustainability, which is far less dominant. I then consider sustainability in another field – chemistry – where it has had significant influence. In this way, it becomes easier to see that the dominance of a discourse is not preordained, but a product of local and historical circumstances.

Lean production refers to the production of products and services at the lowest cost and in the fastest time possible. Its origins can be traced to researchers working at the Massachusetts Institute of Technology who used the term to describe Toyota's production system. Since then, lean has come to be a dominant discourse in supply chain management, embedded in institutionalized supply chain practices in sectors as diverse as retail, aerospace, construction, finance, health, and government (Samuel et al., 2015).

A discursive approach helps to explain how the discourse of lean became dominant (Hardy et al., 2020a). It was first articulated in an authoritative text – *The Machine That Changed the World* (Womack et al., 1990) – whose authors were highly respected researchers. The book translated practices used by Toyota in a local, Japanese context into universal principles that could be adopted in car plants around the world, as well as legitimizing them with reference to lower cost and higher quality (Oliver and Hunter, 1998). The book was widely distributed among academic and business audiences and became one of the most widely cited references in supply chain management (Holweg, 2007). Insofar as countless other texts reproduced the original ideas with a relatively high degree of fidelity, lean acquired an enduring, widely shared meaning. The result is a large corpus of texts that draw on one another in well-established ways, converge in their descriptions of lean principles, and recommend similar practices. Lean is also supported by alternative discourses such as Just-in-Time, Total Quality Management, Six Sigma, and Business Process Engineering, which help to reinforce it. Even criticisms concerning the lack of a clear definition of lean and equivocal findings regarding its impact do not fundamentally undermine the discourse since they are explained by the need to implement practices properly or adapt them in some way. Either way, there is little threat to the dominance of the discourse of lean – merely adjustments to it.

If we compare the discourses of lean and sustainability in supply chain management, we can see some notable differences. While sustainable supply chain management started to emerge around the same time, it is far less dominant. Only as many as 10 percent of researchers study it and relatively few companies have supply chains that are truly sustainable (Pagell and Shevchenko, 2014). Part of the explanation from a discursive perspective is that there is no single, widely distributed, authoritative text whose ideas are faithfully reproduced in subsequent texts. One possible candidate for such a text might be *Our Common Future* (WCED, 1987), which introduced the concept of sustainable development more generally and described how it could be achieved. However, it has not been particularly influential in texts in supply chain management. Moreover, when it is taken up in other texts, its ideas are interpreted in conflicting ways with as many as 300 different definitions of sustainability (Ramsey, 2015). Additionally, there is competition from alternative discourses such as profitability, to which sustainability is typically subordinated (Carter and Rogers, 2008). The result is that sustainability is far less prevalent than lean in supply chain management (Hardy et al., 2020a).

The fate of sustainable supply chain management might lead one to think that the precariousness of this discourse is unavoidable, but this is not the case. In another article (Maguire and Hardy, 2019), we show that the discourse of sustainability has had considerable influence in chemistry. Sustainable or 'green' chemistry seeks to eliminate chemical risks by substituting hazardous products and technologies with safe alternatives, thereby creating a green market for innovations (also see Maguire and Hardy, 2016, 2019). Since emerging in the 1990s, there are now green chemistry programs at universities around the world (ACS, 2017). Green chemists have been responsible for nearly 4,800 academic papers, almost 1,000 industrial innovations and 12,400 patented inventions (Howard-Grenville et al., 2017). Moreover, sustainability and economic goals have been amalgamated to stimulate a growing industry with the market value of green chemistry technologies estimated at $100 billion (Trucost, 2015).

This success has been achieved in ways that are reminiscent of the discourse of lean in supply chain management. An authoritative text – the field's first green chemistry textbook (Anastas and Warner, 1998) – articulates 12 principles underlining the commitment to harm elimination. As a textbook, it has been widely cited and distributed to chemistry students around the world, and the 12 principles have been incorporated into a wide range of academic and practitioner texts to promote the creation and adoption of safer chemicals. Journals, conferences, and centres of research excellence dedicated to green chemistry have been established, which go on to produce their own texts. The result is a large corpus of texts promoting the 12 principles, coupled with widespread research, teaching, and business practices dedicated to enacting them (Howard-Grenville et al., 2017).

Box 2.2 provides a comparison of the three discourses. It helps to explain why sustainability is less dominant in supply chain management, but more successful in chemistry. It also shows that the stabilization and sedimentation of a discourse vary in degree and scope – their dominance (or lack thereof) is contingent on the historical and local settings in which they arise.

BOX 2.2   COMPARISON OF THREE DISCOURSES

	Lean production	Sustainable supply chain management	Green chemistry
Emerged	1990s	1990s	1990s
Effects	Lean practices have permeated across supply chains in many types of organization and industry	Limited uptake of sustainable supply chain practices	Significant growth of sustainable practices across chemistry research, teaching and business
Authoritative text	*The Machine That Changed the World*	*Our Common Future*	*Green Chemistry: Theory and Practice*
Text producers	Text producers were respected researchers in a central position in the academic domain	Text producer (Gro Brundtland) was a global political figure but not part of the sustainable supply chain domain	Text producers were respected chemists with government, business, and academic experience
Text distribution	The authoritative text was widely distributed and taken up in academic and business texts	The authoritative text was less likely to be taken up in sustainable supply chain texts	The authoritative text was widely distributed and taken up in academic and business texts
Text consumption (intertextuality)	The authoritative text was consumed with a relatively high degree of fidelity – key principles are reproduced	The authoritative text was consumed in different ways with as many as 300 definitions – key principles are unclear	The authoritative text was consumed with a relatively high degree of fidelity – key principles are reproduced
Other discourses (interdiscursivity)	Compatible with profitability; supported by other discourses	Subordinated to profitability	Compatible with profitability
Body of knowledge	A clearly delineated body of knowledge that explains and normalizes certain practices	The body of knowledge is unstructured and contradictory	A clearly delineated body of knowledge that explains and normalizes certain practices
Subject positions	Those responsible for researching and managing lean occupy visible, central positions	Those responsible for researching and managing sustainability are usually in peripheral, niche positions	Those responsible for researching and managing green chemistry are increasingly occupying visible, central positions

The Local Enactment of a Dominant Discourse

Another way to probe the apparent solidity of a dominant discourse is to investigate how it is accomplished in local conditions. In this section, I examine how the dominant discourse of strategy (Box 2.3) played out at GlobalTel (a pseudonym) – a European telecommunications company between 2000 and 2003 (Hardy and Thomas, 2014).

BOX 2.3   THE DOMINANT DISCOURSE OF STRATEGY

The term 'strategy' comes from the Greek stratēgia, which means the art of command, while the verb stratego means to 'plan the destruction of one's enemies through effective use of resources' (Bracker, 1980: 219). The term has been traced back to the Roman empire if not earlier. It appeared in English in the seventeenth century (Grandy and Mills, 2004). However, throughout this period, it remained associated with political or military ends – not business objectives.

It was only in the twentieth century that the discourse of strategy began to infiltrate the business world (Knights and Morgan, 1991). The separation of management and ownership coupled with the emergence of the multi-divisional form in large companies with diversified markets gave rise to new forms of business communication. Senior managers needed to be able to talk to both shareholders and divisional managers and to focus attention on the growing complexity of competing in multiple markets.

Existing managerial discourses, such as Taylorism and Mayo's human relations, were inadequate for this task – they were primarily designed for internal communication and focused on the effective organization of material and human resources, rather than external market factors. Strategy, which had worked so well in the military sphere during the two world wars (at least for the allied powers), offered a way forward.

By the 1960s, the discourse of strategy grew through the production, distribution, and consumption of academic texts, such as those authored by influential Harvard academics like Chandler (1962), Andrews (1971), and Porter (1985). The growth in business education, particularly the MBA, meant that these texts were distributed widely to university students and business practitioners. The basic ideas for formulating strategy were unproblematically consumed in a wide range of other texts such as consulting reports, course outlines, case studies, and media reports. Today, strategy is brought into being by a huge corpus of different types of texts that reinforce each other as to its meaning, purpose, and benefits. Collectively, they promote a particular set of practices that are widely accepted as the way to go about making a strategy.

Dissenting authors have emerged, such as Pascale (1984) and Mintzberg (1987), as well as strategy-as-practice scholars (Whittington, 1996; Jarzabkowski, 2004). However, for the most part, these texts reproduce the discourse insofar as they acknowledge the existence of 'strategy' even as they try to challenge it. Any debate remains largely confined to academia and pertains only to the edges of the concept. Is strategy planned or does it emerge? Is it something that organizations 'do' or something they 'have'? Is it good or bad? The concept itself remains inviolable and the discourse continues to grow and intensify.

To talk about organizations with reference to their strategy is completely normal and non-controversial. In fact, it is hard to think of any successful business – or many other types of organizations for that matter – without reference to its strategy. Even failure is typically attributed to strategy, albeit a bad, ineffective, or absent one. Accordingly, strategy is a dominant discourse. It represents a clearly delineated body of knowledge that is widely shared, and which has had a huge impact on organizational practice. However, while there may be general agreement about the discourse of strategy and even support within an organization for a particular strategy, this does not explain how a monolithic 'strategy' is enacted in a particular time and place. As we see in this study (Hardy and Thomas, 2014), a finely grained, discursive approach shows how some aspects of a strategy are fortified as they are put into practice, while others are destabilized.

In the late 1990s, GlobalTel had been a world leader in the expanding mobile phone market. However, during 2000, its mobile phone division posted an operating loss. That same year, a new strategy was announced, encapsulated in the phrase: 'be first, be best and be cost effective.' It comprised two components. *Be first, be best* referred to technological leadership derived from employees' engineering skills – a continuation of the strategy that had helped establish a leadership position in the industry and that was supported by a professional discourse that circulated in the company. *Be cost effective* referred to making cutbacks and reducing operating costs to maintain shareholder value in the context of prevailing market conditions. It was supported by a wider market discourse circulating in the industry. Our aim was to ascertain whether and how this strategy was accomplished and, more specifically, whether both components were implemented according to the apparent intent of the original announcement.

We collected publicly available documents on the company for the period 2000–2003, when the strategy was being implemented, including annual reports, analysts' reports, company website material, in-house magazines, books, articles and technical reviews, as well as media reports. Our aim was to collect as many (English-language) documents as possible by a range of authors from inside and outside the company. Even though we only had textual data, we were able to identify *accounts* of practices such as closing factories, filing patents, etc. Our analysis of these accounts indicated that practices associated with both components of the strategy were carried out (Box 2.4), although reports indicated that those associated with being cost effective endured through the three-year period while those associated being first and best appeared to peter out.

BOX 2.4   SUMMARY OF PRACTICES

	Account of practice in talk and text	Relation to strategy
'Be first, be best'		
Innovation	Company lists new products and technology in press releases with repeated use of 'first' in headline	Technological leadership is important
Generation of patents and intellectual property rights	'[The company] views its existing and future patents as an important and growing source of revenue … [It] has more than 10,000 granted patents worldwide. This makes us one of the strongest patent holders in the … industry' (Annual report)	Technological leadership is associated with patents
Training	The front page of the course schedule for training sessions run for employees in different countries has the heading 'Global services: Be first, be best'	Technological leadership is achieved through training

	Account of practice in talk and text	Relation to strategy
Creation of a new subsidiary	'[The subsidiary] offers complete 2.5G and 3G technology platforms to manufacturers of mobile phones and other mobile devices … The technology is based on [our] global standardization leadership and our exceptional IPR portfolio' (Annual report)	Technological leadership is achieved through formation of a new subsidiary
Change in working practices	'How do we empower our engineers? We need to delegate more. We employ engineers to do a job so let them just get on and do it, that's really important' (Workshop participant)	Technological leadership is achieved through engineering skills
Existing working practices	'When we develop products, the technology was developed [in-house] … and if there were quality issues, we would work with them to overcome them in production because we are all engineers' (Interview)	Technological leadership is achieved through a quality control mindset among engineers
Be cost effective		
Cost-cutting program	'Our 'Back-to-Profit' program, announced … in July 2000, is under implementation and on target' (Annual report)	Cutbacks are part of a delineated strategy
Specific jobs are cut	'We've cut, transferred and outsourced a lot of jobs … the bottom-line profit at the moment is not good. But … we'll be breaking even in 2003' (Interview)	Cutbacks are achieved through job losses
New positions	'The COO [chief operating officer] is part of new structure' (Company magazine)	Cutbacks are achieved through changes in structure

	Account of practice in talk and text	Relation to strategy
Announcement of cuts	'[W]e are now taking necessary measures. We have to drive efficiency much harder' (chief executive officer quoted in press release)	Cutbacks are necessary
The Efficiency Program	'Anticipating shifts in market conditions in late 2000 and throughout 2001, we changed the shape of our business – rapidly. We quickly identified and implemented a range of measures to transform [the company] into a more efficient, integrated and responsive organization. These changes were coordinated through the Efficiency Program' (Annual report)	Cutbacks are part of a delineated strategy and are justified with reference to the market
Development of low-cost platform	'I mean to say at the moment we're working on getting a low cost ... platform out ... we're going to do it slightly differently, reduce the cost and maybe with different processes' (Interview)	Cutbacks are achieved through changes in work practices

Source: Adapted from Hardy and Thomas (2014: 329–330).

It appeared, then, that being cost effective was privileged over being first and best during the implementation, as far as practices were concerned. We therefore continued our analysis by examining how the two components of the strategy were talked and written about. We found that more 'discursive work' went into presenting cost-cutting practices as being part of the company's strategy than practices associated with being first and best. The way we conducted this analysis was, first, to identify five forms of discursive work that went into presenting practices as being part of a strategy in the various texts (Box 2.5).

We then compared the two sets of practices in terms to identify which forms of discursive work were utilized in presenting them as part of the company's strategy. In the case of the various cost-effective practices, all forms were used. *Tailoring* occurred as accounts explained how specific employees were transferred or dismissed in relation to particular plants. *Packaging* repeatedly linked individual practices to an overall strategy of being cost effective.

BOX 2.5   FORMS OF DISCURSIVE WORK

Form of discursive work	Description
Tailoring	The strategy takes shape as practices are materialized – texts refer to practices being enacted in relation to particular people, activities and places.
Packaging	The strategy is given substance as texts bundle together disparate practices and present them as a single strategy.
Scheduling	The strategy is temporalized as texts tie practices to specific timelines, benchmarks, and endpoints, as well as creating a sense of urgency.
Bulking up	The strategy is fortified as texts talk about enacting practices in ways that emphasize its strength and force.
Holding to account	The strategy is reinforced as texts hold particular actors to account for carrying out certain actions.

Source: Adapted from Hardy and Thomas (2014: 331).

Scheduling set out clear timelines for specific cost-cutting activities. There was considerable *bulking up* with talk about the need to take tough decisions and to act aggressively when it came to cutting costs. The chief executive officer was *held to account* as he was repeatedly asked to explain what cuts he intended to make to deal with the falling share price. In contrast, less discursive work went into presenting practices associated with being first and best as being part of the strategy. Some *tailoring* took place as a new subsidiary was spun off to develop innovative mobile platform technology and being first and best was *packaged* as important to technological achievements. However, we could find no evidence of scheduling, bulking up, or holding to account.

The study of GlobalTel shows that the dominant discourse of strategy does not have homogenous, predetermined effects at the local level – in being discursively and practically accomplished, irregularities may appear. Being cost effective was given precedence over being first and best – in both talk and practice – even though both had been presented on an equal footing in the original announcement. It also shows how other, underlying discourses were involved. Being cost effective was legitimated with reference to the market discourse, strengthening both the market discourse and the subject positions of external stakeholders, such as financial institutions and shareholders. In contrast, the professional discourse was undermined, weakening the subject position of the engineers working for the company.

Dominant Discourses and Self-repair

Another interesting question to consider is what goes on behind the scenes of a dominant discourse – how does it maintain its dominance and what happens if it fails? I examine this issue by returning to the discourse of risk and exploring what happens when risks *cannot* be identified through the application of the prevailing body of risk knowledge. This situation is not as unusual as one might think – modern society has been held accountable for a wide range of 'novel' risks that are not amenable to scientific analysis (Beck, 1992; Arnoldi, 2009). In these cases, attempts to apply 'science and technology create as many uncertainties as they dispel' (Giddens, 1999: 4). So, what happens when the discourse of risk fails to measure up to its job of calculating risks? How does it repair itself and retain its dominance?

The study (Hardy and Maguire, 2020) concerns bisphenol A (BPA), which is a chemical found in a wide range of products, including baby bottles, water bottles, and food can linings. In 1993, BPA was categorized as an endocrine-disrupting chemical, meaning that it could potentially adversely affect the hormone systems of humans and animals to cause reproductive and developmental problems. The concept of endocrine disruption was new – it had only emerged a few years earlier and the existing body of risk knowledge failed to answer the question of whether BPA caused endocrine disruption or, indeed, whether endocrine disruption caused harm. Accordingly, BPA was a good candidate for further research into what happens when the dominant discourse of risk fails to establish an object's meaning as to whether it poses a risk or not.

We collected texts on BPA in two countries – Canada and Australia – between 1993 and 2013. The two countries had similar systems for assessing chemical risks and were of a manageable size. We identified articles on BPA in *Science* and *Environmental Health News* (an aggregator of media coverage), as well as from the national broadcaster and a leading newspaper in each country. We downloaded documents from the websites of scientists, government regulators, chemical manufacturers, retailers, and non-governmental organizations (NGOs), and conducted interviews with representatives of each group. As a result, we were able to assemble a database of talk and text about BPA authored by diverse actors over a 20-year period.

We commenced our analysis by examining how the key actors talked (or wrote) about BPA – did it pose a risk? We found considerable equivocality regarding BPA's meaning in relation to risk, which was translated by the various groups into other, more familiar risks that directly affected them. We then documented the risk management actions that each group took to manage their translated risk and noted that, while not necessarily targeting BPA, these actions had an indirect effect on BPA – either strengthening or weakening its meaning as a risk object (Box 2.6).

BOX 2.6   TRANSLATED RISKS, RISK MANAGEMENT ACTIONS, AND EFFECTS

Actors' accounts of risks associated with BPA	Translated risk	Risk management actions	Effect on BPA
Endocrinologists link BPA to toxicologists' methodological bias – they use outdated methods, leading to erroneous research findings	*Professional risk:* threat to the integrity of their profession	More studies using innovative methods; critiques of toxicologists	Studies are more likely to find evidence of harm, which strengthens BPA's meaning as a risk object
Toxicologists link BPA to endocrinologists' methodological bias – they use unvalidated methods, leading to erroneous research findings	*Professional risk:* threat to the integrity of their profession	More studies using traditional methods; critiques of endocrinologists	Studies are less likely to find evidence of harm, which weakens BPA's meaning as a risk object
Chemical manufacturers link BPA to government regulations, which imposes additional costs and restricts opportunities	*Regulatory risk:* threat to their business from regulation	Claims of safety, funds for toxicology research	Safety claims, studies, and continued manufacture weaken BPA's meaning as a risk object
Canadian and Australian retailers link BPA to products that will cause a consumer backlash	*Reputational risk:* threat to their reputation	Withdrawal of products containing BPA	Removal of products containing BPA strengthen its meaning as a risk object
Canadian and Australian NGOs link BPA to products which, if they fail to act on them, will damage the NGOs' image	*Reputational risk:* threat to their reputation	Lobbying for regulations and withdrawal of products containing BPA	Awareness raising and demands for regulation strengthen BPA's meaning as a risk object

Actors' accounts of risks associated with BPA	Translated risk	Risk management actions	Effect on BPA
Canadian regulators link BPA to challenges posed by legacy, endocrine-disrupting chemicals, which, if not addressed, will jeopardize effective chemicals management	*Operational risk:* existing practices threaten chemicals management	New methods for assessing risk conclude BPA to be toxic	Special treatment for BPA and findings of toxicity strengthen its meaning as a risk object
Australian regulators link BPA to emotional debate, public fear, and political pressures which jeopardize effective chemicals management	*Operational risk:* changing practices threaten chemicals management	Traditional methods for assessing risk conclude BPA to be safe	Lack of special treatment for BPA and findings of safety weaken its meaning as a risk object

Source: Adapted from Hardy and Maguire (2020: 691).

Scientists translated the equivocality surrounding BPA into two versions of professional risk. Endocrinologists linked it to toxicologists' use of outdated methods which produced erroneous research findings. They considered their professional integrity to be at risk from this methodological bias. Their actions to manage this translated risk was to continue their research based on new methods and critique the work of toxicologists, both of which strengthened BPA's meaning as a risk object. Toxicologists linked BPA to methodological bias – in this case, endocrinologists experimenting with unvalidated methods – which posed a risk to their professional integrity. In response they continued to use traditional methods, which were less likely to find evidence of harm, and to criticize the work of endocrinologists, thereby weakening BPA's meaning as a risk object.

Manufacturers translated a regulatory risk – the equivocality surrounding BPA meant that regulators might intervene, potentially damaging business conditions. Actions to manage the regulatory risk involved funding research by toxicologists, asserting that BPA was safe, and continuing to manufacture it, thereby weakening its meaning as a risk object. Canadian regulators translated an operational risk to their chemical management program because BPA could not be accommodated by current risk assessment processes. As a result, they used non-traditional risk assessment practices to assess BPA and concluded that it did pose risks. Australian regulators also translated an operational risk, but a very different one. They argued that the politicization of BPA endangered the scientific basis of established risk assessment processes. To manage this risk, they continued to use traditional risk assessment practices and found that BPA did not pose a risk, weakening its meaning as a risk object.

Retailers and NGOs in both countries translated the equivocality surrounding BPA into reputational risks. Retailers were worried about a customer backlash and, so, withdrew products containing BPA from sale. NGOs were worried about losing credibility, members, and donors if they ignored a potentially dangerous chemical found in many everyday products. They took steps to draw attention to BPA, arguing that it did pose a risk and demanding regulatory action. Both these sets of risk management strengthened BPA's meaning as a risk object.

The contradictory effects of the actions taken to manage the various translated risks prolonged the equivocality concerning BPA's meaning. It only fully stabilized as the risk management actions with strengthening effects accumulated sufficiently to outweigh those with weakening effects and, most importantly, the body of risk knowledge was revised to identify BPA as a novel risk. This body of knowledge included not only the results of scientific studies, but also the validation of new scientific methods, the use of new regulatory procedures, new routines for withdrawing products in companies, and the development of consumer advocacy campaigns in NGOs. In its revised form, this body of knowledge was rendered capable of calculating the likelihood and nature of a risk once beyond its scope. During the period between the discourse of risk being brought to bear on BPA and its construction as a risk object, the discourse of risk was not merely 'repaired' but also expanded and intensified to incorporate new categories of risk and draw new objects into its domain.

CONCLUSION

In this chapter, I have discussed how dominant discourses are constituted and shown how influential they can be in terms of constructing bodies of knowledge, subject positions, and power relations. Paradoxically, contingency and fragility are also evident. Dominant discourses are not totalizing. Discourses that may appear to be inevitable and dominant in one setting are not necessarily so in another. Dominant discourses can be picked apart to show contradictions and inconsistencies, especially in local circumstances. Dominant discourses also require maintenance and repair, which may intensify their effects further. The studies discussed in this chapter offer a number of empirical 'pointers' for researchers thinking about employing a discursive approach (Box 2.7).

BOX 2.7   EMPIRICAL POINTERS

- Select relevant, interesting examples – risk, strategy, lean, and sustainability are important in organizations and therefore benefit from closer examination.
- While dominant discourses are stock in trade for many discourse scholars, be careful not to get caught up in a totalizing view of discourse.
- Look out for interesting discrepancies to explore as research questions. The studies in this chapter explore why the discourse of sustainability has more influence in one domain than another, why one component of a strategy overshadows another, and what happens when a dominant discourse fails to provide answers.
- Try to collect texts authored by a wide range of actors to provide a more complete picture, rather than rely on one data source. Make sure you systematically document authorship – who said what.
- Make sure you also log when the text was produced. The timing of texts was important because it allowed us to identify whether practices persisted at GlobalTel and to track changes in the meaning of BPA over time.
- It is possible to derive data on practices from textual data by analyzing accounts of practices in talk and text.
- Compromises may have to be made in the scope and scale of the texts that are collected for a study as, for example, in limiting data collection to English-language texts in the case of GlobalTel or by focusing on Canada and Australia rather than larger jurisdictions, such as the European Union (EU) or United States (US), in the case of BPA.

3. Understanding discursive struggle

Chapter 2 examined dominant discourses – situations where one discourse holds sway and there is the appearance of stability and stillness on the discursive landscape, regardless of what is going on behind the scenes. Some situations are, however, very different – the calm is replaced by visible discursive struggles, scuffles, and skirmishes. These settings are often selected for empirical study because the discursive dynamics are clearly visible and accessible to researchers. A discursive approach is particularly well suited to provide 'insights into the struggle between different strategies for transforming society in different directions through rhetorically oriented analysis of how strategic differences are fought out in dialogue, debate, polemic, etc.' (Fairclough, 2010: 19).

This chapter examines discursive struggles more closely. In the next section, I present two scientific discourses that are often juxtaposed against each other – the legacy discourse of sound science and the newcomer, the discourse of precaution. I then examine how the struggle between them played out among organizations in the context of a new United Nations (UN) Convention addressing toxic chemicals, followed by an investigation of how an individual organization juggled the two discourses in the practices it used to assess toxic chemicals.

DUELLING DISCOURSES: SOUND SCIENCE AND PRECAUTION

The discursive struggle to be explored here concerns the scientific domain, where discourses of sound science and precaution are often positioned in opposition to each other (Maguire and Hardy, 2006). The former is the more established, legacy discourse, predicated on the belief in the infallibility of the scientific method, which can be traced as far back as the 1600s. The latter is more recent and emphasizes the limitations of scientific knowledge.

The discourse of sound science stresses the importance of the scientific method in understanding the physical and natural world. It plays a particularly important role in relation to risk as scientific studies conducted by experts are used to ascertain whether objects are hazardous to humans or the environment. According to the discourse of risk (see Chapter 2), the failure of science to find evidence of harm is generally taken to indicate that an object is safe. If evidence of harm is found, scientists then calculate the risk that the adverse effects will materialize, as well as how much exposure is needed before individuals and/or the environment are adversely affected. To reduce the risk of adverse effects, governments and organizations often impose regulations or rules to restrict exposure to the object in question. The discourse of sound science thus places the burden of proof on would-be regulators to demonstrate clear scientific evidence of an object's harmful effects before implementing restrictions. When scientific studies fail to prove that a product, technology, or activity is harmful, regulation is deemed to be precipitous or disproportionate.

The discourse of precaution emphasizes the need to act on *potential* risks, even when there is scientific uncertainty and a lack of evidence regarding whether an object is harmful (Stirling and Gee, 2002). Precaution can be traced back to the concept of the 'foresight' principle, developed in West German environmental law in the 1970s (O'Riordan and Jordan, 1995). This evolved into the 'precautionary principle,' which started to make its way into environmental laws in the late 1980s. It gained momentum with the UN Rio Declaration on Environment and Development in 1992, whose Principle 15 stated that where there are 'threats of serious or irreversible damage, lack of full scientific certainty shall not be used as a reason for postponing cost-effective measures to prevent environmental degradation' (UNCED, 1992). Precaution is increasingly being incorporated into the policies of the EU and other countries in relation to human health and the environment.

These two discourses are often pitted against each other. Insofar as precaution emphasizes scientific *un*certainty (Stirling, 1999; Stirling and Gee, 2002), it enables regulatory action even when a product's harmful effects are unclear (Wiener and Rogers, 2002). For this reason, many environmental and public health NGOs welcome it because of the reduced need to provide incontrovertible evidence of harm. However, advocates for sound science often assert that precaution is 'junk' science and those promoting it are, at best, uninformed and, at worse, unscientific and anti-science (Miller and Conko, 2001; Pollan, 2001).

Box 3.1 shows the difference between the two discourses in terms of the objects, concepts, subject positions, and conditions of possibility that they construct. In the case of environmental and health sciences, both discourses construct an object of knowledge which is usually a potentially hazardous product, technology, or activity. However, the key concepts associated with this object differ. Sound science associates it with the concept of risk *management* – actions aimed at lowering demonstrated risks to an 'acceptable' level after a rigorous and quantitative process of assessment based on scientific study. The discourse of precaution, although not incompatible with risk management, is more strongly associated with the aim of *eliminating* the risk. The two discourses also create different subject positions. Sound science privileges scientific experts, who are assumed to deliver 'hard' facts to the policy process. Scientists still have legitimacy in the discourse of precaution, but their privilege is diminished since they are often seen as producing limited, uncertain knowledge. Precaution creates a greater role for the public and NGOs, who can legitimately voice concerns about potential risks based on a lower threshold of evidence and advocate for pre-emptive action, especially in the case of vulnerable populations. Governments also occupy a different position. According to sound science, they are neutral consumers of scientific information, arbitrating on demonstrated risks and benefits by acting *after* the facts have been established. According to precaution, governments are arbiters of *potential* risks, acting proactively to defend human and environmental health.

BOX 3.1   COMPARISON OF SOUND SCIENCE AND PRECAUTION

	Discourse of sound science	Discourse of precaution
Object of knowledge	Potentially hazardous products, technologies, and activities	Potentially hazardous products, technologies, and activities
Key concepts	Sound scientific knowledge	Uncertain, limited scientific knowledge
	Demonstrated risk	Potential risk
	Risk assessment and management	Risk elimination
Key subject positions	Scientific experts supply hard facts to the policy process	Scientific experts supply soft, contested claims to the policy process
	Governments act on demonstrated risks and benefits	Governments act on potential risks and benefits
	NGOs can voice concerns about demonstrated risks, but lay knowledge is subordinate to expert knowledge	NGOs can voice concerns about potential risks, and lay knowledge has to be taken into account
Conditions of possibility	Scientific uncertainty justifies inaction; restrictions are likely to come later rather than earlier	Scientific uncertainty does not justify inaction; restrictions are likely to come earlier rather than later

Source: Adapted from Maguire and Hardy (2006: 15).

By shaping meaning through the interplay of different concepts and subject positions, the two discourses create different conditions of possibility for the object of knowledge – the potentially hazardous product, technology, or activity. Sound science justifies inaction – at least until the science unequivocally establishes 'actual' risks. Given that scientific research is time consuming, this gives business more latitude to develop risky products and more time during which they can continue to sell them. Precaution, on the other hand, by foregrounding the limitations of scientific knowledge and emphasizing the concept of potential risk, gives governments the right to act earlier, as well as giving NGOs and the public – those bearing the risks – more right to participate in the process of identifying potential risks.

STAKES IN THE STRUGGLE

In this section, I examine how different actors engaged with the two discourses in attempts to influence a new global regulation – the UN Stockholm Convention on Persistent Organic Pollutants – intended to restrict toxic chemicals (see Maguire and Hardy, 2006). A discourse not only constrains actors by structuring the social space within which they act, it also provides them with resources that they can mobilize in support of their objectives. In this way, actors can promote or challenge discourses by authoring texts in attempts to create certain meanings, leading to discursive struggle. As this study shows, such struggles involve a range of strategies in how actors author and reference texts.

UN Conventions are legally binding agreements that commit signatories to comply with certain norms and standards. The Stockholm Convention established global rules for the production, use, import, export, release, and disposal of a particular type of chemical – those classified as persistent organic pollutants (POPs). These chemicals are highly toxic substances that persist in the environment for many years, travel long distances in air and water, and accumulate in fatty tissues of humans and wildlife (UNEP, 2002). The Convention initially identified 12 chemicals – known as the 'dirty dozen' – as POPs, including pesticides, industrial chemicals, and by-products. The Convention stipulated restrictions on these POPs and specified procedures for adding further chemicals to the list. It was ratified by 151 countries and came into effect in 2004.[1]

The process for negotiating the Convention was initiated in February 1997, when the UN established an intergovernmental negotiating committee (INC) with a mandate to develop an international, legally binding instrument to address POPs. The legal text of the Convention was agreed over five meetings of state and non-state actors that took place between July 1998 and

---

[1]   There are now over 180 parties to the Convention and additional chemicals have been categorized as POPs.

December 2000. State actors are formal participants in the negotiation of UN Conventions – they propose, debate, and, ultimately, adopt the wording of the legal text. Non-state actors such as NGOs and industry representatives attend as observers. They cannot make formal submissions, but they can intervene during plenary sessions with suggestions regarding the evolving legal text. These groups are also prominent in the corridors of each meeting where they set up information booths, distribute discussion documents and position papers, and lobby state delegates.

My co-author Steve Maguire attended three meetings of the INC and conducted 40 interviews with state and non-state actors involved in the negotiations. He also collected texts from the formal negotiating process, including the official draft versions of the legal text of the Convention published after each meeting; papers from the meetings that contained actors' formal submissions proposing modifications to the evolving text; daily meeting reports produced by the *Earth Negotiations Bulletin* which summarizes the interventions by actors regarding the legal text; texts produced by state, industry, and NGO actors in their attempts to influence negotiations; and official UN documentation related to the POPs issue.

To examine the discursive struggle between sound science and precaution, we analyzed the texts produced by four key actors, who took different positions in relation to the two discourses. The EU was the main state actor interested in expanding the scope of precaution, while the US was the main state actor seeking to limit its scope. The International Pollutants Elimination Network (IPEN) – a global network of NGOs – was the main non-state actor trying to expand the scope of precaution. The International Council of Chemical Associations (ICCA), which represents industry stakeholders, was the main non-state actor attempting to limit it. To examine their discursive strategies, we examined the texts they authored. We identified all the instances where the texts referred to one or other of the two discourses and then conducted a subjective analysis of their arguments, their intertextual references, and how they engaged with both discourses.

Texts authored by the EU and IPEN challenged the discourse of sound science by arguing that, rather than removing uncertainty regarding the toxicity of POPs, it created *more* uncertainty. 'Scientific uncertainty results usually from five characteristics of the scientific method: the variable chosen, the measurements made, the samples drawn, the models used, and the causal relationship employed ... [as well as] controversy on existing data or lack of some relevant data' (EC, 2000: 13–14). These actors held sound science responsible for problems associated with POPs – it led to delays in regulatory action during which time POPs had remained in the economy, causing harm: 'Yet, even most serious scientific works often prove to be misleading in the past ... POPs ... were in the past deemed to be so harmless, including by most brilliant scientists, that they were massively employed' (EU, 2000).

They also criticized the assumption of sound science that the risks associated with these dangerous chemicals were manageable: 'We reject the claim that emissions and releases of POPs can be effectively managed and controlled ... A POP has no acceptable emission limit, no acceptable daily intake, and no acceptable level in the environment' (IPEN, 1998).

The US and the ICCA challenged the discourse of precaution for not being scientific enough: '[Industry] faces the prospect of having some chemicals, chemical groups, and entire technologies banned or strictly controlled as a result of government decisions that seem to apply the precautionary principle in a way that disregards important science' (ICCA, 2000a). Their texts promoted sound science by arguing that regulations had to be guided by 'the best scientific evidence to craft provisions to produce real reductions of the risk of POPs to health and the environment' (US, 2000a) and to 'promote actions that are feasible and practical' (ICCA, 2000b).

At times, actors reconciled the two discourses in their texts, albeit giving primacy to their preferred discourse. The EU talked about science in ways that expanded the scope for invoking precaution by, for example, drawing attention to the fact that scientists themselves often called for more precautionary action. Texts produced by IPEN demanded more scientific research, but with the caveat that precaution was 'an overarching principle informing each step of the decision-making process' to which science and traditional risk assessment practices were subordinated (WWF, 2000). The US and ICCA also attempted to reconcile science and precaution but giving primacy to the former. These actors were prepared to 'support precautionary language that is understood to be based in science' (US, 2000b). Precaution could be exercised, but only within the context of sound science. 'Risk assessment [based on science] is entirely consistent with the application of the precautionary principle. Indeed, the precautionary principle cannot be applied *without* a risk assessment' (ICCA, 2000a, emphasis in original). Similarly, the US (2000b) argued that 'precaution must be exercised as part of a science-based approach to regulation, and not as a substitute for such an approach.'

The texts of these actors also invoked other, authoritative texts that promoted specific meanings of precaution. The EU and IPEN regularly referred to legal texts that promoted the idea of precaution as an emerging 'principle' of international law, such as the EU's *Communication from the Commission on the Precautionary Principle*, which made explicit reference to eight international instruments to assert that precaution had 'become a full-fledged and general principle of international law' (EC, 2000: 10). Texts produced by IPEN recommended that 'delegates should recognize the precautionary approach as an emerging principle of customary international law' (WWF, 2000). The texts of these two actors also referred to authoritative texts that promoted strong definitions of precaution. So, although they referred to the Rio Declaration, which was a relatively weak formulation limiting precaution to serious or irreversible threats to the environment and only justifying cost-effective measures (Sandin et al., 2002), they also referenced the 2000 Cartagena Protocol on Biosafety which promoted a far stronger formulation. IPEN's texts evoked the 1998 Wingspread Statement – a strong NGO-authored version of precaution.

In contrast, the texts of the US and ICCA were less likely to refer to texts that suggested that precaution was a legal principle and, in fact, preferred not to use the term 'principle' at all. Their texts tended to refer to a precautionary 'approach,' which had none of the far-ranging implications of a legal principle. They frequently referred to the Rio Declaration's definition, which not only was weaker, but had been consensually agreed upon by the wider international community. There was, argued the US and ICCA, no need to open up the meaning of precaution: 'some of the proposals that we have heard appear to be an effort to renegotiate Rio 15. The US strongly believes that this is not the forum to engage in that inherently political discussion' (US, 2000c). In this way, these actors attempted to delimit and fix the weaker meaning of precaution.

This analysis allowed us to distil the patterns in the similarities and differences among the strategies of the four actors (Box 3.2). Not surprisingly, we found that the texts of the actors promoted and justified their preferred discourse and challenged the alternative. However, at times, the texts reconciled the two discourses, but did so in ways that subordinated the opposing discourse to their preferred one. We also found that actors referenced other authoritative texts strategically – choosing those that either promoted or restricted precaution, as well as those that opened up or closed down meanings.

Having ascertained that the actors used similar discursive strategies, albeit with reference to different discourses and texts, we then examined the outcome of this struggle. In the first step of this analysis, we consulted the final version of the UN text and conducted some straightforward counting, which showed that precaution was mentioned many more times than science. A deeper, qualitative analysis showed that when science was mentioned, its uncertain nature was emphasized, and it was subordinated to precaution. For example, science figured prominently in the provision for adding other chemicals to the list of POPs – an expert, scientific body screens nominated chemicals using various 'science-based' criteria to conduct a traditional risk assessment. However, the final decision on whether to add a nominated chemical was to be taken by the political body – the Conference of the Parties – *not* the scientific experts. Box 3.3 summarizes the way in which discourse of precaution was embedded in the Convention.

BOX 3.2 SUMMARY OF DISCURSIVE STRATEGIES OF ACTORS

Actors seeking to expand scope of precaution		Actors seeking to limit scope of precaution	
EU	**IPEN**	**US**	**ICCA**
Texts challenge the discourse of sound science by claiming it produces uncertainty and can lead to delays in action	Texts challenge the discourse of sound science by claiming it produces uncertainty, leads to delays in action, and is inappropriate for addressing POPs because they pose unmanageable risks	Texts challenge the discourse of precaution by claiming it is impractical	Texts challenge the discourse of precaution by claiming it is impractical for addressing POPs because it can lead to unmanageable and impractical regulations
Texts reconcile the two discourses by constructing precaution as scientific and subordinating key features of sound science to precaution	Texts reconcile the two discourses by constructing precaution as scientific and subordinating key features of sound science to precaution	Texts reconcile the two discourses by constructing sound science as precautionary and subordinating key features of precaution to sound science	Texts reconcile the two discourses by constructing sound science as precautionary and subordinating key features of precaution to sound science
Texts invoke:	Texts invoke:	Texts invoke:	Texts invoke:
• Rio Principle 15 to legitimate precaution • Other international legal texts (e.g., Cartagena Protocol) to emphasize the precautionary 'principle'	• Rio Principle 15 to legitimate precaution • Other international legal texts to emphasize the precautionary 'principle' – a legal principle • Wingspread Statement to highlight an even stronger formulation of precaution	• Rio Principle 15 to emphasize a precautionary 'approach' and challenge its status as a legal principle, as well as secure discursive closure around a weak formulation of precaution that has been consensually agreed	• Rio Principle 15 to emphasize a precautionary 'approach' and challenge its status as a legal principle, as well as secure discursive closure around a weak formulation of precaution that has been consensually agreed

Source: Adapted from Maguire and Hardy (2006: 20).

BOX 3.3   PRECAUTION IN THE STOCKHOLM CONVENTION

- The Preamble acknowledges that 'precaution underlies the concerns of all the Parties and is embedded within this Convention.'
- The Objective states: 'Mindful of the precautionary approach as set forth in Principle 15 of the Rio Declaration on Environment and Development, the objective of this Convention is to protect human health and the environment from persistent organic pollutants.' The Objective is generally understood within international law to be an overarching article that guides interpretation of the substantive articles and provisions of a treaty.
- Explicit reference to precaution is found in Annex C (which applies to POPs that are formed and released unintentionally). Precaution under-pins all 13 factors, and the Annex also draws attention to how scientific knowledge is subject to change, thus highlighting its uncertain and provisional status.
- Within the agreed process for adding other chemicals to the list of POPs, the technical threshold value of the persistence criteria for adding POPs to the Convention is set at a more precautionary level, as advocated by the EU and IPEN (although this is counter-balanced by the technical threshold value of the bioaccumulation criteria, which is set at a less precautionary level, as advocated by the US and ICCA).
- The agreed process for adding other chemicals to the list of POPs states that a 'lack of full scientific certainty shall not prevent the proposal [to list a chemical as a POP] from proceeding.' It obligates parties to take 'due account' of 'any scientific uncertainty' and to make decisions to list a chemical as a POP 'in a precautionary manner.'
- Provision is made to permit chemicals that do not meet the technical criteria of being a POP to be nonetheless categorized as POPs.

The Stockholm Convention thus incorporates the discourses of precaution and sound science in such a way that, while both are evident, precaution has been privileged, creating new conditions of possibility (Box 3.4). Prior to the Stockholm Convention, there were no global regulations restricting POPs, leaving industry free to continue producing and selling products containing these chemicals in other countries even if they were subject to domestic regulations. The Convention banned or restricted 12 chemicals and provided a way to add other chemicals to the list of POPs (another 18 chemicals have since been added), enabling governments

BOX 3.4   CONDITIONS OF POSSIBILITY: BEFORE AND AFTER STOCKHOLM

Prior to the Stockholm Convention	After the Stockholm Convention
No global regulation of POPs	12 chemicals designated as POPs are banned or restricted
	A procedure is specified for adding other chemicals to the list of POPs
	This procedure explicitly accommodates scientific uncertainty and obligates decisions to be made in a precautionary manner
Domestic markets in POPs exist in some countries	Domestic markets in banned POPs no longer exist due to harmonized regulations among states that are parties to the Convention
International markets in POPs are unrestricted, except through heterogeneous domestic controls on import and export	International markets in banned POPs do not exist between states that are parties to the Convention
Markets in products with POPs-like features but about which there is scientific uncertainty continue to function while scientists study them	Markets in products with POPs-like features are more likely to be deliberated and regulated earlier because of the lower threshold of evidence required

Source: Adapted from Maguire and Hardy (2006: 22).

to act proactively even in the face of scientific uncertainty, and empowering NGOs and the public to lobby for action based on a lower burden of proof.

In sum, this study provides an example of how the emergence of a new discourse led to discursive struggle among actors. Both new and legacy discourses provided resources for these actors, who drew on them in different ways as they produced and distributed texts designed to influence outcomes. Actors seeking to expand the impact of the new discourse did not simply promote it, they also produced texts that reconciled it with the legacy discourse, albeit with the latter in a subordinate position. Similarly, actors seeking to limit the impact of the new discourse did not simply dismiss it but attempted to reconcile it with the legacy discourse. Both sets of actors drew on other authoritative texts depending on whether they expanded or restricted the reach of the new discourse. Out of this discursive struggle, new conditions of possibility arose.

JUGGLING THE STRUGGLE

The discussion so far has focused on discursive struggles among different organizations. But what does the struggle mean for an individual organization?

To learn more, I refer to a study (Maguire and Hardy, 2013) of the Canadian government, which introduced a Chemicals Management Plan (CMP) in 2006 to address the risks posed by chemicals to Canadians and the environment.

The first step of the CMP was a review of 23,000 existing substances, which prioritized 200 chemicals for more detailed risk assessment. This involved government scientists analyzing information on each chemical's properties, hazards, uses, releases to the environment, and routes of exposure to humans, which was collected from scientists and other stakeholders (such as manufacturers and NGOs). The government also solicited advice on specific questions from an advisory panel of 12 experts. Various documents were produced during the process: a draft assessment report presented the initial findings; a summary of key issues was circulated to stakeholders for comment; these comments were presented in a summary document; and a final assessment report made a definitive conclusion. If a chemical was found to be toxic, further consultations were undertaken that could eventually result in regulations to restrict its manufacture, use, storage, transport, and/or disposal.

We compared the assessment of two chemicals – vinyl acetate monomer (VAM) and BPA. VAM is an industrial chemical used to manufacture a variety of polymers and found in paints, adhesives, and personal care products. Scientific findings suggested that long-term exposure to vinyl acetate could cause a carcinogenic response regardless of the level of exposure. This 'non-threshold' mode of action led to an automatic conclusion of toxicity in the draft assessment report. However, the final report concluded that VAM was toxic only above a certain, threshold level of exposure. Since this threshold was not exceeded in Canada, VAM did not meet the criteria for toxicity and no regulatory measures were required. BPA is found in a wide range of products, including baby bottles, water bottles, and food can linings. As Chapter 2 discussed, some scientific studies suggested that it was an endocrine disruptor, interfering with the hormone systems of humans and animals to cause reproductive and developmental problems. Both the draft and final assessment report concluded that BPA was toxic leading to a ban on baby bottles containing BPA in 2010 – making Canada the first country in the world to take such action.

We selected these two chemicals because they epitomized the struggle between sound science and precaution and because of the way in which their meanings changed during the assessment process. Both chemicals were already in use in the Canadian economy on the assumption that they were safe. VAM 'became' risky insofar as the draft assessment report found it to be toxic at any level of exposure. However, by the final assessment report, it had become safe again. In contrast, BPA became – and remained – risky to the extent that Canada restricted its use – something that no other jurisdiction had done at that time.

We collected publicly available texts from the government that described the practices used in the CMP, as well as government, NGO, and industry texts pertaining to VAM and BPA. We started by coding these texts to identify the different practices used in the CMP to assess all chemicals. From the various descriptions, we inferred eight distinct practices: referencing, anchoring, categorizing, sequencing, particularizing, innovating, questioning, and pluralizing (Figure 3.1). The practices clustered into two distinct bundles, which we labelled as *normalizing*, which corresponds to the discourse of sound science, and *problematizing*, which corresponds to the discourse of precaution.

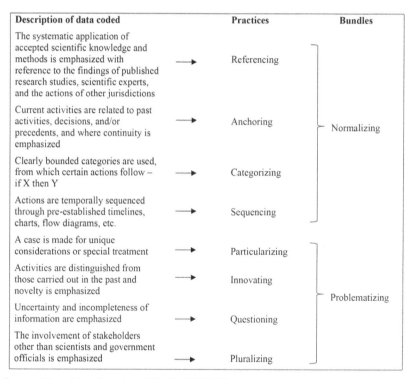

Description of data coded	Practices	Bundles
The systematic application of accepted scientific knowledge and methods is emphasized with reference to the findings of published research studies, scientific experts, and the actions of other jurisdictions	Referencing	
Current activities are related to past activities, decisions, and/or precedents, and where continuity is emphasized	Anchoring	Normalizing
Clearly bounded categories are used, from which certain actions follow – if X then Y	Categorizing	
Actions are temporally sequenced through pre-established timelines, charts, flow diagrams, etc.	Sequencing	
A case is made for unique considerations or special treatment	Particularizing	
Activities are distinguished from those carried out in the past and novelty is emphasized	Innovating	Problematizing
Uncertainty and incompleteness of information are emphasized	Questioning	
The involvement of stakeholders other than scientists and government officials is emphasized	Pluralizing	

Source: Adapted from Maguire and Hardy (2013: 237).

Figure 3.1   Summary of practices

We then examined the texts pertaining specifically to VAM and BPA to see which practices were used in each case. In the case of VAM, we found considerable evidence of normalizing but not much problematizing. In the case of BPA, there was more evidence of problematizing (Box 3.5).

BOX 3.5 COMPARISON OF PRACTICES USED WITH VAM AND BPA

	VAM	BPA
Draft assessment report	*Normalizing* • Referencing of various texts and reports • Anchoring/categorizing: a longstanding policy that non-threshold carcinogens are categorized as toxic *Problematizing* • Particularizing: VAM is a priority meriting special assessment • Questioning: information about mode of action is incomplete	*Normalizing* • Referencing of various texts and reports *Problematizing* • Extensive particularizing: BPA is a priority meriting special assessment; it affects vulnerable subpopulations • Extensive questioning of uncertainty of BPA's effects
Document summarizing key issues for stakeholders	*Normalizing* • Referencing of other texts • Anchoring/categorizing: non-threshold mode of action results in toxicity conclusion *Problematizing* • Questioning: non-threshold mode of action cannot be precluded	*Normalizing* • Little evidence *Problematizing* • Extensive questioning of uncertainty of BPA's effects • Innovating: novel risk management actions are needed • Pluralizing: there is a need to work with diverse stakeholders
Panel advice	*Problematizing* • Particularizing: VAM singled out in a specific question regarding its assessment	*Problematizing* • Particularizing: BPA is singled out in a specific question regarding its assessment
Summary of public comments	*Normalizing* • Extensive referencing of new scientific texts • Extensive anchoring/categorizing: chemicals categorized as non-threshold carcinogens are classified as toxic	*Normalizing* • Referencing of scientific texts • Anchoring by relating back to government texts on precaution

	VAM	BPA
Summary of public comments (continued)	*Problematizing* • Little evidence	*Problematizing* • Extensive questioning and mention of uncertainty of BPA's effects • Innovating: government claims to be a leader in assessment methods and precautionary action • Particularizing: mention of the vulnerable subpopulations that are affected by BPA
Final report	*Normalizing* • Extensive referencing of new data in various texts concerning mode of action and exposure • Categorizing: VAM now has a threshold mode of action • Anchoring: accepted practice for assessing threshold carcinogens is to investigate exposure scenarios	*Normalizing* • Little evidence apart from referencing of texts
	Problematizing • Little evidence	*Problematizing* • Particularizing: BPA affects subpopulations
Web summary	*Normalizing* • Extensive referencing of additional texts	*Normalizing* • Categorizing: boundaries drawn around risk bearers i.e., infants
	Problematizing • Little evidence	*Problematizing* • Innovating: novel risk management measures should be applied • Pluralizing: there is a need to work with industry and acknowledge concerns of Canadians

Source: Adapted from Maguire and Hardy (2013: 243, 245).

In a third stage of analysis, we analyzed the discursive work undertaken to support and contest the conclusions. We examined industry's reactions to the draft assessment reports, which had concluded that both VAM and BPA were toxic by consulting the report that summarized their comments. We then investigated the government's response to industry's criticisms in the same document.

In the case of VAM, industry stakeholders challenged the draft conclusion that VAM was toxic at any level of exposure. They did so by recommending that additional texts should be referenced – most notably the 2008 version of a risk assessment by the EU, which proposed that VAM had a threshold mode of action. In other words, it was carcinogenic only over a certain level of exposure. The government accommodated this criticism and referenced this text in the final assessment report. This led to a different conclusion – VAM *did* have a threshold mode of action, meaning that it could no longer automatically be categorized as toxic. In accordance with normal scientific practice, additional information was now required to ascertain whether the exposure of Canadians exceeded the threshold at which harm was caused. On this matter, industry recommended a range of additional studies that addressed exposure. The government accommodated this challenge by referencing 21 additional texts in the final report and concluding that exposure to VAM was expected to be below the threshold and, therefore, VAM was not considered to be toxic in the Canadian context.

In the case of BPA, industry contested the draft assessment by arguing that some of the texts referenced in the draft report were not scientifically valid and should therefore be excluded. The government rebuffed this criticism, saying the studies were 'rigorously designed, relevant and considered of high utility by the expert panel.' Industry also refuted the government's interpretation of texts that equated the precautionary principle with the need for regulation. The government rebuffed this criticism by asserting its right to act in the face of scientific uncertainty to protect vulnerable Canadians. Additional criticisms by industry that the government's interpretations of texts were value-driven were also rebuffed – not by *denying* that they were value-driven, but by arguing that they were – and *ought to be* – value-driven. In other words, BPA was an exceptional case, where the science regarding its toxicity was uncertain, particularly in relation to a particularly vulnerable subpopulation – babies and infants (because the chemical was found in baby bottles). Accordingly, the government asserted its right to exercise leadership by making innovative, independent judgments about BPA based on the precautionary principle.

The discursive work around the meaning of the two chemicals was thus quite different. In the case of VAM, following an initial conclusion of toxicity in the draft assessment, its meaning subsequently became safe again – one of only two chemicals in over 120 assessed between 2006 and 2010 where the conclusion changed between the draft and final assessment report. Yet this reversal was not controversial and required little contemporaneous discursive work to defend it. It was achieved through normal science and organizational precedent. The discourse of sound science and normalizing practices not only helped to stabilize meanings, but also established a relatively clear target for any discursive work required to change them. An additional text produced in another jurisdiction was referenced which led to the subsequent recategorizing of VAM as a threshold carcinogen which, in turn, led to the referencing of additional texts that addressed exposure. The discursive work had mainly taken place *in the past*. VAM's meaning as safe was held in place by a nexus of pre-existing texts, such as scientific articles, policy documents, and risk assessments from other jurisdictions. Earlier discursive work had created shared understandings. Therefore, there was little need for contemporaneous discursive work to justify the change in VAM's meaning from risky back to safe again.

In the case of BPA, considerably more contemporaneous discursive work was required even though the conclusion did *not* change between the draft and final reports. Compared to VAM, the equivalent texts for BPA were longer, there were more of them, and they involved far more questioning of authors' legitimacy, basic 'facts,' causal models, and methods for generating and validating knowledge. What constituted relevant knowledge, how to produce it, and what to do with it were up for grabs because the discourse of precaution and problematizing practices open up options. If an object is particularized, then it is always possible to afford it further special treatment. If innovating is constructed as necessary, then it is always possible to invent novel ways of dealing with it. If questioning challenges the applicability of a body of knowledge, then it is always possible to expand the scope of this questioning. If interests are pluralized, then it is always possible to find alternative ways to balance stakeholder concerns. Moreover, whereas the additional texts concerning VAM suggested by industry *resolved* the uncertainty, additional texts could only *increase* the uncertainty in the case of BPA. Even additional texts referring to evidence of safety could not 'undo' the existing evidence that indicated BPA might not be safe; they merely added to the controversy. Instead of struggle occurring *within* a paradigm where issues of epistemology, valid evidence, and appropriate value judgments were already settled, there was a struggle occurring *over* a paradigm.

In sum, this study shows the discourses of sound science and precaution that circulate in interorganizational domains influence, and are influenced by, specific practices enacted by individual organizations. It also shows how the practices of an individual organization were influenced by both discourses in a complex juggling act. Finally, the study shows how knowledge production and discursive work were shaped by the two discourses, such that even though the draft finding concerning VAM was overturned – the emphasis on normalizing meant that 'science' took care of business, whereas considerable discursive work was required to problematize BPA, even though the finding of toxicity did not change.

CONCLUSION

Studying discursive struggle shows how new discourses emerge and threaten existing or legacy discourses, with actors having a stake in one or the other. As this chapter shows, new discourses are unlikely to completely eradicate or replace legacy discourses. They create new conditions of possibility, but they also inherit 'the cultural and political capital of older and long-established discourses [even as they] … critique and challenge that very inheritance in their quest to change the institutional status quo in some shape or form' (Reed, 2004: 415). Accordingly, discursive struggles are not straightforward and can give rise to various strategies as discourse plays a dual role: a resource used in the struggle and an outcome of it. For this reason, they are often fascinating empirical settings for researchers.

BOX 3.6   EMPIRICAL POINTERS

- Discursive struggles are good candidates for empirical study – the dynamics are often clearly visible, actors take sides, and they often produce a lot of texts. However, researchers should not assume unfettered agency. While sound science and precaution are often juxtaposed against each other, both operate within a broader scientific discourse in which all actors (and readers) are trapped.
- Researchers can take advantages of settings where a large number of texts are produced. In the case of the Stockholm Convention, the INC meetings were a catalyst for text production. In the case of the CMP, the process of risk assessment of different chemicals resulted in the production of standardized texts that could be compared.
- Researchers can look for ways 'into' a study by identifying discrepancies that they can then pursue with a discursive approach. VAM and BPA were chosen because they were treated differently within the same process. VAM was interesting because the conclusion of the final assessment report differed from that of the draft report. BPA was interesting because, at the time, Canada was the only jurisdiction to restrict it.
- Discourse analysis involves a number of steps. It often starts by systematically combing texts for instances where a phenomenon is mentioned. Then researchers can delve into the way it is written or talked about to identify patterns, which can then be investigated in more depth.
- Analyzing texts does not preclude the study of practices – it can track and analyze them from descriptions and accounts of activities, as in the case of the CMP. However, it cannot show how they were carried

out – observations of meetings and the day-to-day work of government scientists would be needed to collect data on this.
- A discursive approach has limitations as does any research – our analysis of texts could not show the political wheeling and dealing that went on between countries in relation to the Stockholm Convention.
- As with Chapter 2, a discursive approach can be used to study important societal issues such as environmental protection and human health.

4.   Understanding discursive change

In this chapter, I examine discursive change. This focus differs from both Chapter 2 on dominant discourses, where change is minimal, and Chapter 3 on discursive struggle, where change is the result of interactions among multiple discourses. Here, I examine how an individual discourse can change over time by drawing on two studies of the pesticide known as DDT (dichloro-diphenyl -trichloroethane) (Maguire and Hardy, 2009; Hardy and Maguire, 2010). The first study examines the change in the discourse of DDT between 1939 and 1972 and the role of Rachel Carson's book *Silent Spring* in this process. The second study examines changes in the discourse of DDT between 1998 and 2001 resulting from negotiations over the Stockholm Convention (discussed in Chapter 3).

CHANGE IN THE DISCOURSE OF DDT: 1939–1972

DDT is a chemical whose insect-killing properties were discovered in 1939 by a Swiss scientist called Paul Müller. During the Second World War, it was used to protect soldiers from typhus, malaria, and other insect-borne diseases. Its role in saving millions of soldiers' lives won Müller the Nobel Prize for medicine in 1948. After the war, DDT was released into the civilian economy and was widely used on crops and livestock against insects, as well as against flies, cockroaches, and bedbugs. Sales grew and, by the early 1960s, DDT was the top-selling insecticide in the US. At this point, the discourse about DDT claimed that it was safe, effective, and necessary (Maguire and Hardy, 2009).

In 1962, Rachel Carson's book *Silent Spring* criticized the use of chemical pesticides and directly challenged the discourse about DDT, arguing that it was not safe for humans or the environment; it was not effective because insects became resistant to it; and it was not necessary because pests could be managed through biological controls (see Chapter 9 for how we distilled Carson's arguments to these three problematizations). The book was widely read and, over the following ten years, sales of DDT declined by two thirds. In 1972, the Environmental Protection Agency instituted a nation-wide ban to take effect the following year. We investigated the role that *Silent Spring* played in this process of deinstitutionalization and examined whether and how it changed the discourse about DDT (Maguire and Hardy, 2009).

New Patterns of Authorship

In the first instance, we wanted to see whether *Silent Spring* influenced the corpus of other texts that made up the discourse about DDT (see Chapter 8 for how we selected a sample of relevant texts). To examine scientific texts, we identified all PhD dissertations and *Science* articles on DDT between 1939 and 1972 so that we could compare texts before and after the publication of *Silent Spring*. It was not feasible to examine all these long, complicated texts in detail to see if *Silent Spring* had an influence. We therefore used an informal 'proxy' – we looked for changes in the types of studies, which we could infer from reading the abstract. We found that, prior to 1962, the dominant category was studies of insects (84 percent of dissertations, 57 percent of *Science* articles). After 1962, studies of insects declined (27 percent of dissertations, 4 percent of articles), while studies of birds, fish, and mammals and persistence increased to 67 percent of dissertations and 70 percent of articles (from 3 percent of dissertations and 18 percent of articles prior to 1962). These patterns told us something. Studies of insects were likely to be concerned with DDT's efficacy – how well it killed insects. Studies of birds, fish, mammals, and environmental persistence were more likely to address safety – whether DDT had adverse effects. It was therefore possible to infer that *Silent Spring* stimulated the production of scientific texts that were more likely to challenge the existing discourse about DDT.

This conclusion was supported by patterns of authorship. Prior to 1962, 61 percent of dissertations and 43 percent of articles on DDT were authored by entomologists or agricultural scientists, who were more likely to be interested in its use for pest control. After 1962, this proportion dropped to 22 percent and 10 percent, while the percentage authored by biologists, zoologists, ecologists, and eco-toxicologists, who were more likely to be concerned about its safety, increased to 54 percent of dissertations and 65 percent of articles. As these scientists conducted studies and authored texts, they were more likely to challenge the discourse about DDT. Further, their legitimacy and authority increased as a result of the articles they authored, enabling them to challenge the previously dominant subject position of entomologists and contribute new insights to the body of knowledge about DDT.

We also wanted to examine whether *Silent Spring* influenced public and media texts. In the case of public texts, we relied on secondary sources (Lear, 1997; Coit Murphy, 2005), which showed that as members of the public read the book, they also began to author texts by writing letters to Carson, her publisher, *The New Yorker*, CBS television, as well as newspapers and government agencies. Most of these letters voiced support for Carson's criticisms of DDT. For media texts, we analyzed editorials on DDT in the *New York Times*. Prior to 1962, we found that editorials praised DDT's insect-killing properties.

In July 1962, an editorial reported directly on *Silent Spring*, acclaiming it for initiating a public debate about DDT. An analysis of texts authored by environmental NGOs such as the Environmental Defense Fund and Audubon Society also showed they referenced – and affirmed – *Silent Spring* (Long, 1962; Henkin et al., 1971).

Silent Spring was clearly influential – it was taken up in a positive way in a wide range of texts authored by a range of new authors (see Chapter 9 to learn how it was taken up in a negative or adversarial way). By authoring these texts, a great many actors now had a voice on DDT – a new 'public' subject position had been created. As the public voice grew louder, another new subject position emerged – the 'environmental politician' – who not only represented the public in federal and state legislatures, but also authored their own texts supporting *Silent Spring*, such as the Ribicoff (1966) and Mrak (1969) reports, as well as some 40 bills presented to state legislatures across the US. Collectively, these new subject positions came to constitute an environmental lobby that acted as a counterweight to powerful agricultural interests defending DDT.

Our initial analysis indicated that *Silent Spring* was widely distributed and consumed by being taken up in diverse texts in ways that appeared to support its arguments. Moreover, new patterns of authorship, collectively and over time, created new subject positions – environmental scientists, concerned members of the public, and environmental politicians – who were more likely to be critical of DDT.

New Meanings

Our next step was to track whether Carson's arguments survived being taken up in other texts. To conduct this phase of the analysis, we identified specific texts where we could 'drill down' to analyze meaning more closely and to see exactly *how* these texts restated Carson's arguments. We compared the 1962 and 1972 editions of two widely used textbooks on ecology and applied entomology. Box 4.1 shows how the ecology textbook reproduced the problematization of DDT's safety in relation to the environment, but qualified the argument concerning human safety, which was 'not yet demonstrated.' The issue of DDT not being effective was minimized and its necessity was largely ignored (the applied entomology textbook showed a similar pattern).

BOX 4.1   COMPARISON OF EDITIONS OF ECOLOGY TEXTBOOK

Odum, 1959 (2nd edition)	Odum, 1971 (3rd edition)	Significance
'DDT, ecology of' is the only entry in the index and is indexed to two pages (530)	'DDT, in food chains' is indexed to two pages; 'DDT, poisoning of birds by' is indexed to one page; 'DDT, worldwide pollution by' is indexed to one page (561)	The problematization of environmental safety is reproduced: DDT's presence in food chains and poisoning of birds is highlighted in the index
There is no reference to *Silent Spring* which had yet to be written	'and the poisoning of entire food chains was dramatically brought to public attention in 1962 by Rachel Carson's famous book' (445)	The 'poisoning of entire food chains' is asserted without qualification and with explicit reference to *Silent Spring*
Environmental pollution is one paragraph (425–426)	Environmental pollution is addressed in a new chapter of 18 pages (432–450); within it, the 'Insecticides' section is entirely devoted to DDT and similar insecticides – 'these substances have produced one of the world's most serious pollution problems' (446)	A new chapter places particular emphasis on DDT, the negative impacts of which are accepted without qualification and characterized as 'one of the world's most serious pollution problems'
There is no mention of human safety in discussions of DDT and other pesticides	'While direct effects … on the hormone balance in man have not yet been demonstrated, concentration levels in human tissue are now high enough that such effects, and also cancer and deleterious mutations, *could* occur in the future (446, emphasis in original)	The problematization of human safety survives in qualified form: a potential threat is acknowledged
The 'excessive use of insecticides is creating other problems such as … the development of resistance in pests themselves' (426)	'Unheeded warnings of an entomological backlash (i.e., pest outbreaks) actually induced by spraying were voiced in the 1950s' (445)	The problematization of efficacy survives but is minimized: resistance is described in both editions but in passing reference only
Biological control of insects is indexed to two pages (527)	Biological control of pests is indexed to two pages (559)	No evidence that problematization of necessity survives translation: limited coverage of biological controls in both editions

Source: Adapted from Maguire and Hardy (2009: 16).

We also examined *New York Times* editorials on DDT between 1962 and 1972. They showed a similar pattern: they restated concerns about environmental safety, qualified threats to human health, and ignored efficacy. Interestingly, they subverted the argument regarding DDT's necessity by promoting its substitution, not with the biological controls advocated by Carson, but with other chemicals criticized in *Silent Spring*. Finally, we studied the text of the 1972 legislation banning DDT and found that it too reproduced challenges to DDT's environmental safety, but qualified, minimized, and subverted the other concerns.

When we consider the corpus of texts on DDT – or, at least, a sample of it – the evidence suggests that not all of Carson's original arguments or problematizations survived. *Silent Spring* was not uniformly successful in changing all aspects of the discourse about DDT. In fact, the subsequent subversion of the problematization of necessity in other texts – by proposing chemical rather than biological substitutes – may have meant that the 1972 ban was more acceptable to the chemical and agricultural industries than it otherwise would have been. They might have lost the battle over DDT, but they had not lost the war over chemical pesticides in general.

In sum, this study highlights the vagaries and complexities of discursive change. It emphasizes that discourse emerges from a collection of texts rather than an individual text. Even though Carson produced an articulate, persuasive text that was widely read, it did not change the discourse concerning DDT by itself or in all the ways that Carson intended. The deinstitutionalization of DDT was a more complex affair – *Silent Spring* generated new kinds of texts and authors which, collectively and over time, helped to create new subject positions and a new body of knowledge concerning DDT that challenged its safety although not its efficacy and necessity.

CHANGE IN THE DISCOURSE OF DDT: 1998–2001

This section examines how the meaning of DDT changed during the meetings of the Stockholm Convention (Chapter 3), which began in 1998. By this time, most countries had banned DDT and it had been identified as a particular type of toxic chemical – a POP. Its use was confined to a few developing countries for controlling mosquitoes that spread malaria. At the beginning of the negotiations, DDT was treated in the same way as all the other POPs – it was to be eliminated as one of the 'dirty dozen.' Yet, when the legal text was finally agreed, its use was allowed under certain conditions, unlike any of the other POPs. See Box 4.2 for a summary of the changes in DDT's meaning that occurred over the five meetings of the Convention's INC. To understand why the discourse changed and why DDT was singled out for special treatment, we decided to focus on the role of the different discursive spaces created by these meetings and the different narratives that actors told in them (Hardy and Maguire, 2010).

BOX 4.2   SUMMARY OF THE STOCKHOLM CONVENTION MEETINGS

INC-1: Montreal, Canada, June/July 1998	DDT was rarely mentioned except as one in the list of POPs. There was no discussion in plenary of DDT being a candidate for special treatment apart from one mention by the World Health Organization (WHO) which 'acknowledged the need to use DDT in particular cases' related to malaria. The World Wildlife Fund (WWF) proposed a target deadline of 2007 for the elimination of DDT. No malaria NGOs attended. *The meeting 'enjoyed a smooth and relatively trouble-free start. Delegates met with a clear spirit of cooperation, mutual purpose, shared responsibility and voiced their determination to tackle what is universally acknowledged as a very real and serious threat to human health and the environment [POPs]' (Earth Negotiations Bulletin,* 15(10), July 6, 1998: 2).
INC-2: Nairobi, Kenya, January 1999	DDT was rarely mentioned except as one of the chemicals on the list of POPs. There was no discussion of a special status for DDT apart from Physicians for Social Responsibility saying the phase-out of DDT should not compromise malaria control. No malaria NGOs attended. *The meeting was characterized by much cooperation and consensus: 'Overall, many delegates characterized INC-2 as a success' (Earth Negotiations Bulletin,* 15(18), February 1, 1998: 23).
INC-3: Geneva, Switzerland, September 1999	The possibility of exempting DDT in the case of malaria was specifically mentioned. Representatives of two malaria organizations attended, one of whom referred to an open letter in plenary that argued against the elimination of DDT. Environmental NGOs continued to argue for elimination but without a fixed timeline. WWF, which had proposed a 2007 global phase-out date for DDT, withdrew it in plenary. Developing countries were divided. *There was a lack of consensus concerning DDT: 'negotiations haven't really begun yet and the issues are still being framed' (Earth Negotiations Bulletin,* 15(27), September 14, 1999: 30).
INC-4: Bonn, Germany, March 2000	The lack of consensus endured. South Africa proposed placing DDT in Annex B (to be restricted) rather than Annex A (where it would be eliminated) but did not secure agreement. Environmental NGOs continued to advocate placing DDT in Annex A. *The legal text remained 'heavily bracketed and developed and developing country positions [were] deeply divided' (Earth Negotiations Bulletin,* 15(34), March 27, 2000: 1).

INC-5:	Environmental NGOs continued to advocate placing DDT in Annex A. South
Johannesburg, South	Africa and the EU proposed keeping DDT in Annex B but clarified that DDT
Africa, December	production and use would be eliminated by all states except those registering with
2000	the Convention Secretariat. This proposal was adopted in plenary.
	The legal text of the Convention was agreed, and DDT was the only chemical
	on the list of POPs scheduled for restriction (Annex B) rather than elimination
	(Annex A), permitting DDT's 'continued production and use subject to a number of
	constraints' (Earth Negotiations Bulletin, 15(54), December 12, 2000: 42).

Source: Adapted from Hardy and Maguire (2010: 1370).

Discursive Spaces at the Stockholm Convention

As already discussed in Chapter 3, the legal text of the Convention was negotiated over five meetings between June 1998 and December 2000 before being signed in Stockholm in 2001. These meetings created a temporary 'discursive space' (Hajer, 1995), which is 'a site of contestation in which competing interest groups seek to impose their definitions of what the main [problems] are and how they should be addressed' (Jacobs et al., 2003: 442). In fact, during the meetings, three interconnected discursive spaces formed, which we refer to as plenary, corridors, and media. Each was associated with different rules and understandings regarding appropriate forms of text production, distribution, and consumption (Box 4.3).[1]

BOX 4.3   SUMMARY OF DISCURSIVE SPACES

	Plenary	Corridor	Media
Description	The official plenary sessions of the meetings where the text is formally negotiated and agreed by state actors – government officials from different countries	The corridors surrounding the meetings, where the booths of various environmental and public health NGOs and other stakeholders are set up	The media coverage of the meetings by journalists attending the event who publish their observations of the proceedings as well commenting on official media statements and unofficial briefings

[1]   For a discussion of other discursive spaces at treaty negotiations, see Schüssler et al. (2014).

	Plenary	**Corridor**	**Media**
Rules and understandings regarding access to the discursive space and discursive activity in it	State delegates speak before NGOs, they can suggest amendments to the legal text, they do not reopen discussions on agreed text Accredited NGO representatives may speak after state actors, they can make statements but not suggest amendments to the legal text; they may not refer to state interventions positively or negatively, and they cannot distribute materials by placing them on seats; their privileges may be removed if they break these rules	Accredited NGOs can set up tables and kiosks to distribute materials; they can hand materials directly to and talk with delegates in the corridors	Press conferences are given by state delegations, NGOs, and UN agencies and are typically accompanied by written summaries NGOs often engage in media stunts that contain dramatic, emotional images
Text producers	State delegates and accredited NGOs	Mainly accredited NGO representatives	Diverse actors: state delegates, UN officials, state delegates, NGOs, as well as outsiders, such as journalists
Types of texts produced and distributed	Verbal interventions and conference room papers	Position papers, often with specific suggestions for the wording of the legal text, scientific reports, brochures and pamphlets, slide shows, advocacy videos, and informal conversations	Letters to editors, press releases, scientific journal articles, media reports, and websites
Text consumers	Plenary participants	State delegates and the media	The public, scientists, state delegates, and external policy makers

	Plenary	Corridor	Media
Main purpose of text production	To formally amend the evolving legal text	To inform and/or influence state delegates	To publicize positions; inform and/or mobilize actors beyond the meetings
Data sources	The legal text, conference room papers, *Earth Negotiations Bulletin* meeting reports, summary reports, interviewee accounts, observations of plenary sessions	Materials collected from information booths, observations of lobbying activities, the 'in the corridor' sections of *Earth Negotiations Bulletin* meeting reports, and interviewee accounts	Letters, press releases, media reports, and interviewee accounts

Source: Adapted from Hardy and Maguire (2010: 1373).

The identification of these discursive spaces helped us to identify the texts that we needed to collect. In addition to conducting 40 interviews, we collected official draft versions of the evolving legal text of the Convention; the conference room papers, which contained formal submissions proposing modifications to the evolving legal text; the daily meeting reports produced by the *Earth Negotiations Bulletin*;[2] and the closing summary report produced by the UN and agreed by state actors at the end of each meeting. We also collected materials distributed at the information booths set up in the corridors, as well as media texts such as letters to editors and media accounts.

Narratives of DDT

We then explored the narratives told in these discursive spaces over the period of negotiations. A narrative is a 'meaning structure that organizes events and human actions into a whole, thereby attributing significance to individual actions and events according to their effect on the whole' (Polkinghorne, 1988: 18). It consists of 'temporal chains of interrelated events or actions' (Gabriel, 2004: 63) that lead (or fail to lead) to some value-laden outcome (Cobb and Rifkin, 1991), in which various identities feature, such as heroes, villains, and victims (Zilber, 2007; Whittle et al., 2009). Actors draw on narratives 'to give

---

[2]   The *Earth Negotiations Bulletin* is published by the International Institute for Sustainable Development, Canada. It summarizes the previous day's proceedings – both formal and informal meetings – and lists the current day's events. It is considered to provide objective reports of UN negotiations.

meaning to specific physical or social phenomena' (Hajer, 1995: 56) and to infuse 'large amounts of factual information … with normative assumptions and value orientations' (Fischer, 2003: 87). Narratives help to make sense of and create legitimacy for certain individuals and activities (Colomy, 1998; Martens et al., 2007). They are performative (Gergen, 1994) and provide alternative visions of the future that help to bring about change (Fletcher et al., 2009).

We identified three different narratives of DDT (Box 4.4). The initial narrative *– DDT as Evil Threat –* was promoted prior to the first meeting primarily in NGO texts. It was embedded in texts from all three discursive spaces during the first two meetings insofar as the focus was on all POPs, with no mention of exempting DDT. Both the first two meetings were described as being marked by cooperation and consensus in relation to DDT and the other POPs, and 2007 was proposed by the World Wildlife Fund (WWF) as a target date for phasing out DDT.

BOX 4.4   SUMMARY OF NARRATIVES

DDT as evil threat (initial narrative, circa June 1998)	DDT as hero (counter-narrative, from 1999)	DDT as necessary evil (concluding narrative, December 2000)
Coherent identities constructed in the narrative		
POPs are the *evil threat*	Malaria is the *evil threat*	POPs are an *evil threat*; malaria is another *evil threat*
DDT is a POP and, therefore, an *evil threat*	DDT is the *hero* because it kills the mosquitos that spread malaria	DDT is a *necessary evil* because it kills the mosquitos that spread malaria
Women, children, and wildlife in all countries are the *victims*	African women and children are the *victims*	Women, children, and wildlife in all countries are *victims* of POPs;
	Environmental NGOs are *villains* because they want to eliminate DDT	African women and children are also *victims* of malaria
		WHO is a wise *sage* whose knowledge on appropriate DDT use will protect victims of both evil threats
Valued end point constructed in the narrative		
Elimination of POPs	Control of malaria	Elimination of POPs without compromising malaria control

Source: Adapted from Hardy and Maguire (2010: 1375).

A counter-narrative emerged around the time of the third meeting – *DDT as Hero*. It was promoted by two small malaria NGOs – Malaria Foundation International and the Malaria Project – neither of which had been represented at the first two meetings. The two organizations launched a high-profile campaign against the elimination of DDT in the media space. It included an open letter eventually signed by over 400 doctors and scientists that supported DDT for controlling malaria. The letter was written by the director of the Malaria Project, distributed through Malaria Foundation International's networks to malariologists, public health experts, and physicians, posted on a website and various list-servers, and mentioned in correspondence published in the *British Medical Journal* (Attaran and Maharaj, 2000). This counter-narrative eclipsed the initial narrative of DDT in the media space at the third meeting. It travelled to the remaining discursive spaces as the letter was distributed to delegates from developing countries, circulated in the corridors, and introduced into the plenary. This narrative introduced a different evil threat – malaria – which caused countless deaths and sickness, particularly among African women and children. DDT was a hero because it was the only effective defence against malaria, and it saved millions of lives. The valued end point was malaria control, which depended on access to DDT. The counter-narrative also introduced a new villain – environmental NGOs that valued the environment more than human health.

The counter-narrative was displaced by a third narrative during the final meeting. While not a hero, DDT was a *Necessary Evil*, whose use should be permitted under certain circumstances since both POPs and malaria were evil threats. The valued end point was still to protect human health and the environment by eliminating POPs, although not at the expense of malaria control. This narrative permeated the plenary of the final meeting, allowing for agreement on the wording, and was embedded in the legal text to allow exemptions for DDT in cases of malaria control, while the remaining POPs were to be eliminated. It created a new identity for the World Health Organization (WHO), which was given the responsibility of ensuring that DDT was used in accordance with guidelines and reviewing global DDT use every three years. WHO was now a wise sage with special knowledge about DDT that would help to achieve the valued end point of protecting victims from both malaria and POPs.

Narrative Effects

The counter-narrative had a significant effect by, first, undermining the consensus surrounding the elimination of DDT that had existed during the first two meetings and, second, providing the basis for the compromise narrative, which was embedded in the wording of the Convention. This legal text created new rules for POPs and for DDT. The counter-narrative also changed the meaning of DDT from evil threat to hero and, although the final narrative altered it again – to a necessary evil – it was enough to exempt DDT from an outright ban (Box 4.5).

The counter-narrative also had a significant impact on some of the organizations that had been involved, especially the environmental NGOs now cast as villains. Interestingly, these organizations consumed the counter-narrative in different ways. WWF interpreted it as a threat and started to withdraw from the debate about DDT. It had devoted considerable resources to developing specialist knowledge on DDT's adverse effects, but after the third meeting, it started to focus on other POPs. Its earlier publications had highlighted the threats posed by DDT to human health and the environment, but later reports downplayed them. WWF also withdrew its proposed date for elimination. Despite having played a central role in championing DDT's phase-out and being a founder member of IPEN, it retreated to a more peripheral position in the field.

BOX 4.5   NARRATIVE EFFECTS

	Before Stockholm	After Stockholm
Rules	No global regulations exist restricting POPs, including DDT	Global regulations address POPs: all are to be eliminated except DDT, whose use is allowed under certain restrictions
Meanings	DDT is understood to be one of the 'dirty dozen'	DDT is understood to be an 'exceptional' POP
	Environmental and chemical safety expertise is understood to be relevant to POPs	Disease control is also understood to be relevant to POPs
Positions in the field	Malaria organizations do not participate in first two meetings	Malaria organization participate from the third meeting
	WHO is present but its role is ambiguous	WHO becomes more central; it has a clear and formally mandated role in the implementation of the Convention
	IPEN is recently founded, largely North American-based and has no particular expertise on DDT	IPEN is well established with more members, including from Africa; it has developed expertise on DDT
	WWF has a central role: it helps found IPEN, has expertise on DDT, and proposes 2007 as a phase-out date	WWF no longer occupies a leadership role on DDT; it has withdrawn its proposed phase-out date

Source: Adapted from Hardy and Maguire (2010: 1381).

IPEN was also vulnerable to the counter-narrative. It was a network of 58 environmental and public health NGOs, launched prior to the first meeting to lobby for the elimination of all POPs, including DDT. However, instead of withdrawing, IPEN used the counter-narrative as an opportunity to reposition itself as an expert on DDT. Its original manifesto, which had not suggested exempting DDT from restrictions, was complemented at later meetings with texts acknowledging that it warranted special treatment and should only be phased out gradually as alternatives became more available and affordable. IPEN distanced itself from WWF despite being one of its founders. Whereas IPEN had designated WWF as the only contact point for DDT during the first two meetings, it listed other member organizations for the last two meetings. IPEN also began to build relations with African countries and actively recruited African-based NGOs as members – only one of IPEN's original member organizations was African, whereas 34 had joined by 2000.

WHO interpreted the counter-narrative as an opportunity. It moved responsibility for DDT from departments concerned with chemical safety and environmental health to a dedicated malaria unit. It sent malaria experts to the final two meetings, instead of environmental health representatives as at the first three meetings. Having issued no press releases during the first two meetings, at the third meeting it issued a press note arguing for a 'balanced' position on DDT. It distributed a pamphlet detailing this balanced approach, together with a glossy information pack reiterating WHO's support for the special treatment of DDT at the last two meetings. It was rewarded by being made responsible for overseeing the use of DDT and became a central player in the Convention.

In sum, the study of the Stockholm Convention shows how the discourse about DDT changed – no longer one of the dirty dozen, it was now an 'exceptional' POP. This change did not happen simply because actors authored texts that told stories, but because these stories permeated the different discursive spaces. The counter-narrative influenced the legal text, despite not being embedded in it. It also influenced the relative positions of organizations in the field. However, we see the significance and variability of consumption – WWF, IPEN, and WHO consumed the counter-narrative in different ways, becoming more or less central as a result.

CONCLUSION

This chapter shows how a discursive approach can provide insight into the complexity and nuances of discursive change. The links between discursive manoeuvring and practical or political outcomes are not straightforward. As Foucault said: 'People know what they do; they frequently know why they do what they do; but what they don't know is what what they do does' (Foucault, 1982: 187). The example of *Silent Spring* shows that, regardless of how convincing a text is, its author cannot control whether and how it will be taken up in other texts. In the case of the Stockholm Convention, we see the influence of the counter-narrative promulgated by two small, apparently powerless malaria organizations on the legal text, but we also see how its impact on other NGOs depended very much on how those organizations consumed it. So, while we see evidence of agency, we also see serendipity and the accumulation of countless discrete actions in a variable and volatile process of discursive change.

BOX 4.6   EMPIRICAL POINTERS

- Some discursive spaces are replete with naturally occurring talk and text, as in the case of the Stockholm Convention. The fact that the Convention meetings brought a wide variety of different actors together in a single place also made it easy to arrange interviews.
- Collecting and analyzing texts is a customized process for researchers using a discursive approach. It takes a mixture of detective work and creativity. For example, tracking down all the PhD and academic articles on DDT relied on systematic data searches, while the letters written by the public were accessed from secondary sources.
- Researchers should select texts strategically. For example, in the original article on *Silent Spring* (Maguire and Hardy, 2009), we selected a second textbook on applied entomology, which might be expected to be more favourable towards DDT. Since it showed the same pattern as the ecology textbook, it reinforced our findings.
- Texts can be collected in different times and places. Having texts where we could trace meanings over time was important in both these studies, while the analysis of the Stockholm Convention showed that different discursive spaces (which existed only temporarily) are also important.
- Conducting research that explores how a text engages with wider collections of texts, rather than simply studying the meaning of a single text, often provides greater insight.
- Conducting research that explores how a text is consumed also provides greater insight. You can learn more about consumption in Chapter 9.
- A discursive approach often means collecting a lot of different texts. If you do, be sure to explain why you selected the ones that you did – for example, how they represent a corpus of texts.
- If you do collect diverse texts, explain how they are all used in your analysis – there is little point in collecting a wide range of texts if you only rely on a small subset of them.

PART II

Levels and issues

The second part of the book explores how discourse analysis can be used to study organizations at different 'levels' of analysis. Multi-level aspects of discourse were presaged in distinctions between 'little d' discourse and 'big D' Discourse, first made by Gee (1999) when he described the former as language in use and the latter as the set of social practices which is reinforced (or undermined) by the use of language (Nickerson and Goby, 2018). Alvesson and Kärreman (2000) used the same terminology to associate discourse with studies of language in context and the Discourse with Foucauldian understandings of bodies of knowledge and power/knowledge relations (Kärreman, 2014). Similarly, Fairhurst and Putnam (2019) suggest that Discourse forms linguistic and behavioural repertoires, while discourse refers to their inner workings as people use talk to position themselves and others in localized interactions.

Some scholars, however, have argued that the distinction between big D Discourse and little d discourse is an artificial construction (Mumby, 2011). The previous chapters in this book have already shown how discourse is woven through multiple levels. Take, for example, the discourse of risk. It circulates at the 'macro' level through standardized practices that are carried out by medical and epidemiological experts around the world based on widely shared agreement about how to measure health risks, as in the case of Covid-19. However, the local discourse of experts, media, and politicians, which varies widely country to country and even state to state, constructs very different meanings for those risks. Consequently, 'micro'-level practices can vary enormously, with some jurisdictions going into lockdown after only a handful of cases, while others open up despite large numbers.

I therefore use the term 'level' advisedly – acknowledging that it is a useful heuristic, but not ignoring its limitations. So, while Part II is divided into chapters focusing on the individual, the organizational, and the interorganizational, I also draw attention to how micro dynamics and the broader discursive landscape permeate each other. The chapters in this part also show how a discursive approach can shed light on a wide range of organizational and societal issues. The issues discussed here range from the plight of the older worker facing unemployment, challenges facing refugees seeking asylum, collaboration among community and industry in the case of HIV/AIDS, and securing agreement from employees on organizational change initiatives.

5. Using a discursive approach to study individual identities

The growth of studies using a discursive approach to investigate organizations has been accompanied by an interest in new conceptions of individual identity (Ybema et al., 2009). Postmodern writers such as Foucault challenged the idea of a stable, unitary, essential subject. Instead of an individual 'having' an identity, individuals draw on and are influenced by the discourses in which they are situated as they construct their identity (Thomas and Davies, 2005). An individual's identity is 'an intersubjectively reached agreement that is historically and culturally negotiated … [and] subject to constant renegotiation' (Bamberg et al., 2011: 178). The 'decentred' subject is 'a contingent historical possibility rather than a universal or essential truth about human nature' (Heyes, 2014: 159). Discourse thus plays an important role in the processes that go into 'making up' people by bringing into being certain categories of identity and particular ways for people to 'be' (Hacking, 1986).

To accomplish an identity, individuals engage in 'identity work' as they perform their identities. This is a complex process. It inevitably involves a form of audience participation (Garcia and Hardy, 2007), where audience members may regulate the identity work or even reject it altogether (Czarniawska, 1997; Alvesson and Willmott, 2002). Further, identity work does not only construct the 'Self,' it also constructs various 'Others' as individuals articulate their similarity to – and differences from – other identities. How we come to understand who we are 'is intimately connected to notions of who we are not and, by implication, who others are' (Ybema et al., 2009: 306). Finally, identity work inevitably involves materiality and embodiment – not only speaking the part, but also looking and acting the part.

Identity work takes place in a particular discursive landscape. By specifying certain subject positions or categories of identity that have meaning and warrant voice in a particular context, prevailing discourses can provide resources that help individuals to enact their identity (Potter and Wetherell, 1987). Accordingly, individuals may try to position themselves in the discourse so that they secure 'rights' to speak and act (Davies and Harré, 1990). In this regard, discourse is productive insofar as it helps create an identity, as well as the individual's subjectivity or experience of 'being' that identity (Heyes, 2014). But discourse also constrains individuals (Hoffman, 2014).

Not all individuals can successfully perform an identity and not all identities can be made to conform to the available subject positions. Only certain subject positions make sense within a discourse and not all subject positions have rights to speak. The self as subject – someone who acts – is also an object – someone who is acted *upon*. This objectification occurs as knowledge is developed about the subject and then used to categorize them and treat them in a particular way. Rather than autonomous subjects wielding discourse to their personal advantage, discourse produces power/knowledge relations within which identities are constructed, subjects are positioned, and bodies are disciplined. Accordingly, a discursive approach requires researchers to focus less on 'analyzing the relations between the author and what he says (or wanted to say or said without wanting to); but in determining what position can and must be occupied by any individual if he [*sic*] is to be the subject of it' (Foucault, 1972: 95–96).

To explore how a discursive approach sheds light on the construction of individual identities, I revisit a series of studies of a 1999 Australian parliamentary inquiry into the challenges facing unemployed workers over 45 years of age (Ainsworth and Hardy, 2007, 2008, 2009, 2012). Public inquiries provide a wellspring of publicly available texts. In this case, they included nearly 200 written submissions, over 1,000 pages of Hansard transcripts from 20 public hearings held in different parts of the country, as well as the final 200-page report. These texts are authored by different actors – the inquiry's committee, which consisted of 12 members of parliament, as well as older workers, service providers (job placement agencies), employer groups and academic experts – all of whom made submissions and/or appeared as witnesses at the hearings. The availability of these different texts enabled us to use a discursive approach to examine facets of the older work identity: who could be one; how they were expected to speak; and what they were allowed to do.

WHO CAN BE AN OLDER WORKER? THE DISAPPEARANCE OF THE FLEXIBLE FEMALE

In this study (Ainsworth and Hardy, 2007), we examined which identities could occupy the subject position of older worker. We started by identifying four different versions of the older (unemployed) worker identity – two male and two female – from texts produced early in the inquiry (Box 5.1). We then analyzed texts produced at the end of the inquiry to find that the two female versions had disappeared, leaving a predominantly masculinized view of the older worker in the final report. We conducted further analysis to try to resolve the mystery of the disappearing females. The hidden, unemployed female was easily written out – there was no government definition of hidden unemployment and, therefore, no statistical evidence to support her existence or make a case for support. She was a 'non-worker' and outside the scope of the inquiry. The hidden unemployed female remained hidden – unknown and unknowable, she was not considered to be a suitable object of inquiry.

BOX 5.1   VERSIONS OF THE OLDER WORKER IN EARLY TEXTS

The white-collar male: An educated former middle manager or profession-al made redundant from long-term career and 'overqualified' for available jobs.

The blue-collar male worker: A skilled or semi-skilled worker with non-transferable skills in a declining industry, previously the male bread-winner but now unemployed having been retrenched from a long-term oc-cupation and/or living in an economically depressed region.

The flexible female: Employed in low-paid, casual, and part-time jobs in the expanding service sector, with a discontinuous work history mainly due to family responsibilities. She typically had low levels of formal education, was classed as unskilled, and in a precarious financial position.

The hidden unemployed female: Seeking work and/or attempting career re-entry or occupational change following a discontinuous work history due to family responsibilities and periods of unemployment.

The disappearance of the flexible female was more complex. It resulted from a range of factors. One reason stemmed from the way in which her flexibility was turned into advantage. Box 5.2 shows an exchange between a female committee member and a male witness who worked for a service provider. Both parties make repeated use of words and phrases such as 'flexible,' 'much more flexible,' 'adapt more quickly,' and 'move around a bit more' in relation to women. This flexibility is then portrayed as an advantage unavailable to older men who are 'locked in' to 'set types of careers.' Men's intransigence and unwillingness to accept low-status jobs meant they were in a more difficult position in finding employment compared to women, who were willing to take jobs that men would not. In this way, the flexible female's more marginal workforce attachment, lower expectations, and concentration in low-paid, low-skill contingent work paradoxically became a signifier of relative privi-lege and success and, therefore, they did not need the support that men did. Older unemployed women were also portrayed as being advantaged because of their ability to hide periods of earlier unemployment: they could attribute it to

BOX 5.2 IT'S EASIER BEING A WOMAN

Committee member: I now want to talk to you about flexible attitudes to work, and part-time work versus casual work. Do you have any information that shows whether or not women are much more flexible than men when it comes to the prospects of working on a part-time or casual basis? Are women like that because they have gone through a life-cycle curve where they have had a full-time job, had a family, then had to go back into the work force and so are more psychologically suited to part-time or casual work? Could you shed some light on that?

Witness: I have certainly found that women are more flexible. They tend to adapt more quickly than men do, particularly men who have been in jobs where it has been a traditional male situation, where they have all worked in the same industry over the years. They expect to stay there and expect their kids to go into that industry. I do not know the entire reason but the things you have suggested are certainly part of the reason. Perhaps it is because women are naturally more intuitive and mentally able to move around a bit more.

Committee member: I am not a psychologist but is it because women are able to be more flexible in the choice of work they do, as you have said? Or is it a lifestyle thing? Is it because women are used to doing part-time work?

Witness: I do not think they have been stuck in as many stereotypes. That sounds odd because being in the kitchen is a bit of a stereotype, but when women have wanted to go out to work, as they have done increasingly in recent times … The whole notion of a career for life is not always locked in as much with women.

Source: Public hearing, Perth.

taking time out of the workforce voluntarily to take up caring responsibilities. Since older men could not – or would not – do this, older women enjoyed greater freedom in crafting a work biography that would help in finding work. Box 5.3 shows an exchange between a female committee member and a male unemployed worker that recasts family and childcare responsibilities that take women out of the workforce as an advantage when it comes to returning to it.

BOX 5.3 MIND THE GAP

Committee member: You have described your resume as being very extensive. I have worked in the personnel industry as well and I have had people tell me that they have omitted the fact that they were a manager of a company and left out a few key threatening positions.

Witness: They got the job?

Committee member: They were able to obtain work. Have you ever tried that?

Witness: Yes, I have tried that as well ... targeted CVs. One of the problems with targeted CVs is that it means there is a big gap, 10 years in this guy's life [if they are out of work], that is not explained.

Committee member: Women can attribute that to childbirth or something, yes. So, you have done that and people say to you. 'Well, why is there a gap here?' I can understand that.

Source: Public hearing, Perth.

Finally, older male workers were deemed to be in more need of support than women because of the traditional association between men and careers. Unemployment was seen as harder for men because paid work was more important to their identity (Box 5.4). A common view expressed during the inquiry was that unemployment erased or reversed previous accomplishments that provided the basis of male self-esteem and, therefore, had a greater effect on men than on older women. This understanding was articulated by both men and women in submissions and witness statements, and it featured heavily in the final report. It led to the conclusion that unemployment inflicted more damage on men and could even lead to wider societal problems, such as violence and mental health problems. Accordingly, the final report stressed the importance of supporting older males, rather than older females.

BOX 5.4   IT'S HARDER FOR MEN

Submission from an older men's discussion group: Mature male unemployment is a more life-threatening condition than mature female unemployment ... Mature male unemployment exposes the marginal emotional dignity which is afforded males in contemporary society. Employment is the last raison d'être for the vast majority of men. It is the crucial focus for male energy, mateship, and self-esteem. Male unemployment at any age is bad. At a mature age premature male unemployment is a sentence of mind, body, and spirit.

Submission from a male unemployed worker: If the head of the family, no longer in gainful employment, suffers from low self-esteem as a consequence and feels that he is left on the scrap heap ... then the whole family suffers and falls apart. His children refuse to listen to him, in fact his whole character changes, as it did in my case, and this often leads marriages to break down.

Male unemployed worker at public hearing: The first three months after losing a job or being made redundant are critical because that is when you need the help, not after you have been out of work for six months or 12 months. This is particularly so for an older worker, and again I will say particularly a male, because I think men are very much shaped by how they see themselves as a contributing member of a paid work force, and women perhaps less so.

> *Female employee of service provider at public hearing:* Along with the self-esteem and grief, the implications for the family, is the dilemma that – and I am talking about the male again, but that is our experience mostly with the male white-collar workers – there can be a really long period of time where they are so angry or they are still in that stage of disbelief.
>
> *Final report:* Australians define themselves through their work. Work provides a sense of identity and a feeling of self-esteem. Many mature-age men, in particular, have a traditional attitude toward work as the 'primary definer of self' … the last 'raison d'être' for the vast majority of men and that sustained mature-age unemployment can create tension in society leading to self-abuse, violence, and crime (House of Representatives, 2000: 56).

In sum, the use of a discursive approach helps to account for the disappearance of female versions of the older worker – in the final report it was older men who were the most disadvantaged and who needed the most support. 'More older males are opting out of the labour market, partly because structural change has made it difficult for them to retain employment or find new work after loss. In contrast, older women have become more active in the labour market as family structures and social attitudes to female employment have changed' (House of Representatives, 2000: 19). The discursive manoeuvres discussed above were not necessarily deliberate, but they were significant. They constructed the older worker in a clearly gendered form, stressing the greater importance of work-based identity for men, reinforcing traditional gender stereotypes, and resulting in recommendations that were likely to rob older women of much needed support in finding work. The fact that it occurred unconsciously through a myriad of individual micro interactions during the inquiry shows the deeply rooted nature of gender stereotypes.

SPEAKING AS AN OLDER WORKER

In this section, I revisit two studies (Ainsworth and Hardy, 2009, 2012) to examine how older workers were expected to present themselves – or perform – during the inquiry. On the face of it, appearing as an older worker in a public inquiry about older workers would seem to involve having rights to speak. This does not, however, necessarily mean that the older worker is a powerful subject position. Accordingly, we used a discursive approach to examine whether and how older workers were able to speak.

Tell Me a Story

Many older workers who had been affected by unemployment wanted to tell their story in their submissions and during the hearings. These stories were also a useful resource for committee members, allowing them to demonstrate that they had direct contact with the subjects of their investigation and humanizing the inquiry. To ensure that older workers did, indeed, tell their story in the hearings, the Chair would typically ask them to 'tell us your story' or 'share your experiences.' In contrast, other witnesses such as experts or representatives of service providers were usually asked to give an 'overview' or 'précis' of their submission. Individuals who resisted providing personalized accounts in favour of more fundamental critiques of the labour market met with limited success.

Box 5.5 shows that when an older, unemployed male identified four fundamental causes of discrimination backed up by extensive research, the Chair immediately redirected attention to the importance of grief counseling as a response to job loss, invoking a more personal reaction on the part of the witness. In another example, when a witness presented a proposal to restructure the current 'work for the dole' scheme, the Chair pointedly said: 'Can you just tell us what sorts of experiences you have had going through your period of unemployment?' The witness complied, and the rest of his appearance was devoted to telling his personal story, rather than referring to the material he had tried to present earlier. Another older worker, who tried to critique social, cultural, and political structures, was immediately asked for her 'personal' thoughts about unemployment (Ainsworth and Hardy, 2009: 1220–1222).

BOX 5.5   HOW DO YOU FEEL?

Witness (an older worker): I would like to draw your attention to four issues which, from my point of view, need to be addressed seriously by the committee. The first issue is the issue of discrimination against the older unemployed. May I recommend to the committee the paper entitled 'Age matters'? Discussion paper on age discrimination by the Human Rights and Equal Opportunity Commission. You have probably run across that ... The second issue is the necessity of involvement of the unemployed in future decision-making processes affecting the unemployed ... My question is: when are you as a government going to ask us as unemployed people for answers ... We have examples in the world, particularly in Ireland, of the unemployed successfully working with the government and with industry in the national economic and social forums ... The third issue is the issue of the value of working for the dole and volunteering for the older unemployed ... I feel that volunteering is an expensive waste of time for the older employed, except that it gives you this good feeling inside of partially fulfilling the work ethic. Otherwise, it is a waste of time for unemployed older people ... The fourth issue is a delicate one, and you will excuse me for raising it but I think that it needs to be addressed on behalf of all the unemployed. I am referring to derogatory remarks made by your parliamentary colleague[s] ... Perhaps, as a committee, you could reflect on that.

Chair: Thank you very much, Mr Dyke. I am a member of the government and ... I have the greatest sympathy for what you have just said, I can assure you. I will not pretend to speak for my government colleagues here. Can I just ask you about grief counseling.

Witness: I speak just from my personal situation. When you are thrown out of work – and I was 48 1/2 at the time and going quite nicely in a stream which I thought would last for quite a few years – it is a totally life-changing situation. It is very much like the grieving process where you go through stages of non-acceptance, anger, and then at last you sort of start to come to grips with it.

We also found that the committee expected a certain kind of story – one that conformed to typical age stereotypes and presented older workers as helpless victims of job loss. Some older workers appearing at the hearings wanted to challenge these stereotypes. They would talk about their experience and expertise, as well as the jobs for which they had applied to show how proactive they had been. In this way, they demonstrated their identity as members of the labour force – older *workers* who were self-reliant in dealing with job loss and securing new employment. They often rejected the idea of volunteering as a way of finding employment on the grounds that they already had a lot of work experience – they needed paid work, not unpaid experience. Committee members challenged such views (Box 5.6) and the final report strongly encouraged volunteering as a route out of unemployment (Ainsworth and Hardy, 2009: 2018–2019).

BOX 5.6   WHO'S GOING TO VOLUNTEER?

Chair: With respect to volunteering, have you been engaged in volunteer activity over the last three years?

Witness (older worker): No, I have not.

Chair: Is that not something that you really want to do, or is there no opportunity to do so?

Witness: I feel that it is possibly a time fill-in.

Chair: That it fills in time rather than anything else?

Witness: Yes ...

> *Chair:* I have actually given jobs to people over the years because of their volunteer work. For what it is worth, there are some people who look at that and say, 'Two days a week doing this; tell us about it.'
>
> *Committee member:* I have had someone in my office for the last six months working as a volunteer because she wants to get back into the work force. I would not undersell the concept of volunteerism, Mr Clark. It is not from a time point of view, and I am not saying that you are in this situation, but for someone who has been unemployed for a long period of time – two, three, or four years; whatever it may be – the biggest danger is going to be a lack of self-esteem and self-worth. If you are in an activity where you are out there making a contribution, be it in a volunteer capacity, that tends to help, at least in terms of your own psychological well-being, so that when you do front up to that interview eventually, you are coming across as a positive individual and you can point to the fact that you are making a contribution through giving your own time. So that is how I look at volunteerism; not from a point of view of, 'Let's do it because I've got nothing else to do; it takes me out of the home and I don't have to watch Days of Our Lives.' It is more about personal well-being.
>
> *Witness:* Yes, I understand that.

Even when older workers told the right kind of stories, many did not survive the inquiry process. We identified 62 stories told by older workers in the submissions and 92 in the hearings. The final report contained only five partial stories (excerpts from longer narratives told in the public hearings), with another six references to stories (where the report noted that a story had been told but did not retell it).

Give Me a Number

Once a story was told, it became the property of committee members who, in their retelling of it, could change its meaning. Box 5.7 shows an example of the use of numbers in a story told by an older worker. As the story was retold by committee members, both the numbers and the meaning of the story changed. It no longer belonged to the older worker and no longer was a story of self-reliance in job-seeking. It now belonged to committee members and was a story of incompetence – by sending off lots of untargeted applications, the older unemployed were applying for the wrong jobs (Ainsworth and Hardy, 2012: 1707).

BOX 5.7 IT'S ALL IN THE NUMBERS

At one hearing, an individual stated that he had applied for 250 jobs. At a subsequent hearing when the story was retold by a committee member, this number changed to 700 – a number not mentioned by any of the previous witnesses – as shown here.

> *Committee member:* Last week in Melbourne we heard evidence from some very long-term unemployed people. Their stories, I guess, were typical of most long-term unemployed: 700 applications, those sorts of things; 140 interviews … (Public hearing, 16 September 1999)

The inflated number formed the basis of a change in the meaning. The original number of applications (250) was used to emphasize that the witness had been proactive in applying for jobs related to his particular expertise. As the story was retold by different committee members in two separate hearings, it took on a very different meaning: the larger number of applications (700) was used to convey incompetence on the part of older workers who failed to target their job-seeking activities effectively.

> *Committee member:* We have had a lot of submissions where people have said, 'I have sent away 700 applications and the decent ones have replied and then there are a whole lot of others who do not even bother to reply' … What can we do to make sure that people do target according to their skills rather than just sending out blanket applications? (Public hearing, 23 September 1999)

This meaning was reproduced as the story was told again during a third hearing, where it was taken up by a service provider, who also used it to signal evidence of incompetence in job-seeking activities on the part of older workers.

> *Committee member:* We have had a number of people come to us who have sent out 500 to 700 resumes … This is just a thought, but perhaps a lot of the jobs they are applying for are not within their area of expertise.

> *Service Provider:* Yes. People have this idea that as long as they are doing something – sending out resumes – they are helping themselves. But, if the resumes are not targeted to that job, the effort could be quite nugatory. (Public hearing, 27 October 1999)

Numbers told by older workers were treated differently to numbers told by actors constructed as experts. These numbers, especially in the form of statistics, were faithfully reproduced. Even statistics that were simplified during the hearings (when statistical information from dense reports in the submissions was presented in simple, 'user-friendly' ways in verbal interactions), their presentation in the final report typically conformed to the original submission. Not only were the specific numbers reproduced from the original submission, so, too, was the meaning of those numbers – they were used to make virtually the same argument in the final report as the original submission. Even when statistics were challenged, the original numbers and the original meaning were reproduced before being disputed (see Ainsworth and Hardy, 2012). The conventions associated with statistical information differed from those associated with personal narratives – the provenance of the former was protected even when contested, while the latter could be appropriated with impunity.

In sum, older workers did have some rights to speak during the inquiry but only if they said the 'right' thing. Theoretically, the inquiry afforded them an opportunity to educate committee members but, in practice, their stories often served as a resource for the committee. They humanized the inquiry and, in some cases, were used to demonstrate arguments that had little to do with the original story. In being allowed to speak, older workers were required to perform an identity chosen for them – primarily one of a victim who was willing to share experiences, volunteer for unpaid work, and admit to job-seeking incompetence.

WHAT SHOULD AN OLDER WORKER (NOT) DO?

The inquiry examined small business ownership as a prospective way out of unemployment for older workers. In this regard, it was permeated by the discourse of enterprise, which promotes competition, decentralizes authority, and privileges the market, thereby supposedly enhancing productivity, quality, and innovation. Enterprise minimizes state intervention and maximizes individual freedom and choice – so long as individuals exercise these privileges in appropriate ways. Enterprise discourse thus prescribes an ideal identity, that of the 'enterprise self,' where individuals become 'entrepreneurs of themselves, shaping their own lives through the choices they make' (Rose, 1989: 226). The discourse of enterprise thus regulates individuals as much as it enables them – by constructing compliant subjects who take responsibility for their own misfortunes (du Gay, 1996).

The enterprising self is presented as accessible to all. Even those stricken with homelessness, joblessness, or other disadvantages can – so proponents argue – escape their predicament if they are willing to remake themselves (Rose, 1989). We were interested to see if this was the case with older workers. Age is a dominant discourse, informing both material and discursive practices in contemporary society – often in a highly constraining way. Old age is typically subjected to the ubiquitous narrative of decline (Gullette, 1997; Trethewey, 2001) as society wrestles with the 'problems' of aging populations

(Ainsworth and Hardy, 2007). 'Successful' aging typically involves removing any bodily markers of it, thereby reinforcing the cultural repression of unattractive, aging bodies (Andrews, 1999). 'There are parallels between age and other body-based systems of social categorization, such as gender or ethnicity, but ageism is different in that hostility is directed against a future self, not a clearly differentiated "other"' (Ainsworth and Hardy, 2004: 232). Given the constraining nature of the discourse of aging, we wanted to explore how the discourses of enterprise and age intersected and whether the entrepreneurial self was accessible to older workers (Ainsworth and Hardy, 2008).

The first stage of our analysis was designed to 'unpack' the discourse of enterprise. We identified four constituent components: commodification, marketing, consumption, and risk. Box 5.8 shows how we inferred these elements from the data, as well as the implications when they intersected with age. We then explored two constructions of the older worker identity that arose from these intersections – 'unattractive products' and 'risky projects.'

BOX 5.8   UNPACKING THE DISCOURSE OF ENTERPRISE

Components of enterprise discourse	How coded from inquiry texts	Implications for older worker identity when enterprise intersects with age	Other implications when enterprise intersects with age
Commodification	References to appearance, products, self-presentation	Older workers are 'unattractive products'	Older workers are held accountable for not self-commodifying, despite the difficulty of hiding age-related markers
Marketing	References to marketing, advertising, promotion (including self-promotion), selling	Older workers do not know how to sell themselves in the job market	Because they are unattractive products, older workers need extra marketing by job-finding agencies
Consumption	References to consumers, individual choice between products and services, purchasing decisions	Older workers make bad consumer decisions such as buying small businesses on impulse	Employers are consumers in the job market; they have the right to choose between products; it is reasonable for them to discriminate on the basis of age

Components of enterprise discourse	How coded from inquiry texts	Implications for older worker identity when enterprise intersects with age	Other implications when enterprise intersects with age
Risk	References to the future, calculating possible consequences of decisions, safety and security, responsible decision making	Older workers as entrepreneurs are 'a risky project': they want too much safety and security and they take irresponsible risks	Small business is not a suitable job for older workers

Source: Adapted from Ainsworth and Hardy (2008: 395).

Unattractive Products

Commodification and marketing linked the discourse of enterprise to the physical aspects of age, constructing the older worker as an unattractive product for prospective employers. Representatives of service providers emphasized that it was harder to place older workers because employers wanted younger faces that would associate the organization with dynamism and change. Service providers could help older workers, but success ultimately depended on them taking responsibility for presenting themselves as youthful. Older workers who failed to attend to their appearance were at fault – having an old face or grey hair or dressing in an old-fashioned way decreased their prospective value in the labour market. As one member of a job placement agency stated in a public hearing: 'I have got really good at dealing with men who have got out-of-date hairstyles … The ladies wearing the wrong colours, wearing navy stockings with suits or whatever is not currently fashionable or wearing the wrong colour lipstick have to adjust.'

Making older workers responsible for their reinvention as younger selves and criticizing their inability to do so had two broader implications. First, it portrayed employers as consumers with the right to free choice in the labour market even if it included discriminating against older workers in favour of younger ones, thereby justifying employer prejudice against older workers. Second, to be marketed effectively, older workers – as unattractive products – needed the help of service providers which, in turn, legitimated the latter's existence (and requests for funding). It also excused any failure on their part to place older workers, given the additional challenges that were involved.

Risky Projects

The intersection of enterprise and age also constructed the older worker as a risky project in the event of using small business ownership as a way out of unemployment. A series of discursive moves (Box 5.9) served to achieve a representation of older workers as unsuccessful entrepreneurs who should be discouraged from attempting small business ownership, even though the inquiry generally promoted it consistent with the idea of the enterprising self. The result of these discursive moves was that older workers were deemed unlikely to succeed as entrepreneurs because they did not have the necessary characteristics, which were exclusive to youth. They were also too risk averse to engage in the 'proper' form of entrepreneurship – starting a business. Instead, they were more likely to 'buy themselves a job' by investing in an existing business. But even when taking this less risky path, they did so in a risky manner – by 'gambling away' large amounts of money (such as redundancy pay). As a result, older workers were in an untenable position – both too risky and too risk adverse. They therefore had to be *discouraged* from being entrepreneurial – the supposedly accessible enterprising self was clearly not available to them.

BOX 5.9 RISKY BUSINESS

Entrepreneurship and Youth

- Entrepreneurship – small business ownership – was a potential means of economic regeneration and upward mobility for disadvantaged groups excluded from mainstream employment.
- Accounts of small business success and failure were couched in psychological terms – as the result of personality traits rather than wider economic structures.
- Successful small business ownership was associated with the willingness to innovate, energy, and optimism – personal attributes associated with youth.
- Older workers did not have these characteristics and, therefore, were more likely to fail as entrepreneurs.

Entrepreneurship and Risk

- The entrepreneurial identity was split into two subidentities – those who started new businesses and those who bought established businesses.

- The former were 'proper' entrepreneurs, while those who bought an established business were inferior.
- Older workers were associated with the less attractive version – they were more likely to purchase an existing business.
- Purchasing an existing business was the less risky option compared to small business start-ups but, when older workers purchased an existing business, they did so in a risky way by 'gambling' their redundancy money.

CONCLUSION

Using a discursive approach to study individual identities in the case of the older worker allows us to see how identities are constructed through micro interactions among actors and audiences. We see the situated identity work by older workers during the inquiry, as well as identity regulation by committee members. We also discover what happens when the discourse of age intersects with another discourse, such as enterprise. We see how gender and age stereotypes are reinforced through the way they are embedded in accumulations of 'accidental' utterances – a series of incremental, largely uncoordinated discursive manoeuvres rather than a grand conspiracy. This is not to say that these utterances are irrelevant – they can have significant policy implications.

BOX 5.10 EMPIRICAL POINTERS

- We can see the opportunities offered by public inquiries for studies using a discursive approach in that they typically involve a collection of texts (submissions, transcripts of hearings, and a report) authored by different actors at different points in time – allowing researchers to view interactions and identity work in action (albeit as captured in texts) and to compare changes in meaning over time.
- There have been a lot of studies of inquiries, but they often focus on the final report, whereas their full potential as research settings can be leveraged by tracing and analyzing connections between multiple texts over time and with reference to different authors/actors.
- Many public inquiries are now streamed, providing researchers with the opportunity to use observations to gather data related to embodiment, further increasing our insights into situated identity work.

- There is also an opportunity for researchers to follow up with 'outcome measures' in the case of public inquiries – to study the recommendations that are implemented and how they are implemented.
- Much of the analysis in these studies can be described as 'finely grained,' such as systematically comparing how the committee chair invited different types of witnesses to start their presentation at hearings or tracing the mention of numbers over time across multiple hearings and submissions.
- There are many resources regarding this type of analysis, including argumentation strategies (Wodak, 1996), topic choice (Pomerantz and Fehr, 1997), word choice (Fowler, 1991, 1996), functional grammar (Halliday and Matthiessen, 2004), and the tenor of texts (Paltridge, 2000).
- The micro level of analysis does not preclude examining how individual utterances are related to and informed by grand discourses as in the case of the discourses of age and enterprise in these studies.
- Discourse analysis can be enhanced by 'unpacking' a discourse to identify its constituent components (as in the case of enterprise) and then by engaging in an interdiscursive analysis, in this case by investigating how age and enterprise intersect.

6. Using a discursive approach to study organizational identities

This chapter examines organizational identities.[1] If we accept the discursive construction of individual identity, we must also accept that organizational identity is established in similar ways (Leclercq-Vandelannoitte, 2011; Taylor, 2011). Organizational identities 'are not socially predetermined but, like individual identities, are constituted through discourse and are fragmented and contingent' (Tregidga et al., 2014). The precarious identities of both the organization and its members are continually 'authored' in an interactive, iterative fashion as meanings are negotiated among internal and external actors (Schoeneborn et al., 2019). Through language and materiality, the organization is made real, emerging as a distinguishable actor: 'It now exists in the world, materially as well as discursively. Its identity is affirmed. It has its own narrative, where it is the hero, and it is enabled to undertake great tasks' (Taylor, 2011: 1278). Organizational and individual identities are linked insofar as organizations are an important site in which individual identities are constructed and the formation of one is constituted by – and has an effect on – the other (Mumby and Stohl, 1991; Deetz, 1992).

Accordingly, it is informative to look at how organizational identities are formed, as well as their interplay with individual identities, within a particular discursive landscape. In this chapter, I examine organizational and individual identities in two domains – refugee determination and HIV/AIDS.

THE REFUGEE DOMAIN

The 1948 UN Universal Declaration of Human Rights asserts that individuals have the right to seek asylum from persecution in other countries. The 1951 Geneva Convention and the 1967 Protocol Relating to the Status of Refugees define refugees as people who have left their own country because of a well-founded fear of persecution for reasons such as race, religion, nationality, and political opinion. Refugees who claim asylum on arriving

---

[1]   In talking about organizational identity, I focus on the research that takes an explicitly discursive approach and not, for example, the research on organizational identity informed by the work of Albert and Whetten (1985).

in a particular country have their cases heard and status determined by government-appointed officials, who decide whether an individual is a refugee with the right to asylum according to the prevailing legislation. Additionally, a range of 'mainstream' NGOs, staffed by paid, professionally trained employees, provide various legal services to asylum-seekers while their cases are being heard and/or settlement services. They also advocate on behalf of refugees and lobby governments in relation to policy. Another important actor in the domain are refugee community organizations – usually small, ethnic-based voluntary organizations run by and for particular groups of refugees – by offering various forms of support and advocacy (Phillips and Hardy, 1997; Hardy and Phillips, 1998).

Woven through refugee discourse are multiple other discourses, such as sovereignty, humanitarianism, paternalism, empowerment, race, crime, etc. Some of these other discourses do not sit easily with each other. For example, there is a struggle between sovereignty and humanitarianism: the former implies that large numbers of 'bogus' refugees or 'economic' migrants must be controlled; the latter emphasizes a refugee's right to protection. Another struggle arises between paternalism, which constructs a view of desperate refugees in need of care, and empowerment, which promotes the idea that refugees are self-reliant and independent. Organizations in the domain engage with these discourses in different ways. Governments often rely heavily on sovereignty to deal with the refugee 'problem' and control borders. NGOs are more likely to promote humanitarianism and, often, paternalism to justify their position and funding. Refugee community organizations may demand empowerment and self-representation in order to speak and act for themselves (Hardy and Phillips, 1999).

Refugee domains therefore tend to be marked by considerable discursive struggle among these organizations. Chapter 3 has already shown how contested domains and discursive struggles are a fruitful setting for researchers using a discursive approach. In this section, I build on these ideas by revisiting a series of studies of the refugee domains in Canada and the United Kingdom (UK) (Phillips and Hardy, 1997; Hardy and Phillips, 1998, 1999) to examine the implications for individual and organizational identities.

Refugee Identities and Discursive Resources

In one study (Hardy and Phillips, 1999), we examined 127 cartoons in Canadian newspapers featuring refugees, which coincided with two important pieces of refugee legislation passing the parliament at the time (1987–1989). Cartoons are naturally occurring, self-contained texts that portray concise representations that, in this case, offered a glimpse into the identities and the resources available to actors in refugee discourses.

We started by examining who or what was portrayed in the cartoons. Our analysis suggested that each cartoon represented one or more of the following: the refugee, the government (which sets refugee policy), the immigration system (which carries out refugee determination), and the public. (NGOs and refugee community organizations, although active in the domain, did not feature in any of the cartoons.) In a second step, we examined *how* each identity was represented, which we distilled into the themes in Box 6.1. We then did a simple count to obtain an overview (indicated by the numbers in Box 6.1). We found that refugees were most commonly constructed as fraudulent, although they were also shown as victims and, sometimes, as both fraud and victim. The government was most often presented as cruel, corrupt, and incompetent. The immigration system was portrayed as being inconsistent and inadequate in dealing with the large numbers of refugees. The public, which featured less often, was depicted as needing protection. This analysis provided an indication of the identities available to those taking up the refugee subject position – the various ways in which refugees were allowed to 'be' – mainly as frauds and, less often, as victims. Other subject positions were also constrained. The government was cruel to refugees but insufficiently competent to protect the public, which required protection. The immigration system was unable to cope.

We then explored the implications of these identities for discursive struggle in the domain. There appeared to be little support for, or confidence in, the government and immigration system. However, the predominant depiction of fraudulent refugees and a public that needed protection provided justification for border controls and enabled the government to draw on the discourse of sovereignty to explain its policies. NGOs did not feature in the cartoons but, nonetheless, could draw on support from humanitarianism and paternalism. If the government was cruel, corrupt, and incompetent, and the immigration system was inconsistent and often too tough, then refugees were vulnerable and needed NGOs to protect them. So, while the refugee as victim was not a common portrayal on which NGOs could draw and the NGOs themselves were absent from the cartoons, they nonetheless had access to discursive resources to justify their position through the way in which the government and the immigration system were represented. In contrast, refugee community organizations – as organizations run by refugees seeking self-representation – faced considerable challenges in invoking empowerment to justify their position since *none* of the cartoons represented the refugee as autonomous, empowered, independent human beings.

BOX 6.1   THEMES OF ANALYSIS

Object	Theme	Number	Definition
Refugee	Fraud	22	Those presenting themselves as refugees are in no danger
	Fraud and victim	13	Those presenting themselves as refugees may be both/either victim and/or fraud
	Victim	11	Those presenting themselves as refugees are at risk from persecution and warrant protection
	Privileged	2	Those presenting themselves as refugees gain quicker access to Canada than other immigrants
Government	Cruel	13	The government is unwilling to take responsibility for refugees
	Corrupt	9	Individuals in the government allow entry to Canada based on personal reasons
	Incompetent	8	The government is unable to administer the system effectively
	Under tension	6	The government is subject to contradictory and unresolvable tensions regarding their responsibility to refugees and the public
Immigration system	Inconsistent	23	The determination system treats some groups, such as illegal immigrants, fraudulent refugees, or individuals with political connections, preferentially
	Inadequate	17	The determination system is unable to prevent large numbers of refugees entering Canada
	Too tough	12	The determination system keeps out people who should be allowed into Canada
	Too lenient	10	The determination system lets people in who should be kept out of Canada
	Too slow	7	The determination system takes too long to render decisions
	Gullible	7	The determination system is unable to distinguish between genuine and fraudulent refugees
	Honourable	1	The determination system carries out its responsibilities towards refugees
Public	Requiring protection	8	The public requires protection from large numbers of refugees entering Canada
	Opposed	4	The public is opposed to refugees entering Canada

Source: Adapted from Hardy and Phillips (1999: 17).

Links between Individual and Organizational Identities

To drill down further on what these identities meant for individual organizations, we conducted two other studies in the UK (Phillips and Hardy, 1997; Hardy and Phillips, 1998). We carried out interviews with government officials involved in refugee determination, members of two mainstream NGOs (Refugee Legal Centre and British Refugee Council), and members of the Refugee Forum, which was a refugee community organization (Box 6.2).

BOX 6.2   ORGANIZATIONS IN THE UNITED KINGDOM REFUGEE DOMAIN

The Refugee Legal Centre provided free, independent legal representation and advice to asylum-seekers during the determination process. It handled the vast majority of individuals who sought refugee status. A case worker from the centre represented the asylum-seeker, while a civil servant from the UK government's Asylum Division determined the status of that individual. In the event of an appeal of a negative decision, the case worker would challenge the Asylum Division's decision. Despite being on the 'opposite' side of the determination process to the UK government on individual decisions, the organization had been set up by the government, which had established it as the sole provider of free legal advice and representation for refugees in 1991, and it was heavily (88 percent) dependent on government funding.

The British Refugee Council had been formed in 1981 to provide a focal point for aid to refugees and to promote refugee rights. It acted as an umbrella organization of over 100 NGOs, including well-known international charities like Oxfam and Save the Children Fund. Approximately one third of the membership comprised refugee community organizations. It employed around 200 people and provided direct services to refugees. It was also an active lobby group campaigning against government policies, although it also depended on government funding for about 60 percent of its budget.

The Refugee Forum was an umbrella association of refugee community organizations formed in 1984 because of, in the words of its director, the 'failures' of mainstream institutions like the British Refugee Council. Its aims included self-organization, self-determination, and direct funding to refugee-led organizations – 'helping refugees to help themselves.' The forum was not directly government-funded and engaged primarily in lobbying activities, although individual member organizations provided legal and settlement services. It remained a loosely federated network operating on a small budget with only two full-time employees.

The Refugee Legal Centre constructed a refugee identity of a helpless client, to whom it dispensed legal services, resisting any notion that refugees should play a role in how the organization administered its services. This was important because it needed refugees to be apolitical clients, and relatively silent ones at that. If refugees were given a voice, they would likely be critical of the government, as well as of the organization's reluctance to take a more political stand in supporting refugee rights more broadly. This would be problematic insofar as the Refugee Legal Centre was heavily dependent on the government, which expected it to toe the line.

> Technically [the Refugee Legal Centre is] an independent organization. Where this falls down in the eyes of the public or of the pressure groups is that it does receive part of its funding from the government and critics say: 'How can an organization that receives funding from the government be independent of the government?' We say that ... we have no say in how the organization runs. It's entirely up to them and their constitution how they carry out their work. That also falls down slightly when you consider that we gave them an ultimatum on how to reform themselves and later withdrew their funding on the basis that they didn't do it. (Civil servant)

Since the government was, by far, the more powerful player of the two, employees of the Refugee Legal Centre admitted they did not engage in much 'table pounding': 'The [employees of the Refugee Legal Centre] don't work in an antagonistic sense, unlike some solicitors who are being paid by the client, who see it as much more confrontational "you're wrong, I'm right" way' (Civil servant). The identity of an apolitical, compliant refugee helped the Refugee Legal Centre to deal with its position of dependency. Dispensing services to clients who accepted them with gratitude avoided difficult questions that might cause problems in its relationship with the government.

The British Refugee Council constructed a very different refugee identity: refugees were not silent clients but a vocal constituency that had to be taken into account. So, while the Refugee Legal Council muted the voice of refugees, the British Refugee Council amplified it. It encouraged refugee community organizations to become members and amended its constitution to ensure that one third of the executive committee were representatives of these organizations. It established a community development team, completely staffed by refugees to help refugee community organizations organize more effectively. The team of six worked with around 70 refugee community organizations on management, governance, fundraising, and training. These practices, in turn, helped to produce a refugee identity that *was* capable and powerful – discourse and practice reinforced each other.

> Certainly, the attitudes of the established agencies have changed; this one [the British Refugee Council] has changed … I think that the strategic planning exercise [on community development] here had an impact … questioning the role of our services. Should we be doing this, or should we be helping a community organization to do it? You have to introduce that questioning so you don't automatically assume that you've got to do it. Your role might be to help a refugee community organization to solve the problem. (Member of the community development team)

The British Refugee Council could construct – and tolerate – a more vocal identity for refugees than the Refugee Legal Centre because it had greater independence from the government. It received some funding from the government but also from other large NGOs. It was expected to lobby for refugee rights and therefore to take a more adversarial position in relation to the government.

The Refugee Forum challenged the established agencies – the latter received the bulk of government funding and paternalistic NGOs undermined any bid for refugees to be seen as empowered and independent. 'The British Refugee Council has been a disaster; when there is any parliamentary debate, the government can always say the British Refugee Council is dealing with the problem' (Refugee Forum member).

The Refugee Forum considered the British Refugee Council to be highly selective in taking an adversarial position to the government – concentrating on specific 'winnable' issues. It also felt that the British Refugee Council ultimately retained a paternalist position in relation to refugees. Accordingly, the Refugee Forum distanced itself from mainstream agencies, regardless of how their interests might appear to overlap. It challenged the government's determination system, supported illegal aliens, and lobbied to cut mainstream NGOs out of the funding relationship by channeling money directly to refugees. It helped to create refugees who were autonomous, competent, capable, and self-reliant. It was highly successful in promoting refugee empowerment through its African Refugees Housing Action Group, one of the first refugee-led housing associations to be registered with the Housing Corporation (a £2 billion, government-funded agency that provided grants for non-profit housing). The forum was also important in embarrassing established agencies into sharing more power with refugees, engaging in initiatives like the community development team, and employing more refugees.

The response of the mainstream agencies was to marginalize the Refugee Forum because of its 'extreme' demands. Nonetheless, the forum *did* have an impact on the domain: 'I tried to look at the Forum as an instrument to get the British Refugee Council running around … the years of criticism made the Council nervous enough to make changes. A lot of change [in increasing refugee participation], we could say we owe to the Forum indirectly' (British Refugee Council employee and former refugee). In other words, the Refugee Forum, despite minimal resources and dubious legitimacy in the eyes of established agencies, did have some influence.

> The Refugee Forum is useful. It stems from the grass roots which results in an enormous commitment which is sometimes more effective than the British Refugee Council. It's more radical, so it can't attract a lot of funding, while the Council has funding but is bureaucratic. Both have their limits. It's important to have the Forum because it challenges the others in the system. It provides a check and keeps them honest. Also, it sometimes identifies the real issues because it doesn't make the same assumptions. (Representative of another refugee community organization)

In doing so, its practices helped to produce more refugees that *were* autonomous, empowered, and independent human beings.

In sum, this study shows how individual identity is constructed, partially at least, by organizations in relation to subject positions provided by wider discourses. It also shows a link between organizational and individual identities – an organization 'needs' identities that align with its own identity, both of which are discursively constructed. Finally, it shows how identities are linked to organizational practices. In constructing certain kinds of individual identities, the organization engages in particular practices that help to produce that identity.

THE HIV/AIDS DOMAIN

In this section, I revisit a study of the HIV/AIDS domain in Canada and the creation of the Canadian Treatment Advocates Council (CTAC) – a collaborative organization involving members of the HIV/AIDS community and pharmaceutical companies launched in 1997 (Maguire et al., 2001, 2004; Maguire and Hardy, 2005). At this time, 6 million people had died of AIDS and more than 30 million people worldwide were living with HIV. In Canada, over 40,000 people had tested positive for HIV and more than 11,000 had died. To explore this domain, we conducted 29 interviews with key actors from both community and industry organizations in Canada. Our analysis showed how the discourse of HIV/AIDS had created new subject positions for individuals which, in turn, created new conditions of possibility for collaboration.

New Subject Positions in the Discourse of HIV/AIDS

Other disease domains at the time typically consisted of a skilled, professional elite – pharmaceutical companies and medical researchers, who produced scientific knowledge and treatment products. Another elite body – physicians – then prescribed these products to patients. Patients were uninformed, sometimes desperate, and therefore potentially vulnerable to pharmaceutical companies seeking to maximize profits. Accordingly, their access to treatments was controlled by doctors and regulated by governments. However, HIV/AIDS was different. First, it was not well understood by the existing medical elite, which was wracked by uncertainty and impotence. Not only did physicians not have the expertise to deal with this new challenge; some were unwilling to treat patients with the disease. Second, it was wrapped up in emotional issues of death and sexuality, and it killed in a horrific way, attracting considerable media attention as it did so. Third, early cases were concentrated in a marginalized, but also organized and politicized, social group – the gay community.

Members of this community soon started to challenge existing understandings of medical knowledge production and treatment delivery (Wachter, 1991; Roy, 1995). In doing so, they rejected the traditional subject position of 'patient.' *Patienter* means to wait in French, as in a physician's waiting room, and *patior* means to suffer in Latin. Those with HIV/AIDS – or, at least, some of them – were unwilling to be patient and suffer in silence. They were not patients but people living with AIDS (PWAs). 'We condemn attempts to label us as "victims," a term which implies defeat, and we are only occasionally "patients," a term which implies passivity, helplessness, and dependence upon the care of others. We are "People With AIDS,"' stated the first of the Denver Principles (www.nmac.org/living-denver-principles), a manifesto created by a group of gay men at the 1983 Annual Gay and Lesbian Health Conference in Denver. Patients had become 'PWAs.'

The manifesto set the scene for the creation of countless community-based organizations that advocated activism and self-empowerment as a way of dealing with the challenges faced by PWAs. The AIDS Coalition to Unleash Power (ACT-UP) was formed in the US in 1987 as a non-partisan group of individuals 'united in anger and committed to direct action to end the AIDS crisis' (www.actupny.org). It adopted the 'Silence = Death' poster to emphasize that PWAs would not be silent and they demanded political action (www .brooklynmuseum.org/opencollection/objects/159258). AIDS Action Now was founded the following year in Canada, demanding improved access to treatment, care, and support for PWAs through grass-roots activism, public demonstrations, lobbying, and research (www.aidsactionnow.org). These organizations and others like them were involved in high-profile demonstrations against governments and pharmaceutical companies. PWAs had become 'activists.'

Many of these activists were 'middle-class, white, HIV-positive gay males who prioritized, above all, the goal of getting "drugs into bodies"' (Grossman, 2016: 726). Unlike social activists, who had a broader political agenda, they focused on opening the black box of medical science (Epstein, 1996). To do so, they became extremely knowledgeable about the various treatments that pharmaceutical companies were developing (Epstein, 1996). Issues like secrecy to protect patents and high pricing placed corporate goals in direct opposition to community objectives. Even compassionate access programs (free access to experimental, unapproved treatments) often led to conflict, with the community demanding greater and quicker access to drugs than the companies were willing to provide. The late 1980s and early 1990s were, then, notable for an unprecedented level of activism by knowledgeable community members against pharmaceutical companies (Wachter, 1991; Roy, 1995). Activists had become 'treatment activists.'

Interestingly, CTAC was formed despite this adversarial relationship. In June 1995, an employee of one of the major pharmaceutical companies called a meeting with individuals from AIDS community organizations to review their relationship. A follow-up meeting in January 1996 discussed the idea of a permanent, national organization and established a taskforce of community members to develop recommendations regarding a constitution and mandate for this new organization. The taskforce circulated its draft proposals in April 1996 at a meeting between the original pharmaceutical company and community members. It was followed by meetings with two other pharmaceutical companies. In June 1996, the structure of a national organization was agreed. CTAC was formally launched in 1997, bringing together members of over 15 HIV/AIDS organizations with representatives of several major pharmaceutical companies. It was largely autonomous – controlled neither by a single community organization nor by industry. Its objectives included the articulation of a united, national voice, the development of treatment advocacy skills at national and provincial levels, and the provision of a central access point for companies to consult with the community on new treatments, the design of clinical trials, and compassionate access programs.

The new organization was dependent upon the emergence of yet another subject position. The identity of treatment activist was not conducive to collaboration – individuals who chained themselves to buildings and hurled fake blood at pharmaceutical company representatives were not obvious partners: 'When time comes for funding a pure activism activity I'm not there. I say, this is not why we're there ... I wouldn't want to fund a really up-front activism' (Pharmaceutical company employee).

As activism was replaced by advocacy, the subject position of 'treatment advocate' emerged. Individuals taking up this identity continued to emphasize access to medical treatments and continued to be highly knowledgeable in medical matters, but they eschewed more confrontational initiatives. 'There was a debate about activist versus advocate because we felt that activist has the ACT-UP connotations of, you know, burning things, and chanting and falling down. The drug companies were scared of that. So, we just changed it to advocate. The reality is advocacy is what we do' (Community member).

Treatment advocates were far more acceptable partners for industry: 'We kind of knew that there were people who would help [advocates] and then we kind of knew there were political activists and the two aren't necessarily the same' (Pharmaceutical company employee). The subject position of treatment advocate thus opened up new conditions of possibility for greater collaboration between community and industry.

New subject positions were also required in industry. Most companies had the identity of 'profiteer' to contend with, given the amount of money being made from HIV/AIDS with millions of dollars in sales from drugs such as AZT and 3TC, as well as protease inhibitors, which ushered in combination therapies and a wide variety of other medicines used to treat the opportunistic infections associated with the disease. 'Yes, we sell services and drugs, and this is our raison d'être, like it or not. They [community members] have a different raison d'être' (Pharmaceutical company employee).

However, profiteering was not conducive to collaboration with a community whose members were dying from the disease. Accordingly, pharmaceutical companies had to take steps to redefine themselves and their employees.

> We were looking for people [employees to work with CTAC] who were really quite open and transparent for the community. Very HIV oriented. In other words, it wouldn't bother them at all to be working in this kind of community and ... open enough to be able to work solidly with them. Those are values ... that would be valued by the community. (Pharmaceutical company employee)

These 'compassionate partners' were far more likely to be able to work with and provide support for the community.

Performing the Necessary Identity Work

The emergence of the new subject positions created new conditions of possibility that increased the chances of successful collaboration. This was a necessary but not sufficient step. CTAC also depended on individuals being able to *perform* the necessary identity work. Community members had to *act* as reasonable, knowledgeable, business-minded professionals. 'We have to make ourselves much more attractive to the private sector, which means there are things that we can't do any more. And one of them may be the kind of aggressive, in your face advocacy that some [community] members have demanded. It just doesn't sell' (Community member). Similarly, employees also had to act like compassionate partners: 'I've been out to their [community] meetings and participated ... I think maybe at times, I can go a little too far over the line but that's me. That's where I want to be anyway, you know … if I wasn't here, I'd be on the non-profit side' (Pharmaceutical company employee).

Accordingly, in the remainder of this section, I discuss the successful performances of individuals who were able to take up these subject positions and negotiate a complex relationship with both community and industry. I also explore why some individuals who wanted to take up particular subject positions were unable to carry out the necessary performances.

In the study (Maguire and Hardy, 2005), we examined the identity work of eight 'champions' of CTAC (four community members and four pharmaceutical company employees). These individuals played an active role in the new organization and were successful in constructing themselves as treatment advocate or compassionate partner.

> One of the fundamental tenets of being a good advocate [compared to an activist] … is that you don't speak for yourself. You solicit the opinion, you inform your constituency about what their options are, you give them your opinion as to what you think they should do, but they can decide different. Anything else is abuse. It's imposing … Advocacy is not about me deciding what I think is best. (Community champion)

Similarly, industry champions insisted that they were nothing like the typical pharmaceutical company employee.

> Some [managers] still felt that if you touched someone with HIV you can get HIV … plus it is a homosexual disease and, you know, all of these taboos. [This] is a male company, of course, a boys' club and all of this type of stuff. [For me] it is not a problem, it is to be demystified. (Company champion)

Much of the identity work of community and industry champions was thus targeted at the Other – their partner in CTAC.

Champions nonetheless still had to speak for and to their constituency. Many community members were still vested in activism. Treatment activists remained powerful actors. By emphasizing that they were advocates and not activists, community champions inevitably distanced themselves from core members of the community – who could easily oppose CTAC.

> If CTAC does sell-out at any one day, my support's gone … I've had frank conversations and I've said: 'I think you're getting too cozy! I haven't seen you say anything pretty awful about [a pharmaceutical company] lately on this issue and before you used to be out there in the front with the battle.' And anger and rage is part of what AIDS is about … If we don't show that emotion, then we're being co-opted. (Community member and treatment activist)

Accordingly, champions also took steps to identify with legitimate identities within the community by emphasizing that they were among those *dying* from AIDS and they acted as unpaid volunteers in self-help PWA organizations.

Industry champions of CTAC also had to be careful not to alienate their senior managers, who held commercial expectations. '[Disagreements between us] have to do with traditional activism. I know sometimes we have to sit down together, and I say, "I'm not and we're not in the activism business. We're a pharmaceutical company"' (Manager). Industry champions therefore had to emphasize those aspects of their identities that resonated with both constituencies. By juggling their identity work, community and industry champions were able to take up the appropriate subject position *and* maintain a connection to their own constituency, while also identifying with the 'opposing' constituency.

We then investigated the identity work of another group of individuals – five members of AIDS service organizations and two employees of particular pharmaceutical companies – who supported CTAC and *wanted* to play a more central role but were unable to do so. In the community, these individuals were not HIV+ and/or were not volunteers, instead holding salaried positions in AIDS service organizations. They found it impossible to participate in CTAC.

> I don't have the virus in my body. I'm not infected with HIV … It reduces my legit-imacy because I don't have the virus in my body and because I'm a paid person who works in this movement … I finally had to out myself and say, 'I don't have HIV … I'm almost the enemy.' (Community member)

Despite being part of the HIV/AIDS community, these individuals were seen as 'living' from the disease, rather than dying from it.

In the industry, employees of companies that were not seen as compassionate were also excluded. Some companies were not acceptable to the community. 'They [a particular pharmaceutical company] are disgusting North American pill pushers who have the American mentality and who try to push pills all the way down your throat until you vomit. Well, the community vomited on them, and in my opinion, they should have vomited harder' (Community member).

The employees of these companies were unable to play a leading role in CTAC even though they had worked for compassionate companies in the past and engaged in considerable identity work to show they shared community goals, as indicated by this individual:

> The perception is that manufacturers of pharmaceutical drugs make a lot of money so what I always try to do is to try and explain to them what my reality is, who my bosses are, what I have to do for a living, how I live versus what they have to do, what my life is. I have kids. I have a house. I have to work here. I have enormous amounts of responsibilities. I have enormous amounts of pressure. So that is my

reality. I know what your reality is, now listen to my reality. You have to humanize this you know. If this is a manufacturer who is completely dehumanized, they cannot understand when you humanize it to my level, and say: 'Look this is my life, I am trying to help you, so please help me. There is a limit to where I can go before I lose my job.' (Employee)

In sum, new subject positions emerged in the HIV/AIDS discourse that increased the conditions of possibility for collaboration *if* the appropriate identity work could be carried out. Champions of CTAC had to engage in a delicate dance where they identified with Self and Other at the same time. Not everyone was able to undertake such performances and take up the necessary subject positions because some aspects of identity were non-negotiable. In some cases, this was physical and material – not having the virus in one's body – and sometimes it was a matter of work history – working as a paid employee rather than a volunteer or working for a particular company.

CONCLUSION

This chapter provides insight into organizational identities, showing how they are discursively maintained and sustained over time. It also shows the complex links between organizational and individual identities, where the former depends upon having the 'right' kind of individual among its employees, managers, customers, and clients. These individuals are then subjected to organizational practices which, in turn, help to 'make' them a particular kind of person. The chapter shows the relationship between the discursive landscape and the construction of individual and organizational identities. Of particular importance are the subject positions available in a discourse. In some cases, as the refugee study shows, these positions are heavily constrained, severely limiting the individual. In other cases, subject positions may create new conditions of possibility, as in the case of CTAC, but not all individuals will necessarily be able to take them up. Finally, the chapter shows the complexity of identity work, which has to be successfully performed to and accepted by multiple audiences.

BOX 6.3   EMPIRICAL POINTERS

* A discursive approach is most insightful when researchers situate local studies in a broader discursive landscape. For example, it is hard to understand what happens in an individual refugee organization without taking into account the struggle between discourses such as sovereignty and humanitarianism or paternalism and empowerment. Similarly, the

formation of CTAC rests on an understanding of new subject positions in HIV/AIDS discourse.

- Obtaining evidence of discourses that circulate widely in society is, however, always a challenge, and discourse researchers often have to be creative. We were able to use a complete set of cartoons on refugees during a particularly significant period (when legislation was passing through parliament) as a 'proxy' for the wider discourse.

- Cartoons are an interesting source of data for discourse researchers. They are publicly available and relatively easy to gather, and it is often possible to collect a whole 'data set' covering all newspapers over a particular period on a particular subject. They are instances of natural 'talk' that can be systematically analyzed and discussed in a relatively limited space.

- Studies using a discursive approach often require the development of ad hoc, customized 'mini-analyses.' For example, to identify CTAC champions, we examined the interviews to see who had expressed support for the new organization. We then ascertained whether supportive individuals followed through by documenting their actions in relation to CTAC from interviews and texts. This showed that some individuals could be classified as 'champions' in that they had followed up with action. Others failed to do so. Rather than dismiss these latter individuals as not being supportive, we went back to their interviews and identified patterns in how they talked about their identity. From this we learned that these individuals had wanted to play a more central role but were unable to do so because they could not assume a legitimate identity – they worked for the 'wrong' company or were not HIV/AIDS+.

- A considerable amount of identity work can be captured through accounts of activities in texts as in these studies. However, studies of how organizational and individual identities are formed can be further enhanced by collecting data on the embodiment of identity work and the physical aspects of setting (e.g., Dale and Latham, 2015; Hultin and Introna, 2019; Hultin et al., 2021).

7. Using a discursive approach to study organizational change

In this chapter, I explore how a discursive approach can contribute to our understanding of organizational change. Following from the conceptualization of organizational identity discussed in Chapter 6, a discursive approach emphasizes that organizations are 'unstable social constructions constituted through acts of languaging' (Brown and Humphreys, 2006: 231). To appreciate fully what this means, we must engage with a perspective known as 'organizational becoming' (Tsoukas and Chia, 2002; Carlsen, 2006), which draws attention to two important aspects of organizations. First, they are not fixed entities, but 'unfolding processes involving actors making choices interactively, in inescapably local conditions' (Tsoukas and Chia, 2002: 577). An 'organization' is an emergent property of change – a temporary pattern constituted by and shaped from micro interactions among actors, situated in their everyday work. Accordingly, change is endemic, natural, and ongoing – the product of situated human agency rather than an exceptional or episodic event. Second, organization is contingent upon language. Structures and processes are held in place through language, while changes in patterns of organizing depend upon new language as new meanings and interpretations of organizational activities are negotiated among actors through their communicative interactions (Hardy et al., 2005; Tsoukas, 2005).

Language only ever provides the *potential* for meaning – specific meanings result from unfolding, contextually embedded social interactions in a non-deterministic way over time. Rather than thinking of a change program as the realization of a particular management plan, it is more helpful to think of it as a 'discursive template' (Tsoukas and Chia, 2002) – a text produced by a particular author whose meaning is interpreted by those whom it addresses. Senior managers may hold privileged positions in terms of their ability to introduce new templates but, ultimately, the meanings of their texts are negotiated with other organizational members. Accordingly, organizational change is a 'multi-authored' process (Buchanan and Dawson, 2007) during which actors negotiate and co-construct shared meanings.

In the remainder of this chapter, different aspects of organizational change are explored in three different studies. The first examines how a new organization is discursively constructed. The second explores how an organization became a different type of organization only to revert back to its original status. The third is an investigation of the micro dynamics of a program to change the culture of an organization.

DISCURSIVELY CONSTRUCTING AN ORGANIZATION

In this section, I present a study of a group of 13 organizations providing employment services in a mid-sized Canadian city (Hardy et al., 1998). They included publicly funded educational institutions, private-sector organizations, and not-for-profits, ranging in size from 20 to 3,000 employees, that provided counseling, training, and support to the unemployed. They had been brought together by the manager of a major funding agency, referred to here as the Employment Office, who wanted them to work together to serve his clients (individuals collecting employment insurance) more effectively. He made an announcement, telling representatives of these organizations that they *had* to work together, but then left them to work out how to make it happen. Having been thrown together by an external party, they felt little connection to each other and, despite monthly meetings for over a year, little progress was made. As a result, a 3.5-day workshop was held over a six-week period to help the group work together. By its end, the group had founded a new organization, developed its mission and vision, articulated major goals, and set dates and assigned teams to achieve them.

The workshop was facilitated by one of my co-authors, Tom Lawrence. It offered the opportunity to explore how this new organization came about. Pre-workshop interviews were conducted with the 13 participants, a research assistant took notes during the workshop, and an open-ended survey was administered at the workshop's close. We then examined how the workshop helped in the discursive production of an organizational identity, as well as the skills and emotions that supported the new endeavour.

Identity

The first two days of the workshop were devoted to developing a mission statement for the group. Through a series of brainstorming, prioritizing, and decision-making sessions, the group worked on a statement to capture their reasons for working together and establish a collective vision of the future. A crisis occurred on the morning of the third day. In reviewing the mission statement that they had developed, participants began to note elements that described the partnership they wanted, but contradicted the responsibilities laid down by the Employment Office. It defined the group more broadly than the original mandate in terms of geographic area, types of unemployed persons served, and scope of political action. The group arrived at an impasse:

accepting their mission statement took them well beyond their remit; rejecting it meant all their work would go to waste. A suggestion was made to name the new collaboration as a way of accepting the mission statement, but this led to conflict over whether such a move was legitimate. A compromise was finally reached when the group agreed to 'try on' a new name – *CityWorks* (a pseudonym) – for the remainder of the day.

Another source of conflict was the question of membership. Having identified themselves as CityWorks, the group wanted to establish membership criteria that differed from the directive of the Employment Office. A variety of alternatives were suggested – from restricting membership to the current participants to accepting any organization that wanted to join – based on a range of arguments, which included restricting competition, broadening political influence, and ensuring efficiency. At the end of the day, a great deal of frustration and some anger had been generated, but no membership policy had been agreed. The final day of the workshop began with more heated discussion. After some debate, a suggestion was agreed that membership should remain open, with the initial membership limited to the founding partners and new members ratified by a two-thirds majority vote.

In trying on the new name and voting to ratify the new membership policy, an organizational identity was constructed for the new collaboration. As one member said: 'I guess it's a question of do we really want CityWorks to exist? Right now, it's kind of pretend. A membership policy means we are real.'

Skills

The conceptualization of skills discussed here focuses on their role as cultural resources constituted in conversations that shape behaviour (Swidler, 1986). Skills represent abilities that are culturally meaningful – abilities that are situated in a cultural context enable individuals to act. The development of individual and collective skills was an explicit part of the workshop. Each of the first three days included a skill development session, including collaborative decision making, building a strategic mission, and conflict management. These sessions provided participants with the opportunity to develop a collective, non-hierarchical approach to problem solving and decision making through such exercises as rotating the assignment of roles (chair, facilitator, task manager, timekeeper, scribe) and specific procedures (brainstorming, bundling ideas, prioritizing).

The process of skill development illustrates their discursive nature. Many of the participants had significant previous training in facilitation and collective decision making but had not used their expertise within this particular group – their knowledge of group dynamics had not been enacted as a cultural resource in this specific context. Consequently, despite well-developed individual abilities prior to the workshop, the group 'lacked' skills until they were collectively articulated and legitimated in the conversations that comprised the workshop.

The collective development of skills ensured that skills were legitimated through conversation and negotiation rather than by fiat. Initial discomfort with the roles and procedures transformed into an open desire to protect the processes to which the group had agreed. Participants' conceptualization of the decision-making skills changed from them being 'the rules imposed by the facilitator' to being seen as 'the way we operate.'

Emotions

The workshop was, at times, a highly emotional experience for participants. Sometimes, these emotions took the form of heated disagreements about the mission and membership. Several members wanted a restrictive membership policy to protect their competitive advantage in terms of access to funding, while others felt that such a policy was unethical. During these discussions, the facilitator deliberately did not intervene, even when participants were openly frustrated and angry. Later, as the identity and skills of the group became more established, participants invoked the identity of CityWorks and used their decision-making skills to bring about more productive resolutions. Of particular importance was the moral basis of the services provided by the group to unemployed persons in the local community. This moral ethic was regularly invoked by participants to supersede the interests of individual members. Although it occasionally prompted clashes about how the interests of the unemployed might best be addressed, it generally served as a catalyst for positive emotional energy and reinforced the formation of a collective identity (see Westley, 1990). Strong, positive emotions were drawn upon to move the group beyond sectional interests since someone would 'remind' them of 'why they were really there.'

In sum, this study reveals some of the micro dynamics as participants negotiated meanings leading to a new organization (be)coming into existence. The group discursively established an identity for the new organization, legitimated appropriate skills, and generated positive emotions for its development and survival through the workshop conversations.

DISCURSIVELY RECONSTRUCTING AN ORGANIZATION

In this section, I examine how, by changing the discourse, an international NGO became a local NGO and, following some unexpected events, became international once again. It provides further examples of discursive work involved in organizational change, as well as showing the scope and the limits of agency.

This study involves an international *Mère et Enfant* (a pseudonym) – an international NGO based in Europe and funded by a European government, which worked on behalf of disadvantaged children and committed to empowering the communities it served. Our interest was in the 'branch' that operated in the West Bank and Gaza (Hardy et al., 2000). The West Bank covers an area of 5,500 square kilometres. At the time, it was mainly rural with about 400 villages and four major towns. Forty percent of its population were refugees, living in refugee camps. The Gaza Strip is a small piece of land (365 square km) occupied by over 800,000 Palestinians, making it one of the most densely populated areas in the world. Around three quarters of inhabitants were refugees living in camps. Around half of the Palestinian population were under 14 years of age. The infant mortality rate was estimated to be 50 deaths per 1,000 live births, often as a result of diarrhoea and acute respiratory infection. Mère et Enfant had been operating in Gaza and the West Bank for over ten years. Its main emphasis was on improving child nutrition and reducing infant mortality by providing medical and nutritional services through a community education outreach program.

To conduct our research, we interviewed the delegate – the manager in charge of the NGO's operations in Palestine, who was a European in charge of 60 local, Palestinian employees. We also interviewed employees, members of the local steering committee, other NGOs, and members of the health department. We conducted a total of 14 interviews in 1997, which lasted between one and two hours, were semi-structured, recorded, and transcribed. The delegate also made available a range of documentation including memos, newsletters, organizational charts, reports, minutes of meetings, funding proposals, and other documents.

Location

The delegate had been preparing the organization for localization, whereby regionally based operations, administered and funded by an *international* NGO, are transformed into a *local* NGO. The localized organization typically has a steering committee comprised of members from the local community and is ultimately responsible for securing its own funding from a variety of sources on a sustainable basis. In this way, it becomes independent and self-sufficient, providing services demanded by the community in which it operates and contributing to regional development and empowerment. Accordingly, localization is a familiar discourse in the humanitarian and development community.

In late 1996, the organization was still seen by members of both the organization and the community as an international NGO. To be constituted as a legitimate, local NGO in the eyes of the Palestinian medical, political, and NGO communities, further changes were required. Accordingly, the delegate introduced the discourse of localization by making a series of statements that the organization was going to be localized and using the Arabic translation of Mère et Enfant. He wrote about localization in internal reports and in the organization's newsletter. He also set about creating a steering committee consisting of community representatives. These actions served to associate the existing organization with a new concept – a *local* NGO.

In September 1996, the delegate called together a number of prospective members of the new steering committee, although he remained in charge of decision making. The following month, in a separate move, the delegate announced the layoff of 15 employees, provoking demonstrations by employees and members of the local community. Although it had no formal authority, the members of the steering committee met, in the absence of the delegate, to discuss the layoffs and issued a statement saying that the employees should be reinstated. The matter then escalated when disaffected employees went to the security forces and made allegations against Mère et Enfant and some of its Palestinian managers. The security forces became involved, calling in some of the Palestinian managers for interrogation and threatening imprisonment and torture unless the employees were reinstated.

By this time, in the eyes of many Palestinians – including the security forces – the organization was a local NGO with its own steering committee, which had recommended the reinstatement of the employees. In other words, the international organization had been discursively reconstituted as a local one through the creation of a steering committee, a meeting of that committee, and a statement by that committee. These discursive acts 'changed' the organization, particularly in the eyes of powerful external actors, even though it remained under the formal control of the delegate and part of the international NGO. As a local NGO, it did not have the political protection afforded by the status of an international agency.

Re-internationalization

To protect his managers from further harassment, the delegate engaged in a number of discursive activities that were designed to re-establish the status of the organization as an international agency. He sent out a series of memos and letters to a range of individuals and organizations, including heads of other NGOs, the Palestinian National Authority, and the security forces, stating that 'with immediate effect, the process of localizing its projects in Palestine – that is of handing over the projects of Mère et Enfant to new owners and managers is suspended.' He also let it be known that 'line management responsibility for the projects of Mère et Enfant in Palestine will be assumed in totality by the delegate and, through him, Mère et Enfant.' He disbanded the steering committee to reinforce the statement that decision-making authority did not reside in local hands. He met with the head of the security forces, as well as prominent members of the Palestinian National Authority, to emphasize the organization's status and the authority of the European headquarters. By the end of November, he had received reassurance from members of the Palestinian National Authority that the NGO was safe from further intervention by the security forces – the organization once again became international.

The delegate's discursive work 'worked' for a number of reasons. In the case of localization, the concept of a local NGO already had a meaning in this context. Many NGOs were localizing at this time and the practice was familiar to individuals inside and outside the organization. The local steering committee was a commonly recognized symbol, while the Arabic version of the organization's name and the various narratives regarding localization written by the delegate resonated with individuals in the local community. Finally, the subject position of the delegate warranted voice – someone in his position had the authority to make such statements and decisions. These factors comprised a circuit of performativity – the symbols, concepts, and subject position had meaning within the particular context and among the relevant actors. As a result, the discursive statements of the delegate 'stuck' – linking organization to the new concept, albeit somewhat precipitously. The emergence of new subject positions, such as the steering committee, gained and exercised voice but so too did the security forces which now had the 'right' to intervene.

The delegate then engaged in a second round of discursive work aimed at *re*-attaching the organization to the concept of an international NGO. The memos, faxes, and meetings communicated a new (or, rather, old) narrative of an international NGO governed from Europe, while the disbanding of the steering committee removed a symbol associated with a local NGO. These discursive statements reassociated the organization with the concept of an international NGO. The original concept still had meaning which, in turn, meant that the delegate still had authority. These discursive (re)statements also stuck, with the result that the steering committee ceased to be a subject position and the security forces ceased to have the authority to intervene.

In sum, Mère et Enfant became a local NGO and then became an international NGO once again as a result of a series of discursive manoeuvres. The 'organization' – its governance, structure, and operations – did not change. The discursive manoeuvres worked because they were appropriately grounded in the prevailing discursive context, where both localization and internationalization made sense, and where actors held subject positions that warranted voice. In this way, there was an interplay between broad societal discourses, specific discursive acts, and outcomes.

CONSTRUCTING CHANGE IN AN ORGANIZATION

In this study (Thomas et al., 2011), we conducted a detailed analysis of the real-time negotiation of meaning during an organizational change initiative in a company referred to as *Utel*, which was a spin-off of GlobalTel (discussed in Chapter 2). In 2001, Utel became an independent organization, employing approximately 1,500 employees mainly in Europe. Previously a division within a larger company that manufactured mobile phones, it was now a company that sold 'knowledge' (platforms and technology) to other phone manufacturers. Senior managers believed that its success hinged on building a new culture that focused more directly on its customers. To this end, they developed a cultural change program involving a series of 80 workshops rolled out across the company (Box 7.1).

BOX 7.1   THE CULTURE CHANGE WORKSHOPS

Each workshop lasted for three hours. It was organized around a 'culture toolkit' consisting of a brochure, a video, and a set of instructions including PowerPoint slides for conducting the workshops.

The brochure, entitled *Utel's Target Culture: Involving Every Employee*, specified a target culture in broad terms that related to four drivers of business success (unity in teamwork, technological innovation, excellent customer service, and leadership) and four shared values (trust, empowerment, commitment, and quality). Given the company's mission – 'to make our customers first, best and profitable through innovation, quality and commitment' – the new culture was expected to be more customer focused. The brochure also described an implementation process involving additional workshops that were to be run by middle managers using the same process.

The video, shown during the workshop, was a ten-minute question-and-answer session between the chief executive officer and another senior manager. It explained why a new culture was needed and provided further information on the drivers and the values that underpinned it. It also presented a view of the implementation of the new culture, as the chief executive officer stated that the 'next step is to involve everybody' through the additional workshops.

The instructions specified the activities for each half-day workshop: (a) a presentation of the target culture using the brochure and accompanying video; (b) a discussion of the relevance of the target culture to the particular group attending the workshop; and (c) a 'stop/start/continue' exercise to identify one behaviour that was hindering cultural change and needed to be stopped, one new behaviour that needed to be started, and one existing behaviour that should be continued.

The first author observed one of these workshops held at a UK plant, recording the workshop and taking notes during it. It was attended by five senior managers (three from the European head office and two from the UK plant) and 31 middle managers (support staff and engineers). Semi-structured interviews were also conducted with 18 participants, who were asked for their views on the change program. We identified two issues for closer investigation – a customer focus as part of the new culture and the implementation process. They were selected because the negotiations around these two issues differed significantly and a comparison of the two promised some useful insights. Accordingly, we extracted all instances of talk about customer focus and implementation from the workshop transcript and placed it in chronological order. We then started our analysis by mapping out precisely how the two sets of negotiations unfolded.

Negotiations around the Meaning of Customer Focus

The meaning of customer focus was described in the culture toolkit, although it changed as it was negotiated by the participants during the workshop. We observed four main strands to these negotiations, each relating to a different meaning: (a) *who is the customer?*; (b) *what is the relationship with the customer*; (c) *are we customer focused?*; and (d) *the need for a commercial focus*. Figure 7.1 portrays how these different strands played out during the workshop, showing that, by the end, the meaning had changed from a need to be customer focused to a need to be *commercially* focused.

In the opening address by a senior manager, the need to achieve a 'common understanding' of *customer focus* is introduced. Another senior manager makes some suggestions as to how a customer focus might be defined in terms of a *relationship* with the customer [1].[1] At this point, a senior manager seeks clarification on *who is the customer* and whether they are talking about the *end user* (the person who buys and uses the phone) or *another business* (another company that sells the phone) [2]. This comment triggers a lively debate concerning *who is the customer*. A senior manager then attempts to return to the nature of relationship with the customer – one in which *the customer is dominant* [3]. This triggers another debate about *who is the customer* and, if it is a business-to-business relationship, how it should be conducted [4].

---

[1]   The numbers in square brackets provide a cross-reference to Figure 7.1.

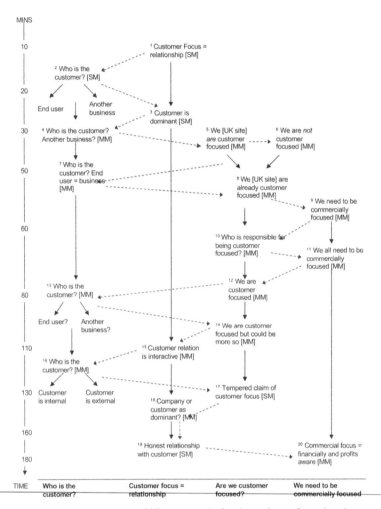

Note: SM = senior manager; MM = middle manager. Left-axis numbers refer to time, i.e., minutes after the commencement of the workshop; the light, dashed arrows indicate the order of interventions, which are numbered; the bold arrows indicate the development of the different meanings; and the phrases at bottom of the figure refer to the different meanings proposed and developed during the workshop.

Source: Reproduced from Thomas et al. (2011: 28).

Figure 7.1   Summary of negotiations around customer focus

One of the middle managers then challenges the assumption that the UK site is not already customer focused [5]. A debate ensues over whether this is the case, shifting the discussion towards claims that the UK site *is already cus-*

tomer focused. This claim is disputed by some participants [6] but is supported by others. During this debate, the discussion returns to *who is the customer*, and becomes further complicated as the *end user is equated with business* [7]. The claim that the UK site is *already customer focused* re-emerges [8].

At this point, the importance of a customer focus is challenged at a more fundamental level as one of the middle managers argues for the *need for a commercial focus* [9]. This comment is followed by a long silence. Another middle manager attempts to shift the emphasis away from the accusation that they lack a commercial focus by arguing that it is sales and marketing staff who are *responsible* for the customer [10], but the discussion soon returns to the need for a *commercial focus* [11] – being close to the customer is only useful if they have a commercial focus. A middle manager asks for a show of hands on who believes that they are already *customer focused* [12], which sparks another debate on *who is the customer* [13], the nature of the *relationship*, and whether the company *is customer focused*.

The discussion around *who is the customer* returns to the earlier debate – whether it is the *end user* or the *business* that sells the phone. It arrives at a denouement with a statement that, although already customer focused, they could be *more so* [14]. This is interspersed with a discussion of the nature of the *relationship* between company and customer, which should be *interactive* [15]. The debate about *who is the customer* continues but switches to *internal versus external* customers [16]. Throughout this discussion, the debate that the company *already is customer focused* reappears [17]. Another middle manager returns to the *relationship* with the customer, questioning whether the customer should be dominant. The debate moves to whether *the customer or company should be dominant* [18].

Following this debate, the video presentation returns to the issue of customer focus, defined in terms of an *honest relationship* [19]. After the video, the stop/start/continue exercise is conducted and the need for a *commercial focus* re-emerges [20], initiated and supported by middle managers. A gradual consensus develops regarding the definition of a commercial focus – being *financially aware* and *profitable*. By the end of the discussion, the group has come to an agreement that a customer focus is less important than the need for a commercial focus.

Negotiations around the Meaning of Implementation

These negotiations were more polarized with two separate, parallel discussions – one involving senior managers and the other involving middle managers – with little engagement between them. Senior managers defined implementation in terms of the next step – a continuation of the workshops – to create awareness of the existing culture and where specific activities were decided by head office. Middle managers tried to fix the meaning of implementation in terms of local actions, which required clear direction, roadmaps, and timelines. Figure 7.2 portrays these negotiations during the workshop.

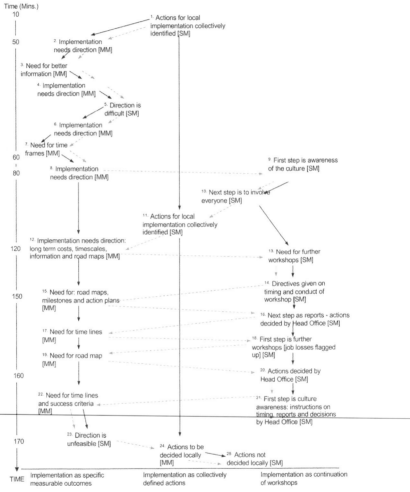

Note: SM = senior manager; MM = middle manager. Left-axis numbers refer to time, i.e., minutes after the commencement of the workshop; the light, dashed arrows indicate the order of interventions, which are numbered; the bold arrows indicate the development of the different meanings; and the phrases at the bottom of the figure refer to the different meanings proposed and developed during the workshop.
Source: Reproduced from Thomas et al. (2011: 30).

Figure 7.2   Summary of negotiations around implementation

At the start of the workshop, a senior manager states that one of the aims of the workshop is a *collective identification* of the *actions* that are needed to implement the change program at the *local site* [1]. Fifty minutes later, a middle manager picks up the issue of implementation, suggesting that it requires a clear *direction*, something which is currently lacking [2]. Another middle manager then suggests that, rather than a lack of direction the issue is a *lack of information* [3], although this is countered by another middle manager as the discussion returns to a *lack of direction* [4]. At this point, a senior manager tries to divert the debate by arguing that it is *difficult* to establish a clear direction [5]. Another middle manager attempts to press for implementation to be defined in terms of the need for *direction* [6]. Some frustration is expressed during this discussion by middle managers. A senior manager attempts to clarify the debate by questioning whether implementation is about setting *time frames* [7]. A middle manager returns to the issue of implementation requiring locally agreed *direction* [8]. A senior manager switches the issue to argue that implementation involves an *awareness of the culture* at the different sites [9]. At this point, a middle manager draws attention to the power of head office: 'You know it's them and us and we always have to do what [head office] says.' A senior manager then defines implementation in terms of the *first step* being an increased *awareness of the existing culture*, which is reinforced by another senior manager.

At this stage, the video is shown. It defines implementation in terms of the *next step*, which is to *involve everyone* [10]. Following the video, a middle manager asks for feedback on whether actions identified in previous workshops were implemented. In response, a senior manager returns to implementation as *collectively identified actions* to be *taken at the local site* [11]. Later, a middle manager again raises the issue of implementation requiring *direction* [12]. A discussion ensues among middle managers that links *direction* to *long-term costs*, *timescales*, *information*, and *empowerment*, and the need for *roadmaps*. However, this definition is ignored by a senior manager, who returns to implementation as requiring *further workshops* [13]. The discussion, among senior managers, turns to the *culture kit*, as directives are issued for the specific *timing* and *conduct* of subsequent workshops [14]. In this way, talk is diverted from the need for a clear direction into instructions about the process for conducting future workshops.

Later, the middle managers return to the need for *a roadmap*, *milestones*, and *action plans* as a necessary part of implementation [15]. At this stage, a middle manager takes up the definition of implementation as *next step* – not in terms of future workshops or greater cultural awareness, as suggested previously by a senior manager, but in terms of setting *action plans*. In response, there is a strong assertion of control as a senior manager defines *next step* as *reports* and *actions* to be *decided by head office* [16], contradicting an earlier point that actions are to be collectively identified. A middle manager returns to the need for a *timeline* [17], while a senior manager returns to the *first step* being the need to conduct *further workshops* by August [18]. The same manager refers, somewhat threateningly, to possible job losses: 'We don't know if you're going to be here in 2003–2004.' Again, a middle manager raises the need for *roadmaps* [19] and, again, a senior manager defines implementation in terms of a set of *activities decided by head office* [20]. This is reinforced by another senior manager who returns to the *first step* requiring greater *cultural awareness*, emphasizing *process* rather than activities, setting out *instructions for timing and reports*, and noting that decisions will be *taken by head office* [21]. There is another attempt to define implementation in terms of *timelines* and *success criteria* by a middle manager [22]. Measuring success is dismissed as *unfeasible* by a senior manager [23], contradicting the earlier video. A middle manager reminds participants that implementation was defined as *collective actions* to be *taken by the local site* [24]. This is directly refuted by a senior manager, thereby contradicting the opening statement at the start of the workshop and the message from the chief executive officer in the video [25].

Communicative Practices during the Negotiations

We examined the two sets of negotiations further. Through an interpretative process involving discussions among all three co-authors, we identified different patterns in how participants engaged in the workshop conversations. We distilled these patterns into the following list of distinct communicative practices (Box 7.2).

We then compared the specific communicative practices used by senior and middle managers in negotiating each of the two issues. In the case of customer focus, a senior manager initially *invites* a discussion of customer focus and *proposes* a meaning by making reference to the culture toolkit; it is a middle manager who *challenges* the initial meaning that the company is not sufficiently customer focused. This meaning is then *reiterated* by other middle managers. Another middle manager *proposes* the new meaning of the need for a commercial focus. This meaning is *reiterated* by other middle managers. Middle managers and senior managers *build* on each other's meanings throughout the workshop. Senior managers also seek *clarification* of middle managers' meanings in ways that open up the negotiation of meaning with statements like 'What do you mean?' There is only one incident where a senior manager attempts to *dismiss* the meaning proposed by a middle manager by saying 'I don't agree with that.' There is also frequent *affirmation* of middle managers' contributions by senior managers.

BOX 7.2   SUMMARY OF COMMUNICATIVE
PRACTICES

Practice	Description
Inviting	Statements that encourage participation by other actors in negotiation of meanings
Affirming	Statements that agree with alternative meanings proposed by other actors
Clarifying	Questions that open up negotiations regarding meanings
Building	Statements that engage with, elaborate, or develop alternative meanings proposed by other actors
Dismissing	Statements that serve to rebuff or ignore alternative meanings proposed by other actors
Reiterating	Statements that return to and repeat meanings
Deploying authority	Statements that contain directives that eliminate alternative meanings proposed by other actors
Invoking hierarchy	Statements that refer to superiors in order to justify the elimination of alternative meanings proposed by other actors
Reifying	Statements that invoke the culture toolkit to represent a particular, non-negotiable meaning
Proposing	Statements that introduce a new meaning
Challenging	Statements that reject or critique alternative meanings proposed by other actors
Undermining	Statements that criticize other actors in order to discredit their proposed meanings
Holding to account	Statements that demand action from other actors (or question a lack of action) in ways that undermine or discredit their proposed meanings

Source: Adapted from Thomas et al. (2011: 26).

In the case of implementation, despite an initial *invitation* to middle managers to participate in identifying implementation actions, senior managers repeatedly assert the original meaning of implementation as indicated in the culture toolkit. When middle managers attempt to *propose* alternative meanings of implementation, senior managers repeatedly *dismiss* them and *reiterate* their original meaning. In addition, they *deploy authority* by drawing on their position to silence middle managers – many interventions involve direct orders to subordinates. They *invoke hierarchy* by referring to other members of the top echelons of the organization to back up their meaning of implementation. Senior managers regularly *reify* the culture toolkit to present implementation as having a non-negotiable, fixed meaning rather than using it to facilitate the negotiation of different meanings. They refer to the culture toolkit (in the case of the video), point at it (in the case of the PowerPoint slides on the timeline), and wave it about (in the case of the brochure) to justify adhering to the specified implementation plan, rather than modifying it in light of points raised by middle managers. As the workshop progresses, senior managers escalate their coercive communicative practices, deploying them simultaneously as when a senior manager *dismisses* a request to change the timing of the workshops, *reiterates* the meaning proposed by another senior manager, *invokes hierarchy*, and *reifies* the culture toolkit all at the same time.

Middle managers employ some of the same communicative practices they used in the case of customer focus. For example, they initially *challenge* the senior managers' meaning and *propose* an alternative one, which they continue to *reiterate*. However, they do not engage in any *building* and, in response to continued attempts by senior managers to reproduce their preferred meaning of implementation, middle managers try to *undermine* it and *hold* senior managers *to account* by demanding action. As senior managers increasingly reinforce their preferred meaning of implementation towards the end of the workshop, middle managers appear to give up trying to negotiate its meaning and, around the two-hour mark, the number of middle managers' interventions starts to decline.

Comparing the various communicative practices in the two sets of negotiations (Box 7.3) shows how a discursive template can be negotiated among participants or simply hammered home. In the case of customer focus, the meaning that emerged from the workshop was multi-authored. The use of affirming, clarifying, and building by senior managers allowed middle managers to build on their meaning, as a result of which new knowledge concerning the need to be commercially focused was developed collaboratively during the workshop. In the case of implementation, senior managers used more coercive communicative practices by dismissing middle managers, deploying their authority, and invoking hierarchy coupled with the reification of the original meaning of implementation as laid out in the video and brochure. This led middle managers to resist by challenging, undermining, and holding superiors to account. The result was stalemate – no new ideas for implementation were developed.

BOX 7.3   COMPARISON OF COMMUNICATIVE PRACTICES

Communicative practice	Customer focus		Implementation	
	Senior managers	Middle managers	Senior managers	Middle managers
Inviting	X		X	
Affirming	X			
Clarifying	X			
Building	X	X		
Dismissing			X	
Reiterating		X	X	X
Deploying authority			X	
Invoking hierarchy			X	
Reifying			X	
Proposing	X			
Challenging		X		X
Undermining				X
Holding to account				X

In sum, the study shows how meaning is negotiated. Conversations around change dialogue can be productive (Tsoukas, 2009), as in the case of a commercial focus. But this is not always the case, as in the stand-off over implementation. Moreover, it is possible for the same conversation to be both productive and unproductive in terms of generating shared meanings. The study also shows how particular communicative practices affect negotiations – sometimes facilitating the co-construction of meaning and, sometimes, reinforcing existing meanings. Senior managers are in a privileged position to propose a particular discursive template and to use certain practices that reinforce their preferred meanings. However, that does not mean that other actors will necessarily accept them.

CONCLUSION

This chapter provides insight into how organizational change is discursively accomplished as organizations are 'talked into existence and the basis is laid for action' (Taylor and Van Every, 2000: 58) through 'ongoing authoring acts situated in everyday work' (Carlsen, 2006: 132). A wide range of discursive activities were conducted in the three cases. At CityWorks, we see the importance of discursively constructing an organizational identity, as well as skills and emotions. Mère et Enfant shows how wider discourses – localization and internationalization – set the scene for the delegate's activities. In Utel's workshop, we lean more about the micro dynamics of how the meaning of a change program was negotiated.

BOX 7.4   EMPIRICAL POINTERS

- The study of texts and interviews is supplemented by observations in the cases of CityWorks and Mère et Enfant. This allows greater insight into the micro dynamics of how meanings are negotiated in real time and in situ.
- Naturally occurring talk in real time – such as meetings and workshops – are excellent sites for finely grained analyses using a discursive approach.
- Such analysis shows how multiple strands of negotiation can be threaded through a single 'conversation.' In the case of Utel, it would be difficult to conclude whether the workshop was participative or not since the micro interactions of which it was constituted contained elements of both participation and hierarchy.
- Analyzing data using a discursive approach often involves an iterative process of distilling patterns and reducing complexity. For example, in the case of Utel, we started with the entire workshop transcript and selected all the talk referring to customer service and implementation. We put it in chronological order and logged who made each statement. We then clustered individuals into three groups – engineers, administrative staff, and senior managers – to see if there were different patterns among them. We then reduced this to senior and middle managers because we could see significant differences. Having traced the flow of negotiations and interpreted them in the form of arguments related to customer focus and implementation, we distilled them visually by producing Figures 7.1 and 7.2. Finally, we identified a discrete set of communicative practices that we could compare across the two issues.
- One of the great juggling acts of a discursive researcher is to distil patterns to the extent that they can be translated into findings that are sufficiently general as to have relevance to other settings while, at the same time, not reducing complexity to such an extent that all the richness is squeezed out of the data.

- Workshops are a useful setting for researchers adopting a discursive approach – they represent a series of naturally occurring, structured interactions that can be observed in real time. In the case of Utel, these workshops were repeated in a similar fashion throughout the company. While we did not claim that all workshops produced the same negotiations of meaning, we were able to justify the in-depth study of a single workshop.

8. Using a discursive approach to study organizational fields

In this chapter, I show how a discursive approach can be used to investigate organizational fields. Here, the focus is on the interorganizational level of analysis – what is happening among organizations rather than (although often in addition to) what is happening inside them. The term organizational field has been defined in various ways (Wooten and Hoffman, 2017; Zietsma et al., 2017), but is generally accepted to be 'a social arena in which individuals and organizations partake of a common meaning system and interact more frequently with one another than with actors outside of the field' (Scott, 1995: 207–208). It is often used interchangeably with 'institutional field,' which is a collection of organizations that 'constitute a recognized area of institutional life' (DiMaggio and Powell, 1991: 148) based on exchange or market relationships and/or social issues (Zietsma et al., 2017). Much of the work on organizational/institutional fields has been conducted by institutional theorists who are interested in the emergence, persistence, and decline of institutions. These are 'social structures that have attained a high degree of resilience [and are] composed of cultural-cognitive, normative, and regulative elements that … provide stability and meaning to social life' (Scott, 2008: 48). Accordingly, they take the form of organized patterns of action, such as marriage, as well as formal organizational structures, such as the church (Zucker, 1987).

A discursive approach argues that institutions are constructed primarily through the production of texts (Phillips et al., 2004). Accounts of actions and the ideas they generate are transmitted across time and space through texts, which are the main way of transcending 'the essentially transitory character of social processes … [and crossing] separate and diverse local settings' (Smith, 1990: 168). Specific actions and practices may form the basis of institutionalized processes but, in being observed, interpreted, and then written and talked about, or depicted in some other way, texts are generated. When these texts draw on one another in well-established and understandable ways, they present a unified view of some aspect of social reality, which becomes reified and institutionalized (Phillips et al., 2004). In other words, as a dominant discourse emerges, it tends to produce institutions, as in the case of the dominant discourses of risk, strategy, and lean discussed in Chapter 2 (Box 8.1).

BOX 8.1 THE DOMINANT DISCOURSES AND INSTITUTIONS

	The discourse of risk	The discourse of strategy	The discourse of lean
Examples of organized patterns of action	The use of institutionalized techniques to calculate the probability of a negative event occurring multiplied by the consequences if it does	The use of institutionalized models to identify internal strengths and weaknesses and external threats and opportunities to formulate strategy	The use of institutionalized production methodologies to create value and eliminate waste in the manufacture of products/delivery of services
Examples of formal organizational structures	Society of Risk Analysis, Basel Committee on Banking Supervision	Strategy Institute, consulting companies	Lean Enterprise Institute, Lean Global Network
Cognitive elements	Risk is an objective phenomenon that can be calculated	Strategy is a competitive position in an industry or a plan of action to achieve organizational goals	Lean creates the most value for the customer at the minimum cost
Normative elements	Risk helps to normalize uncertainty	Strategy is associated with success	Lean is associated with success
Regulative elements	Codes of risk compliance, exposure levels	Share markets, reporting to external stakeholders	Lean six sigma, lean certification

In this chapter, I return to research discussed in earlier chapters to show how a discursive approach can be applied to the study of organizational fields. I examine the creation of new institutions, as well as changes in the degree of institutionalization in different fields. Finally, I explore how the metaphor of an ecology may offer additional insights in exploring interorganizational dynamics from a discursive perspective.

NEW INSTITUTIONS IN AN ORGANIZATIONAL FIELD: THE CANADIAN TREATMENT ADVOCATES COUNCIL AND THE STOCKHOLM CONVENTION

CTAC, discussed in Chapter 6, was a new, collaborative organization that brought together actors in an organizational field – the Canadian HIV/AIDS treatment domain (Maguire and Hardy, 2005; Maguire et al., 2001, 2004).

CTAC represents not just a new organization but also a new institution that changed practices in the field (Box 8.2).

BOX 8.2   NEW PRACTICES IN THE CANADIAN HIV/ AIDS TREATMENT DOMAIN

Field-level practices	Before CTAC	After CTAC
Interactions between community and pharmaceutical companies regarding treatment issues	Ad hoc meetings	Regular, ongoing meetings with dedicated team of CTAC representatives, as well as annual meetings and specialized workshops
Primary arena for national community policy discussions on treatment	Canadian AIDS Society's HIV Therapies Committee	CTAC
Community development of treatment advocacy skills	Ad hoc and minimal at provincial level	CTAC has an explicit mandate to develop and train new generation of treatment advocates at national and provincial levels
Main contact for government for collective community view on treatment issues	Canadian AIDS Society	CTAC, Canadian AIDS Society
General pattern of consultation and information exchange on treatment issues in the field	Decentralized, ad hoc	Centralized, regularized
Prominent community actors on treatment issues	Members of Canadian AIDS Society's HIV Therapies Committee; individuals associated with various PWA organizations; various freelancers	Members of CTAC, which are mainly from PWA organizations; Canadian AIDS Society is an observer, not a voting member, and its HIV Therapies Committee has been disbanded
Representation of community organizations	Representational roles are unclear: Canadian AIDS Society does not have systematic representation of other organizations; freelancers are not accountable to any organization	CTAC members are representatives from all provinces, the three largest urban PWA organizations, haemophiliacs, aboriginals, and women
Mandate for providing advice to industry on treatment issues	Actors have no formal mandate to provide advice to industry on treatment issues	CTAC is mandated to consult and exchange information with pharmaceutical companies

Source: Adapted from Maguire et al. (2004: 663).

CTAC was made possible as new subject positions emerged in the discourse of HIV/AIDS in the form of treatment advocates and compassionate pharmaceutical companies (see Chapter 6). As individuals took up these subject positions, they overcame barriers to collaboration that existed both in traditional disease treatment domains and as a result of the conflict between HIV/AIDS activists and industry. However, only some individuals were able to take up these subject positions. In the community, they tended to be individuals who had the disease and volunteered in AIDS organizations with a wide geographic scope. In industry, they were individuals who had a history of working with the community and held liaison positions in more compassionate companies. In other words, the individuals that helped establish CTAC did not 'possess' the power to set up a new institution but, rather, occupied positions in the field that granted them the potential for agency.

The Stockholm Convention on POPs discussed in Chapters 3 and 4 (Maguire and Hardy, 2006; Hardy and Maguire, 2010) shows the formation of a new global regulation governing toxic chemicals. As discussed in Chapter 3, it represented a struggle over a legacy discourse of sound science and a newly emerging discourse of precaution, which emphasized potential risks and facilitated pre-emptive action in the face of scientific uncertainty regarding potential harmful effects. The new global institution was clearly marked by the emerging discourse of precaution, which helped to create new conditions of possibility, although it still bore the traces of the legacy discourse.

A discursive approach thus emphasizes the *possibilities* that come with new institutions, rather than suggesting that they have a deterministic impact. Despite overwhelming support for the elimination of all POPs prior to the Convention, the final text allowed DDT to be used for malaria control, as its meaning changed from being an evil threat to a necessary evil. This change was instigated by two malaria organizations, who were able to leverage a particular discursive space to tell a new narrative about DDT. In addition to influencing the regulatory impact of the Convention, the position of several key organizations in the organizational field changed. However, it is important to note that these effects were not straightforward: the narrative of the malaria organizations did not survive the final plenary and NGOs reacted to the same counter-narrative in vastly different ways.

These two studies challenge the idea that new institutions emerge from the reflexive, politically skilled actions of 'exceptional' individuals, who are not only able to step outside the prevailing conditions of the field to imagine something completely new but also are able to overturn the status quo to achieve it. A discursive approach emphasizes how new subject positions emerge as discourses change, from which some – but not all – organizations or individuals are able to act in ways that were not possible before. In situating the agent in the organizational field in this way, it becomes clear that actors do not simply 'have' the power to change organizational fields; rather their agency 'is ultimately determined by the internal rules of the field' (Chalaby, 1996: 695), as well as their ability to conduct the necessary identity work to occupy particular positions in it.

INCREASING INSTITUTIONALIZATION IN AN ORGANIZATIONAL FIELD: GREEN CHEMISTRY

In the case of green chemistry (Maguire and Hardy, 2016, 2019; Howard-Grenville et al., 2017; Hardy et al., 2020), discussed in Chapter 2, we saw how this discourse has made significant inroads into mainstream chemistry. As the discourse has permeated this organizational field over the last 30 years, new practices have become increasingly institutionalized. New research practices emphasize collaboration among chemists, toxicologists, and environmental scientists at the design stage of chemicals in order to find safe alternatives to hazardous products and processes. As more research projects have been initiated using these practices, institutions in the form of centres of research excellence and new journals have been established. Teaching practices have been modified to incorporate toxicology and environmental science into the chemistry curriculum, ensuring that students learn not only about a chemical's intrinsic functional properties, but also its hazards.

Green chemistry has thus become increasingly institutionalized in terms of organized patterns of action in research, teaching, and commerce. Similarly, new organizational structures have become institutions. The Green Chemistry Institute, launched in the US in 1997, has since integrated into the mainstream chemistry institution – the American Chemical Society. The Canadian Green Chemistry Forum was created within the Chemical Institute of Canada in 2003. In Europe, SusChem was launched in 2004. In the business arena, institutions like the Green Chemistry and Commerce Council, a multi-stakeholder collaboration set up in 2005, promote the commercial adoption of green chemistry principles (Howard-Grenville et al., 2017; Maguire and Hardy, 2019).

A discursive approach explains this growing institutionalization by arguing that changes in the discourse introduced by green chemists inverted the relative importance of exposure and hazard in relation to chemical risks (Maguire and Hardy, 2019). Whereas traditional chemistry avoids risk by limiting exposure to chemical hazards, green chemistry focuses on eliminating the risk altogether (Maguire and Hardy, 2016). This distinction is significant because it changes the object of the discourse – the chemical molecule – and how it is 'known.' Traditional chemists know the molecule in terms of its structure and function – it is a site of discovery and potential innovation. It is left to other scientists – toxicologists and environmental scientists – to identify potential hazards and ascertain acceptable levels of exposure to them. As a result, within the discourse of mainstream chemistry, the object posing the risk is not the molecule but activities that result in an unsafe degree of exposure. The solution therefore lies in regulations that limit exposure. In other words, traditional chemists need not worry about risk – their role is to innovate through their discoveries. Someone else (other scientists or regulators) takes care of chemical risk by identifying and stipulating restrictions on exposure.

In contrast, green chemists know the molecule in terms of properties, functionalities, *and* hazards because of the incorporation of toxicology and environmental science into teaching and research practices. Accordingly, the problem shifts from unsafe exposure to unsafe molecules. The solution to this problem is research by green chemists, who are 'naturally' risk conscious and whose innovations are the source of safer alternatives. In changing how the object of knowledge is known, the organization field in which it is situated also changes as new subject positions emerge and new practices are carried out. Green chemists become more predominant in the field since they are the source of innovations designed to eliminate chemical risk. Regulators become less central since innovations are adopted – not through enforced compliance, but voluntarily as a result of market factors (Maguire and Hardy, 2019) (see Box 8.3 for an example).

BOX 8.3   THE EXAMPLE OF PLASTICS

Plastics are ubiquitous in our society although they are associated with significant chemical risks. Many of the raw materials for plastics are toxic. Its manufacture depends upon non-renewable petroleum, thereby contributing to climate change, as well as involving high temperatures and pressures that expose workers and communities to risks of explosions. At the end of their life, most synthetic plastics end up as waste that does not biodegrade, but instead contaminates landfills and habitats.

According to the traditional discourse, the object that poses the risk is not the molecule per se but activities that result in an unsafe degree of exposure. As a result, regulations are introduced to limit exposure. For example, to deal with carcinogenic effects of vinyl chloride, the US Department of Labor's Occupational Health and Safety Administration regulations stipulate that no employee may be exposed to concentrations greater than 5 ppm averaged over any 15-minute period; and signs must be posted with a clear warning. Risks of explosions are managed by establishing lower and upper explosive limits for vinyl chloride in the air. To deal with risks associated with additives such as phthalates, the EU restricts their concentration in toys and childcare articles to 0.1 percent by weight. Waste streams are regulated to limit the concentration of hazardous substances, as well as by imposing labeling, record keeping, and monitoring obligations on waste producers. The management of risk depends heavily on having regulators in a central position where they can measure toxicity and control exposure.

The discourse of green chemistry emphasizes the elimination of chemical hazards by creating new chemical molecules, substances, and processes that are 'benign by design' throughout the entire plastics life cycle. Green chemists are the source of many innovations that remove the chemical risks associated with plastics. Examples include making plastic from renewable biomass (plant-based material), rather than petroleum, using micro organisms to biosynthesize materials, avoiding toxic intermediate chemicals as well as high temperatures and pressures, and using enzyme, derived from bacteria, to break down plastics at the end of their life. As green chemists become more central in the field, they become a potential source of new, safer technologies which are adopted by industry because of their market potential, rather than being mandated by regulators.

Source: Adapted from Maguire and Hardy (2019: 163).

DECREASING INSTITUTIONALIZATION IN AN ORGANIZATIONAL FIELD: DDT

Changes in discourse can also dismantle institutions. The study discussed in Chapter 4 (Maguire and Hardy, 2009) examined the deinstitutionalization of DDT, following the publication of *Silent Spring* (Carson, 1962). It showed how a text that problematized existing meanings concerning DDT's safety, efficacy, and necessity was taken up in countless other texts authored by other actors. Collectively, these new patterns of authorship, as well as the way in which they translated meanings in *Silent Spring*, resulted in a change in the discourse. As the discourse changed, institutionalized practices of DDT use declined.

The discursive approach in this study was explicitly designed to contribute to institutional theory. Accordingly, data collection aligned with key concepts from this research domain, namely the cognitive, regulative, and normative pillars through which legitimacy and conformity are secured (Scott, 1995). The cognitive pillar is based on a shared understanding or knowledge about the nature of social reality with the result that conformity occurs automatically and unconsciously because of fundamental understandings about the world. The regulative pillar refers to the authority of certain actors to formally constrain behaviour, including the ability to establish rules, monitor, and coerce compliance. The normative pillar influences behaviour by defining what is appropriate or expected. It consists of values and norms that produce legitimacy and conformity based on beliefs that it is the right thing to do.

We collected texts that provided insight into each of these pillars. For the cognitive pillar, we focused on the scientific literature which provides understanding about what DDT 'is.' This literature consists of a massive number of texts. Accordingly, we targeted PhD dissertations to capture the frontiers of scientific knowledge and articles in *Science* to capture additions to scientific knowledge. Using the *Proquest Dissertations and Theses* and *Reader's Guide to Periodical Literature* databases, we retrieved dissertations and articles from 1939 to 1972 with DDT in their title or as a keyword. We also selected two recognized textbooks in ecology and applied entomology (see Chapter 4).

Texts related to the regulative pillar were relatively straightforward – we collected the texts of federal regulations and administrative rulings affecting practices of DDT use between 1939 and 1972. Texts related to the normative pillar were more complicated. Secondary data – a study by Coit Murphy (2005) of the large numbers of letters written by the public in response to *Silent Spring* – allowed us to draw conclusions regarding the public becoming a new category of author of normative texts, but we did not have access to the individual letters. We therefore collected *New York Times* editorials mentioning DDT between 1939 and 1972, which provided a surrogate for public opinion and gave us a manageable number of texts that we could systematically compare over time. We also analyzed three reports on DDT produced by government advisory committees (PSAC, 1963; Ribicoff, 1966; Mrak, 1969). Their recommendations did not have any legal weight or direct legislative impact (and therefore were not considered to be regulative texts), but they did make normative statements about the appropriateness of DDT use.

By collecting and analyzing texts aligned with the three institutional pillars, we were able to explain the process of deinstitutionalization from a discursive standpoint. First, new patterns in the authorship of scientific texts weakened the cognitive pillar as existing 'facts' about DDT were increasingly contested by scientists outside the discipline of economic entomology. As new breeds of scientists published their studies, they came to occupy a powerful new subject position that challenged the authority of economic entomologists. Second, a growing volume of texts concerning the ethics of DDT authored by the public, the media, and politicians weakened the normative pillar supporting DDT use. It led to the emergence of new subject positions related to an environmental lobby that started to challenge the dominance of existing agricultural interests. Finally, legal texts increasingly restricted DDT during the 1960s and the newly formed Environmental Protection Agency soon removed the regulatory pillar by banning the use of DDT completely.

RECONCEPTUALIZING ORGANIZATIONAL FIELDS: THE CASE FOR AN ECOLOGY

This chapter has shown that research using a discursive approach helps to shed light on various aspects of organizational fields. However, the concept of an organizational field can itself be problematic. The metaphor sets boundaries around discursive landscapes that fix them in time and space, making it difficult to understand the nuances and complexities of change. As a result, studies often overemphasize the role of agency in changing fields, as in the case of 'institutional entrepreneurs' (see Hardy and Maguire, 2017). These individuals are credited with somehow being able to adopt 'a reflective position towards institutionalized practices and ... envision alternative modes of getting things done' (Beckert, 1999: 786). This results in researchers concentrating on the political acumen, strategic thinking, and coalition-building abilities of exceptional individuals. Even the body of work that examines how institutions are accomplished through communicative means (see Cornelissen et al., 2018) tends to accentuate the skilful use of language on the part of certain actors. This emphasis on individual exceptionalism ignores the decentred nature of the subject that underpins a discursive approach. Consequently, critics argue that the 'conception of competent agency' remains paramount in institutional research, taking for granted 'the exercise of conscious, sovereign calculation to achieve desired ends with appropriate means' (Cooper et al., 2008: 675; also see Willmott, 2011).

To avoid some of these problems, we adopted the concept of an 'ecology of risks' in the study of BPA discussed in Chapter 2 (Hardy and Maguire, 2020). Our use of the term ecology is informed by disciplines such as political ecology, cultural ecology, and ecological anthropology. It refers to a complex system in which humans and non-humans are connected, and which is apprehended through 'a post-positivist understanding of nature and the production of knowledge about it' (Bridge et al., 2015: 7). Consistent with a discursive approach, it denotes a view of the material environment, not as pregiven or predetermined, but as consisting of myriad objects whose meaning can be constructed in different ways (Watts, 2015). Rather than try to identify a field of organizations, we focused on an ecology constituted by the risks translated by organizations as they converted uncertainty over BPA into more familiar risks over a 20-year period.

Initially, the ecology of risks in which BPA was situated was relatively small. Endocrinologists translated the uncertainty surrounding BPA into a risk to their professional integrity because of what they believed to be toxicologists' outdated methods. Toxicologists translated it into a different version of professional risk – unproven methods used by endocrinologists.

Manufacturers translated the uncertainty into regulatory risk because of the threat of government restrictions. Over the years, other organizations started to translate uncertainty concerning BPA into more familiar risks. Canadian regulators translated an operational risk – they were worried that existing risk assessment processes could not accommodate BPA. Australian regulators translated a different operational risk – they believed the risk lay in how BPA was becoming politicized, threatening the scientific basis of effective chemicals management. NGOs in Canada translated a reputational risk – they were worried that the failure to lobby against BPA would damage their reputations. Canadian retailers also translated a reputational risk associated with customer backlash. Australian NGOs and retailers soon followed suit as they, too, translated reputational risks. By 2013, the ecology of translated risks in which BPA was situated included multiple versions of professional, regulatory, reputational, and operational risks.

The actions taken to manage these translated risks had an indirect effect on BPA. The actions taken by toxicologists, manufacturers, and Australian regulators to manage their professional, regulatory, and operational risks weakened BPA's meaning as a risk object. Toxicologists continued to use orthodox methods to study BPA, which often did not provide evidence of harm. Manufacturers managed regulatory risk by funding toxicologists' studies and repeatedly denying there was any risk. Australian regulators managed their operational risk by maintaining their commitment to existing risk assessment processes, resulting in a finding that BPA did not pose a risk.

A growing number of other risk management actions strengthened BPA's meaning in relation to risk. Endocrinologists' actions to manage professional risk was to critique toxicologists and to continue to use experimental methods, which led to more evidence of harm. Canadian regulators managed their operational risk by fast-tracking the risk analysis of BPA leading to a conclusion that it did pose risks. Retailers managed reputational risk by withdrawing products that contained BPA and promoting 'BPA-free' products. NGOs managed their reputational risk by campaigning against BPA – raising public awareness, mobilizing opposition, and lobbying politicians. As these actions accumulated and reinforced each other, BPA's meaning – as a novel risk – started to stabilize.

The focus on an ecology of risks provides a glimpse into a far more fluid, fragile, multi-dimensional space than is possible with the concept of an organizational field (Box 8.4). In the case of BPA, the ecology was constituted by the translated risks rather than the interests of actors. The same category of actor could translate different risks or different versions of the same risk, as with the case of scientists and regulators. Organizations then took action in relation to their translated risk affecting BPA indirectly, rather than acting directly on BPA on the basis of predetermined interests. For example, manufacturers continued to manufacture BPA and maintain it was safe *because* they translated regulatory risk. Had they translated reputational or strategic risk, their risk management actions might have been different. They might have developed safer alternatives to BPA and even argue that BPA *did* pose risks to encourage customers to switch to new products. In other words, rather than actors with fully formed identities whose pre-existing interests determined their actions, interests and actions emerged from the object of knowledge – the translated risk. The divergent actions of regulators were explained by the different versions of operational risk they translated, not by radical differences in policy contexts or industry lobbying in the two countries. Moreover, when risk management actions reinforced each other, it was not because they had been deliberately mobilized or politically aligned. There was, for example, no evidence of an organized coalition among Canadian NGOs, retailers, and regulators even though their actions to manage their various translated risks reinforced each other in strengthening BPA's status as a risk object. Thus, the ecology was constituted by cumulative, local risk translation efforts, rather than any grand strategy.

BOX 8.4   COMPARING THE CONCEPTS

	Organizational field	**Ecology**
Boundaries	Fixed	Fluid
Object of analysis	Organizations/stakeholders in the field	Object of knowledge of the discourse (in this case, BPA)
Subjectivity	Fully formed subjects initiate action	Discursively formed subjects whose actions influence their subjectivity
Actions	Action by an organization is based on its interests and identity (which tend not to change)	Action by an organization is based on the object of knowledge and the meaning it has for the actor (which can change)
Effect	Mainly intended as the result of strategic, coordinated actions, although countervailing actions of other actors may result in unintended consequences or failure of actions	Unintended, indirect; an accumulation of localized actions may produce synergistic effects
Agency	Conscious, calculated, often unfettered	Contingent, partial, contextual

CONCLUSION

This chapter has argued that a discursive approach can be used to study organizational fields and processes of institutionalization and deinstitutionalization. As such, it is a useful tool in the analysis of interorganizational dynamics. The conceptualization of institutions as discourse shows the fragility of organizational fields and the limits to the agency of the organizations located in them by emphasizing that actors are 'of' the field rather than in (or out) of it. The chapter argues that the metaphor of an ecology is more attuned to these aspects than the metaphor of a field, offering different ways of thinking about the interactions among organizations and better able to accommodate ad hoc, non-deterministic change.

BOX 8.5   EMPIRICAL POINTERS

- A discursive approach is consistent with interorganizational dynamics because of the way in which discourses circulate beyond individual organizations. As such, there are opportunities for discourse scholars to contribute to institutional theory.
- In terms of data collection, both approaches make use of archival texts. It is not hard, then, for discourse scholars to ensure the collection of relevant texts that resonate with institutional theorists, such as 'field-level' texts that provide evidence of the institutional pillars, as shown in the study of DDT.
- However, collecting data that show dynamics affecting an entire field can be difficult to acquire. Researchers may need to be creative by seeking out secondary sources or other 'proxies,' as in our study of DDT.
- Both organizational discourse theory and institutional theory are concerned with practices; researchers should ascertain whether they can gain adequate evidence of practices from texts or whether they also need observations.
- A discursive approach offers an understanding of the fragility of organizational fields and the limitations of the agency of supposed institutional entrepreneurs.
- One way to maintain a less deterministic orientation in research is to reconceptualize the idea of a 'field' in which 'actors' (with pre-existing identities and interests) are located and instead to think of 'objects' around which an 'ecology' forms and about which particular kinds of 'knowledge' are developed, as in the case of the ecology of risk.

PART III

Future challenges

In this final section, I examine some of the future challenges facing researchers who want to use a discursive approach to study organizations and discuss how they might address them. The chapter on consumption addresses the tendency to grant too much agency to certain individuals or organizations in shaping discourse. It argues that we can tackle this challenge by studying the consumption of texts, which helps to guard against overplaying agency. Chapter 10 explores how investigating different forms of resistance provides further insight into the limits of authorial agency. Chapter 11 investigates reflexivity and challenges researchers to be sceptical not only of the issues they study, but also of the knowledge they produce. Finally, I explore the challenge of dealing with materiality within the context of discursive research. I make the case that future studies will need to take a sophisticated account of materiality in light of recent debates.

9. The consumption of discourse

Many discourse researchers concentrate on what goes into producing an influential text – genre of text, frames, rhetoric, narratives, etc. This tends to draw attention to the production of texts and to associate authorship with agency. The appeal of a powerful, agential author is not surprising – many domains of linguistic study are concerned with what makes language effective and how it can be used to bring about change. However, producing a text, by itself, is unlikely to bring about discursive change, no matter how compelling and convincing it may appear to be. The reason for this is that, if we consider agency as actions or interventions that produce a particular effect, any such effect depends upon particular meanings enduring over time, becoming widely shared and being embedded in organizational practices. This requires more than a single text. In other words, meanings must pass from one text to another. This is not straightforward since the meaning of a text is neither unequivocal nor inherent; it is *negotiated* between the text's author and its readers (Czarniawska, 1997) as the text is consumed, which involves being read, interpreted, and then reinscribed or taken up in other texts (Hardy, 2004). During this process, meanings often change as they are decontextualized from the original, local circumstances of their production and recontextualized by being inscribed in other texts or situated in specific practices (Taylor et al., 1996).

In other words, a lot can happen between the production of an initial text and subsequent events – meanings may be wilfully or inadvertently translated by consumers of the text, becoming diluted, intensified, transformed, or even eliminated as they are successively taken up in other texts. Accordingly, an important challenge for researchers is to investigate patterns of consumption in order to avoid the pitfall of glorifying agency. The remainder of this chapter discusses how this challenge can be addressed by tracking meanings over time and studying the role of translation.

MEANINGS OVER TIME

Studies that explore meanings over time investigate whether and why certain meanings 'take' when others do not by examining what happens to meanings *after* a text is produced. In doing so, they consider the consumers of the text and what they do with it (Cuganesan et al., 2007). One study that demonstrates the importance of taking consumers into account is the investigation of the role of Rachel Carson's (1962) book – *Silent Spring* – in the deinstitutionalization of DDT (Maguire and Hardy, 2009) discussed in Chapters 4 and 8.

Silent Spring was widely consumed – it was taken up and reinscribed in a wide range of other texts. More than 500,000 copies of the book had been sold by April 1963 which, in turn, sparked large numbers of letters from members of the public to Carson, her publishers, and the media (Coit Murphy, 2005). The book was consumed by scientists with reviews appearing in scientific journals such as *Ecology* and *Science*, as well as various opinion pieces. It featured in texts produced by NGOs such as the Environmental Defense Fund and National Audubon Society, as well as those authored by members of the agribusiness and chemical industries. *Silent Spring* also appeared in texts produced in the political arena. Portions of the *New Yorker* serialization were read directly into the *Congressional Record* and various legislative reports and regulatory documents referred to claims made in the book.

Clearly, *Silent Spring* was taken up in a wide range of media, public, scientific, political, and regulatory texts, but this did not guarantee that its meanings would endure. Our study was designed to explore whether specific meanings in *Silent Spring* survived this process of consumption. To do so, we first had to establish what those meanings were. We therefore analyzed the content of the book in detail – summarizing the content of each chapter and distilling these summaries into three problematizations of the existing discourse concerning DDT which asserted that it was safe, effective, and necessary (see Figure 9.1). In other words, three key meanings in the book were that DDT was *not* safe, effective, or necessary. It is important to note that these meanings derived from *our* consumption of the text and represent our interpretation of its meaning. They were not necessarily what Rachel Carson had intended to highlight when writing the text. Nonetheless, they provided a useful basis for further investigation since we could then trace them over time by examining whether and how they were reproduced in subsequent texts.

Having identified the three problematizations, we went on to identify a sample of 'counter-texts' authored by various actors. These texts certainly consumed *Silent Spring*, but they did so with the apparent aim of undermining its meaning and dampening its effects. For example, the National Agricultural Chemicals Association produced a pamphlet called *Fact and Fancy* that directly countered Carson's 'allegations' with the industry's 'facts' (NACA, 1962). The National Pest Control Association sent a collection of negative reviews of *Silent Spring* to its members with the following lines (see Lear, 1997: 435):

Hunger, hunger, are you listening
To the words from Rachel's pen?
Words which taken at face value
Place lives of birds above those of men.

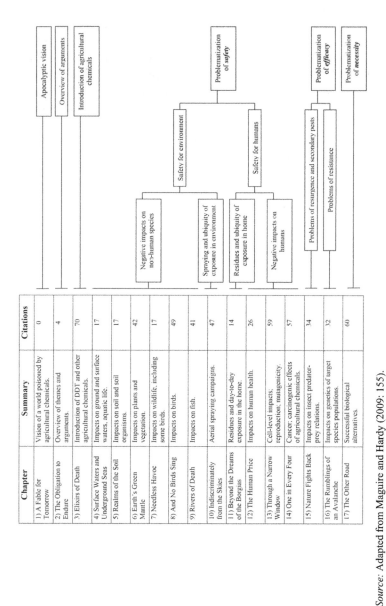

Source: Adapted from Maguire and Hardy (2009: 155).

Figure 9.1   Problematizations in Silent Spring

Chemical manufacturer Monsanto (1962: 9) parodied the opening chapter of *Silent Spring* with a description of plagues and starvation that would occur without pesticides. Dr Robert White-Stevens of American Cyanamid warned during the CBS documentary: 'If man [*sic*] were to faithfully follow the teachings of Miss Carson, we would return to the Dark Ages, and the insects and diseases would once again inherit the earth' (CBS, 1963). *Time*'s review of *Silent Spring* referred to Carson's 'emotional and inaccurate outburst' (September 28, 1962: 48). Many other texts were highly critical of the book and its author. While authors of these texts had clearly consumed *Silent Spring*, they did not reproduce its meanings – on the contrary, they refuted and repudiated them. However, insofar as the use of DDT was voluntarily abandoned and then banned within ten years of the publication of *Silent Spring*, it seemed reasonable to conclude that these counter-texts had limited success in undermining Carson's problematizations.

We also examined whether the problematizations survived less hostile consumers. As reported in Chapters 4 and 8, we selected a sample of texts to investigate in more detail: two textbooks, *New York Times* editorials, and three government reports. We then conducted qualitative coding of whether and how they discussed DDT's safety, efficacy, and necessity and if they diverged from Carson's problematizations. The general pattern across these texts indicated that the problematization of DDT's environmental safety survived consumption – it was taken up in ways that reinforced and reproduced the original problematization. The problematization of DDT's safety for humans survived, but in qualified form – as a *possible* threat. The problematization of efficacy was minimized in that texts often failed to report on it, while the problematization of necessity was subverted as texts reported that DDT could be substituted with other chemicals, rather than the biological controls advocated in *Silent Spring*.

By identifying this pattern of consumption, we were able to gain further insight into the deinstitutionalization of DDT. The survival of the problematization of DDT's safety (albeit in qualified form in the case of human safety) indicated that counter-texts had failed to undermine this key meaning, with the result that users started to abandon DDT and regulators eventually banned it. However, the subversion of the problematization of DDT's necessity meant that deinstitutionalization was less of a threat to manufacturers and the agricultural lobby because they could replace it with other chemical pesticides. Tracking meanings over time shows that the act of authoring *Silent Spring* was not an unfettered, predetermined act of agency. Instead, it was a cumulative, iterative, and sometimes indeterminate process involving a corpus of sequentially authored texts in which some – but not all – meanings survived.

The consumption of discourse

TRANSLATION

A useful resource in studying consumption is the concept of translation, which derives from the work of the French philosopher Michel Serres (Czarniawska and Sevón, 1996; Brown, 2002). It has been used in actor-network theory (Callon, 1984; Latour, 1986) and institutional theory (Czarniawska and Sevón, 1996; Zilber, 2006). The notion of translation draws attention to the way that meanings inevitably change as they travel in space and time (Taylor, 2011). 'To translate is to transform, and in the act of transforming a breaking of fidelity towards the original source is necessarily involved' (Brown, 2002: 7).

Some researchers have focused on actors who deliberately and strategically translate meanings to achieve intended effects (e.g., Lawrence, 2017). However, a discursive approach to translation is more interested in its unintended and indirect effects, as in Chapters 2 and 8, which showed how the uncertainty associated with novel risk BPA was translated into more familiar, organizational risks. In this case, the construction of BPA as a novel risk occurred through the cumulative and indirect effect of countless local translations – it was not a result of a deliberate strategy of translation by a powerful actor.

This is not to say that the aggregated effects of multiple translations are insignificant – they led to restrictions on the use of BPA in Canada as well as the withdrawal of products by many retailers. Another example of the cumulative effects of translation concerns the way in which public risks, such as unemployment, old age, and illness, have been translated into individual risks in recent years, making private citizens responsible for risks that used to be assumed by the state (Vaz and Bruno, 2003; Hacker, 2006). The individual has increasingly become viewed 'as an active agent in the risk-monitoring of collectively produced dangers; risk-information, risk-detection and risk-management is more and more constructed and designed as a matter of private responsibility and personal security' (Elliott, 2002: 305). Economic risks once borne by organizations have also become privatized and individualized (Neff, 2012) through various forms of casualization (Gephart, 2002). Risk translation redistributes responsibility and accountability, changing 'the locus of decision-making, and ... who has the obligation – to "do something"' (Hilgartner, 1992: 47). Individuals shoulder more of the risk burden, while the obligations of governments and organizations to help citizens and employees deal with risk are diminished (see Hardy et al., 2020).

In sum, a discursive approach is attentive to how meanings change as they are translated during the consumption process. It does not preclude the study of deliberate translation strategies, but it is attuned to how translation may occur as an uncoordinated accretion of localized, individual actions. In this way, the investigation of the consumption of texts and translation of meanings protects against an overemphasis on agency, while still allowing for the exploration of significant shifts in power.

CONCLUSION

A discursive approach to studying organizations may start with an investigation of the production of texts – who authored them, what they said, and how they said it. But, if this analysis is complemented with an exploration of how texts are distributed and consumed, additional insight can be gained. The study of consumption comprises an analysis of whether the text is taken up in other texts (or practices) and whether meanings survive this process or whether they are translated in some way – either deliberately or inadvertently. Obviously, this complicates the empirical challenge as studies require a longitudinal element and multiple analyses. Nonetheless, the results are worth it. In Box 9.1, I distil the empirical studies discussed so far in the book into 13 case studies to show the role played by consumption in each.

BOX 9.1　SUMMARY OF CONSUMPTION IN CASE STUDIES

Case study	Chapter	Consumers	Translation of meaning	Outcome
BPA	2, 8	Scientists, manufacturers, NGOs, retailers, regulators consume texts on BPA	Chemical risk is translated into diverse organizational risks	BPA is constructed as a novel risk but only over time and through indirect actions
Canadian HIV/ AIDS domain	6, 8	Members of the HIV/ AIDS community and pharmaceutical industry consume texts informed by the discourse of HIV/ AIDS	The meaning of patient is translated into PWA, activist, treatment activist, and treatment advocate; the meaning of profiteer is translated into compassionate partner	New subject positions become available that facilitate the creation of a new organization, although not everyone is able to take them up

Case study	Chapter	Consumers	Translation of meaning	Outcome
Chemicals management in Canada	3	Government scientists consume texts on two chemicals – VAM and BPA – informed by discourses of precaution and sound science	Precaution is taken up more often in the case of BPA compared to VAM and is translated so as to rebuff criticism and justify restrictions	The discursive work required to translate the two discourses into organizational risk assessment practices differs
CityWorks	7	Members of CityWorks consume the text (announcement) of the manager of the Employment Office concerning working collaboratively	Meaning of the collaboration is translated and enhanced through the discursive construction of an identity, skills, and emotion	A new collaborative organization is created
DDT (1939–1972)	4, 8	A wide range of actors consume *Silent Spring*, which problematizes DDT's safety, efficacy, and necessity	The problematization of environmental safety is translated with a high degree of fidelity; human safety is qualified, efficacy is minimized; necessity is subverted	The reproduction of the problematization of environmental safety helps to explain the de-institutionalization of DDT; subverting necessity makes it easier for industry to accept
DDT (1998–2001)	4	Malaria organizations, NGOs, state actors, and media consume texts on DDT and author different narratives about DDT	Meaning of DDT as evil threat is translated into DDT as hero and as a necessary evil; NGOs consume and act on narratives in different ways	DDT is exempted from the ban and restricted, rather than eliminated like other POPs; WWF becomes less central; IPEN and WHO become more central
GlobalTel	2	Employees consume texts on the new strategy authored by managers informed by a market and a professional discourse	The market discourse is translated with more fidelity; the translation of the professional discourse weakens it	The strategy changes from emphasizing both cost-cutting and technological leadership to concentrate on the former

Case study	Chapter	Consumers	Translation of meaning	Outcome
Green chemistry	2, 8	Actors consume texts on green chemistry	The traditional emphasis on managing risk is translated into eliminating risk	Chemical molecules become known differently, creating a new subject position for green chemists, as well as new practices
Mère et Enfant	7	Members of the Palestinian community consume texts authored by the delegate	The meaning of localization is translated as intended but precipitously, leading to a second cycle of discursive activity	Organization becomes a local NGO and then becomes an international NGO once again
Older workers	5	Committee members consume texts authored by older workers, experts, and service providers informed by the discourses of age, gender, and enterprise	Female versions of the older worker disappear; stories of competence in work search are translated into stories of incompetence; the enterprising identity is translated into unattractive products and risky projects	Recommendations are aimed at older males; age stereotypes are reinforced; older workers are prevented from using small business ownership as a route out of unemployment
Refugee domain	6	Organizations consume texts on refugees, informed by discourses of humanitarianism, sovereignty, and paternalism	Different organizations translate a range of meanings of refugee	Different refugee and organizational identities are constructed; the meaning of refugees as empowered is absent
Stockholm Convention	3, 8	State and non-state actors consume texts informed by discourses of precaution and sound science	The meaning of precaution is translated in more/less strong ways by different actors	Precaution is predominant in the legal text resulting in new conditions of possibility for regulating POPs

Case study	Chapter	Consumers	Translation of meaning	Outcome
Utel	7	Participants at the workshop consume the text outlining the workshop and the planned culture change	The meaning of customer focus is translated into a commercial focus; middle managers translate a new meaning of implementation	The new meaning of a commercial focus is shared by both senior and middle managers; the new meaning of implementation is not

10. Resistance to discourse

The study of resistance is another way to address the challenge of overestimating agency. Murphy (1998: 504) defines resistance as 'a process through which meanings are prevented from becoming fully fixed, meanings remain open, partial, and contingent.' It builds on the investigation of consumption discussed in Chapter 9 since it also tracks meanings over time and, particularly, why imposed meanings fail to 'stick' and how alternative meanings emerge. In this regard, studies often take a 'relational' view by examining struggles between dominant and marginalized actors to show how resistance creates 'an alternative and contrast to dominant practices therefore preventing prevailing norms, meanings, practices, and discourses from becoming entirely fixed or hegemonic' (Wilhoit and Kisselburgh, 2019: 873). Many studies of resistance focus on organized attempts to undermine prevailing meanings and practices but, as I show here, discursive approaches are also attuned to less obvious forms of resistance that are more in keeping with Foucauldian ideas. To explore how a discursive approach can incorporate both forms, I first examine Foucault's conceptualization of resistance in relation to a study of Ghanaian refugees and then explore two forms of resistance in a telecommunications company.

POWER–RESISTANCE RELATIONS IN THE REFUGEE DOMAIN

Power and resistance have often been treated separately in the social sciences, with the exercise of power seen as domination, while resistance takes the form of distinct actions taken to challenge it (Hardy and Clegg, 1996). Foucault's work led to a reconceptualization of this relationship insofar as he presents both power and resistance as diffuse, co-constitutive, and multi-dimensional. There 'are no relations of power without resistances: the latter are all the more real and effective because they are formed right at the point where relations of power are exercised' (Foucault, 1980: 142). On the one hand, regardless of apparent privilege, power is never complete but, rather, always open to the possibilities of resistance. On the other, resistance can only operate through prevailing systems of power/knowledge and may, in fact, end up reinforcing and reproducing those systems.

Chapter 1 referred to Foucauldian 'webs' of power relations that create bodies of knowledge and subject positions, influencing what can be said and who can say it. It emphasized that power is not only constraining – it can be productive, although not easily manipulated by individual actors. Refugee systems (discussed in Chapter 6) are a useful setting in which to explore such webs of power and resistance (Box 10.1).

BOX 10.1 REFUGEE DETERMINATION SYSTEMS: WEBS OF FOUCAULDIAN POWER

The 1948 UN Declaration of Human Rights asserts that everyone has 'the right to seek and enjoy in other countries asylum from persecution.' Refugees have left their own country because of 'a well-founded fear of being persecuted for reasons of race, religion, nationality, membership of a particular social group or political opinion.' Only a small number of the millions of displaced persons around the world claim asylum in Western countries. Many of these countries have refugee determination systems to decide their status – whether they are refugees and whether they will be granted asylum.

Limitations of Sovereign Power in the Refugee Determination System

Western governments have the authority to determine who is a refugee and usually try to control refugee numbers. However, the international flow of asylum-seekers is beyond the ability of any single government to control. It is influenced by events in distant countries, such as war, famine, disease, political upheaval, climate change, etc.

The Refugee Subject Position

The 'refugee' exists as a category recognized through determination processes. It is a subject position in refugee discourse, although with limited rights to speak.

Power/Knowledge in the Refugee Determination System

The knowledge on which individuals are determined to be refugees is fragmented and politicized. It is impossible to 'know' the facts of an individual case. The determination system represents a set of techniques that accords certain facts and information regarding refugees the status of 'truth.'

Resistance in the Refugee Determination System

Overturning refugee determination systems is difficult, although groups can exercise power through these systems as local struggles improve the chances of being accepted as a refugee.

A case study of Ghanaian asylum-seekers in Canada (Hardy, 2003) provides further insights into this conceptualization of power and resistance. Immigration to Canada from Ghana began in the late 1950s following the latter's independence from Britain in 1957. In the 1990s, numbers of immigrants increased to more than 1,000 individuals a year, a large proportion of whom applied for refugee status (Owusu, 1996; Firang, 2011). However, relatively few were determined to be refugees by the Canadian refugee system. As a result, members of the Ghanaian community decided to resist the system that was denying entry to their compatriots.

> I thought [we] … should organize, to do the research and get the documentation, and convince the government, or whoever does the refugees' determination, of the real situation which is driving people to this country. That way they couldn't accuse us of being bogus or queue jumpers … The Canadian government and the NGOs think that as far as Africa is concerned, Somalia is the only refugee-producing country. They can only see refugee-producing countries where there is open warfare, and people are killing themselves. (Member of the Ghanaian community)

One step taken by these individuals was to provide information to the Canadian government on the political situation in Ghana to reinforce the validity of Ghanaian claims for asylum.

> In the initial stages [interactions with government officials] were full of resentment but it was part of a long-term strategy. People take time to accept new ideas. Also being black from a third world country meant they had certain stereotypes. But we kept on and we succeeded in organizing a series of cultural meetings with the [Canadian] Immigration and Refugee Board and our community to highlight certain cultural differences. From there it evolved on its own and we had a good relationship especially under the previous administration … Initially the [Board's] Documentation Center tried to dispute our facts but now I think they accept them. (Member of the Ghanaian community)

Ghanaians worked with NGOs to 'educate' Canadian officials and the media regarding the 'true' situation in Ghana.

> [The Ghanaians] have their own correspondence with the minister's office in Ottawa. They've made a number of representations to immigration officials. They

have their own contacts. They constantly talk to people at the documentation center, which advises board members on the conditions in their country. One of the last country profiles on Ghana was full of mistakes, which they corrected. (NGO representative)

Ghanaians seeking asylum were provided with education, information, and support, such as mock panel hearings to coach them on how to handle the determination hearing.

The people taking the decisions don't know the situation. So, we started to docu-ment it and got [Ghanaian] volunteers to follow claimants through the system, go to hearings with them, explain the system to and their rights to them and, at the same time, help them document their situation ... [The Ghanaians also] developed credibility to the point where they now are working on a collegial basis with [civil servants]. (NGO representative)

Ghanaians slowly gained a voice within the system. The acceptance rate of Ghanaians applying for refugee status increased from less than 7 percent in 1987–1988 to over 30 percent in 1990–1991. By coming to understand the refugee determination system and learning how to operate more effectively within it, Ghanaians were in a stronger position to exercise power through it – albeit in the form of small, local struggles concerning the determination of individual refugees. As Foucault points out: 'Freedom does not basically lie in discovering or being able to determine who we are but in rebelling against those ways in which we are already defined, categorized and classi-fied' (quoted in Sawicki, 1991: 27). The Ghanaians' actions thus illustrate a Foucauldian view of resistance: they created 'knowledge,' enabling them to exercise power through the web of power relations that constituted the deter-mination system and increasing the chances that it would produce a positive identity – genuine refugees. This resistance did not overthrow, dismantle, or even change the system to which they were subjected, but it did afford them a degree of security in a safe country.

FORMS OF RESISTANCE AT GLOBALTEL

A significant amount of research has studied resistance in the form of organ-ized 'insurrection,' where the dynamics are often visible and well documented (Mumby et al., 2017). This has, however, sometimes been at the expense of studies of low-key resistance or 'infrapolitics,' which involves practices that are 'individual and hidden, covert, anonymous or nonattributable and/ or ambiguous in their oppositional intent' (Mumby et al., 2017: 1164). In this section, I compare both forms of resistance by revisiting GlobalTel (Hardy and Thomas, 2014) discussed in Chapter 2.

This study traced the two components of GlobalTel's strategy over a three-year time frame: cutbacks to maintain shareholder value, referred to as being cost effective, and technological leadership, referred to as being (technologically) first and best. The former drew on a wider market discourse circulating in the industry. The latter drew on a longstanding professional discourse in the company associated with its leadership position derived from patents, new product development, and technological innovation. Chapter 2 discussed the discursive work and organizational practices enacted by management in relation to each component, which saw the strengthening of cutbacks and reinforcement of the market discourse and the weakening of technological leadership and the professional discourse. Here, I discuss the role of resistance to each of these strategic components and compare the different forms that it took.

Visible instances of organized resistance to cost cutting arose as powerful actors drew on alternative discourses to counter the market discourse. The prime minister drew on a discourse of egalitarianism to question the large salaries of the senior executives who had recently announced massive job losses in order to undermine the latter's cost-cutting proposals. Union leaders, at a rally protesting the cuts, invoked a nationalist discourse to criticize the outsourcing of jobs to low-wage countries. A government minister also drew on a discourse of nationalism, when he blamed the layoffs on 'an Americanization of [our] industry, in which profit and upturns in the stock market control the whole process' (media report). However, despite obvious acts of coordinated resistance by relatively powerful groups, they had little impact. When we looked for evidence of whether these activities changed the meaning of cost cutting, we could find little indication that the alternative discourses were widely taken up or that they displaced the emphasis on the market discourse. Cost-cutting practices continued and, in fact, intensified despite these attempts to resist them.

When we examined resistance to being first and best, we found far more complex dynamics. When discussing this component of the strategy, employees drew on sporting and military discourses circulating in the media as they compared GlobalTel's performance with its close rival – CompTel (a telecommunications company of similar national importance in a neighbouring country). The two companies were regularly juxtaposed to praise the 'winner' and scorn the 'loser.' When GlobalTel was the winner, employees attributed it to being first and best technologically – the professional discourse eclipsed the market discourse. However, when GlobalTel was seen as losing to its competitor, employees started to debate the meaning of being first and best. Did it mean superiority in terms of the technological features of the phone, as with GlobalTel, or did it mean being best in relation to customers as appeared to be the case with CompTel? Box 10.2 provides an example of how, during such exchanges, the meaning of being first and best changed as it was disconnected from the professional discourse and the company's engineering skills and folded into the market discourse – being best in terms of customers. However, by undermining the professional discourse in this way, employees also unwittingly undermined their own professional skills – the market discourse that they were now privileging was the same discourse that threatened their jobs through cuts.

> ## BOX 10.2   CHANGING THE MEANING OF BEING FIRST AND BEST
>
> *Employee:* And the other point on [being] the first – CompTel wasn't first with GSM [a new technology].
>
> *Senior manager:* No.
>
> *Employee:* But they're making substantial amounts of money …
>
> *Senior manager:* Yeah.
>
> *Employee:* And we need to keep that reality in mind.

Box 10.3 compares the two forms of resistance at GlobalTel. In the case of being cost effective, there was evidence of organized resistance in the form of insurrection – highly visible, collectively organized efforts by politicians and unions to change the discourse away from the market to protect jobs in the name of egalitarianism and nationalism. However, although these alternative discourses were introduced, there was no evidence that they left any long-term traces in terms of different meanings or practices. In other words, they did not change the debate about the need for cutbacks. The market discourse, which necessitated these cuts, continued to hold sway. In contrast, the meaning of being first and best was changed through multiple instances of unorganized, uncoordinated, unintentional resistance which, ironically, threatened the jobs of the very employees whose discursive manoeuvres changed its meaning.

BOX 10.3 COMPARING FORMS OF RESISTANCE

	Be cost effective	Be first, be best
Form of resistance	Insurrection	Infrapolitics
Original discourse	Market	Professional
Inferred meaning of the original discourse	Success depends upon cutbacks, which are necessary in current market conditions	Success depends upon technological leadership, which depends upon engineering skills
Alternative discourses proposed	Nationalism, egalitarianism	Sport, war, competition
Source of alternative discourses	Government, unions	Media
Change in meaning from alternative discourse	Cutbacks should not be carried out because they are unpatriotic or unfair	CompTel is the winner – being first and best to market is more important than being first and best technologically
Evidence of other actors taking up the alternative discourse	None	Employees and managers
Impact on original discourse	The relevance and importance of market discourse is strengthened	The relevance and importance of professional discourse is weakened; market discourse is strengthened
Impact of resistance on strategy	Negligible: actors continue to accept the meaning of cutbacks as inevitable and (possibly) beneficial	Significant: actors question whether (their own) professional engineering skills are important to company's success

Source: Adapted from Hardy and Thomas (2014: 332).

CONCLUSION

Resistance is a complex phenomenon. It can both challenge existing power relations and reproduce them. It is always situational and contextual. It can be collective or individual. It can involve organized groups drawing on alternative discourses in intentional attempts to change meanings and it can occur gradually and iteratively as meanings are changed almost by accident in local, transversal struggles. It has multiple possible outcomes, not all of which may be intended or necessarily bring about 'better' outcomes (Mumby et al., 2017). Box 10.4 summarizes the nature of resistance and its outcomes in each of the case studies discussed in the book. It shows considerable variation in whether the resistance was organized or not, who conducted it, if it was intended, and whether it was successful.

BOX 10.4 SUMMARY OF RESISTANCE IN CASE STUDIES

Case study	Chapter	Nature of resistance	Outcome
BPA	2, 8	Resistance took the form of an uncoordinated struggle among actors – some of whose risk management actions strengthened BPA's status as a risk object, while others weakened it	Resistance to the construction of BPA as a novel risk failed
Canadian HIV/ AIDS domain	6, 8	Individuals resisted the identity of patient and attempted to take up other identities, such as treatment advocate	Some individuals were successful in taking up these identities and went on to play a role in CTAC; others were unable to take up the necessary subject positions
Chemicals management in Canada	3	Industry actors formally resisted the findings of government regulators through submissions made during the process	Resistance was more successful in the case of VAM than BPA; the discursive work in response to the resistance varied in the two cases
CityWorks	7	The workshop that gave rise to CityWorks was a form of resistance to the directive from the Employment Office, but it was largely emergent and unintended	The resistance was successful in that CityWorks was created in ways that exceeded the directive from the Employment Office
DDT (1939–1972)	4, 8	Resistance took the form of counter-texts by industry and political actors who opposed the move to restrict DDT	The resistance failed insofar as DDT was banned, but was successful in that it was substituted with other chemical pesticides
DDT (1998–2001)	4	Low-power actors (malaria NGOs) resisted the initial narrative of DDT as evil threat and promoted a counter-narrative	The resistance was successful in that DDT was restricted rather than banned, even though the counter-narrative did not endure to appear in the legal text of the Convention
GlobalTel	2	Resistance occurred in the form of both organized insurrection and infrapolitics	Resistance in the form of infrapolitics had more impact in changing meaning than insurrection, although it was not necessarily intended

Case study	Chapter	Nature of resistance	Outcome
Green chemistry	2, 8	Green chemists resisted the discourse of chemistry	Green chemists were successful in creating and institutionalizing an alternative discourse of green chemistry
Mère et Enfant	7	The security forces resisted the dismissal of staff; the delegate then effectively resisted his own, earlier discursive work	The delegate's resistance was successful in that Mère et Enfant became an international NGO again, which caused the resistance by the security forces to fail
Older workers	5	Some individuals resisted moves by the Committee to force them to tell stories	This uncoordinated resistance was largely unsuccessful
Refugee domain	6, 10	The Refugee Forum resisted mainstream NGOs; Ghanaian refugees resisted the determination system and low approval rates	Both groups had some success but did not overturn existing power relations in the refugee domain
Stockholm Convention	3, 8	Resistance by different actors to the new discourse (precaution) and the legacy discourse (sound science)	Resistance to the legacy discourse appeared to be more successful in that the language of the legal text was highly precautionary
Utel	7	Resistance to senior managers by middle managers regarding the meaning of customer focus and implementation	The resistance succeeded in changing the meaning of a customer focus to a consumer focus and in getting senior management to share the new meaning; it was not successful in the case of implementation

11. Reflexivity in research on discourse

Reflexivity is another challenge for researchers. It involves questioning what is taken for granted and exposing the hidden assumptions, meanings, and power relations that underpin particular understandings of 'reality.' In this chapter, I discuss two forms of reflexivity. The first concerns the way reflexive practices serve to problematize the phenomenon under investigation, often with the aim of unsettling more established versions of reality and generating alternative ways of thinking (Grandy and Mills, 2004). The second is radical or self-reflexivity (Cunliffe, 2003; Langley and Klag, 2019), where researchers interrogate their own involvement in the production of knowledge and researchers turn 'the reflexive gaze onto ourselves' in order to question 'the "truth claims" we make and the ways we have constructed reality' (Thomas et al., 2009: 316).

A discursive approach lends itself to both forms of reflexivity. By emphasizing how power relations circulating through discourses produce bodies of knowledge, this approach is well placed to disturb conventional wisdoms. By highlighting the fragile and decentred nature of identities, it sheds doubt on the idea of an objective, expert researcher who is somehow able to step outside of discourse in order to comment upon it. By focusing on the role of texts, it acknowledges that researchers are accomplices in processes of knowledge production. However, being reflexive is not necessarily straightforward. Accordingly, in this chapter, I examine ways in which researchers can be reflexive when using a discursive approach – in terms of both problematizing reality and being self-reflexive.

PROBLEMATIZING REALITY

Reflexive practices that help to paint alternative, unorthodox pictures of what we consider to be 'reality' are part and parcel of a discursive approach. By acknowledging that language constructs rather than reveals, discourse scholars look beyond what appears to 'be' to examine how it *came* to be. Accordingly, empirical studies that rely on a discursive approach are designed to challenge the conventional wisdom concerning the phenomenon under investigation, as well as the theorizing used to make sense of it. Box 11.1 summarizes how the studies discussed in this book problematize some aspect of reality.

BOX 11.1 EXAMPLES OF PROBLEMATIZING 'REALITY' IN CASE STUDIES

Case study	Chapter	Phenomenon being problematized	Findings
BPA	2, 8	Risk is objective	Novel risks are constructed over time, by diverse organizations and often in unintended ways
Canadian HIV/ AIDS domain	6, 8	Actors have fixed identities which, in the HIV/AIDS domain, results in conflict between community and pharmaceutical companies	Some individuals in both community and industry were able to take up newly emerging subject positions that allowed them to collaborate
Chemicals management in Canada	3	Science determines whether chemicals are toxic	Discursive work by regulators to determine whether chemicals are toxic varies, depending on discourses such as precaution and sound science, as well as on normalizing versus problematizing practices
CityWorks	7	Organizations have fixed identities	Organizations are discursively constructed
DDT (1939–1972)	4, 8, 9	Silent Spring led to the ban on DDT	The impact of Silent Spring was complex and only achieved by being consumed by multiple actors who changed some of its meanings
DDT (1998–2001)	4	A chemical (DDT) has a singular meaning	The meaning of DDT changed over the course of the Stockholm Convention
GlobalTel	2, 10	A dominant discourse is monolithic and deterministic; resistance is organized	A dominant discourse (strategy) is locally enacted in nuanced, diverse ways; organized resistance does not necessarily endure
Green chemistry	2, 8	A discourse is uniform and homogenous across different domains	The nature and impact of the discourse of sustainability depends on the circumstances of its production (and differs in green chemistry compared to supply chain management)
Mère et Enfant	7	Organizations have fixed identities	Organizations can be discursively constructed and reconstructed

Case study	Chapter	Phenomenon being problematized	Findings
Older workers	5	Public inquiries are arenas where subjects of an inquiry have a voice	Power is exercised by public inquiries in highly nuanced ways to shape what subjects (older workers) can say, do, and be – the subject of an inquiry is also the object of that inquiry
Refugee domain	6, 10	The refugee identity is objective and fixed	Refugee identities vary, depending on other discourses and organizational identities
Stockholm Convention	3, 8	Dominant legacy discourses cannot be displaced	The legacy discourse (science) was subordinated to the new discourse (precaution); both proponents and opponents had to reconcile the legacy and the new discourse
Utel	7	Conversations are either participative or not, depending on hierarchical relations among managers and employees	Hierarchical relations played out in different ways during the same conversation (workshop)

These case studies show the value of a discursive approach in looking behind the rhetoric and providing ways to unpick a wide range of organizational issues. Achieving this form of reflexivity is at the core of empirical studies based on a discursive approach. For example, paying particular attention to the social, political, and historical context in which particular discourses emerge allows us to gain insight into alternative knowledges, identities, and meanings that might have been, even when a dominant discourse makes them seem impossible. Comparing multiple meanings and exploring discursive struggles shows the precarious and conflicted nature of reality. Incorporating multiple voices, especially those normally ignored by more traditional research methods or who have been silenced by a particular discourse, helps to reveal different versions of reality as diverse experiences are identified and shared. Studying discursive change is a useful way to shed light on power and privilege that might otherwise be hidden.

SELF-REFLEXIVITY

The second form of reflexivity – self-reflexivity or radical reflexivity – requires us to 'deconstruct our own constructions of realities, identities, and knowledge, and highlight the intersubjective and indexical nature of meaning (i.e., accounts are ongoing discursive social accomplishments taking place in shared, taken-for-granted interactions between people)' (Cunliffe, 2003: 986). In other words, as researchers, we are situated in certain discourses through which power/knowledge relations circulate and from which we cannot escape. 'No longer all-knowing, all-seeing, objective and omnipotent, the researcher is forced to re-examine his or her relation to the research process and the "knowledge" it produces' (Hardy and Clegg, 1997: S5).

Informed by developments in sociology, anthropology, and postcolonialism, self-reflexive work in OMT has used a range of techniques, including autoethnographies, confessionals, narratives, fiction, and drama to subject the subjectivity and experiences of the researcher to greater scrutiny (e.g., Van Maanen, 1988; Chang et al., 2013; Prasad, 2014; Levy, 2016; Manning, 2018; Rhodes, 2019; Black, 2020; Pullen et al., 2000). The aim of such research is to draw attention to a series of complex dynamics. First, the reflexive researcher recognizes themselves as a subject constructed in and through the research project: we do not simply 'bring the self to the field,' we also 'create the self in the field' (Reinharz, 1997: 3). Second, it acknowledges that the researcher and the research subject collectively negotiate meaning. This means that the two identities 'co-evolve in a process of continuous interplay from which they give meaning both to one another and to the relationship in-between' (Gilmore and Kenny, 2015: 59). Third, reflexive researchers allow the voices of diverse research subjects to be heard (Alvesson et al., 2008), while also acknowledging the power relations involved in the relationship between those doing the research and those being researched (Hardy and Clegg, 1997). To achieve its aims, self-reflexivity requires the researcher to attend to two aspects of the research process: authoring reflexive research accounts and engaging in reflexive research practices.

Authoring Reflexive Texts

Cutcher et al. (2020) identified some common discursive practices used in writing theoretical articles about organizations and management, as well as some of the pitfalls each involves in relation to self-reflexivity. Box 11.2 summarizes and adapts these practices for authors writing up empirical studies who wish to be self-reflexive, as well as adding some words of caution.

BOX 11.2 AUTHORING REFLEXIVE TEXTS

Discursive practice	Categories	Caution
Choice of language	Technical	Author hides behind the 'scientific method' or 'transparency'
	Provocative	Experimental writing is used but it may be inaccessible and/or alienate mainstream readers
Presentation of Self	Expert	Author pulls rank in order to claim authority
	Vulnerable	Author draws all the attention to him/herself at the expense of the research subject
Presentation of Other	Silenced	Author treats the research subject in an essentialist way, or simply ignores them
	Championed	Author acknowledges the marginalized position of the research subject but then speaks for or over them
Contextualizing knowledge production	Absent	Author ignores the context in which the text is authored and treats knowledge as 'true' and universal
	Present	Author is aware of the context but assumes that they can rise above or stand apart from knowledge/ power relations

The language used in writing a research account has significant effects (see Rhodes, 2019). Many articles and books rely on a technical or 'scientific' style of writing – describing issues in measured tones, working through arguments carefully and prosaically, and using carefully defined terms. This is often the professional 'default' position of authors, but it can obscure the politics of knowledge production. To address this, some research accounts rely on more experimental forms of writing – using a provocative or alarmist writing style to draw attention to certain contradictions, ironies, or hypocrisies. However, insofar as they draw on esoteric literary traditions from outside the field, such accounts may also be accessible only to elite, like-minded academics. A more practical disadvantage is, while such efforts may convince researchers who are interested in reflexivity, other readers may dismiss important insights simply because of how the article is written.

Another discursive practice is the way in which the author constructs an identity for themselves in the article – what Cutcher and colleagues (2020) refer to as 'selfing.' It often involves positioning the author as an expert – a scientific researcher whose claims are supported by objective data – or, sometimes, as a veteran of the field, whose claims are supported by virtue of tenure, experience, and seniority. Much like technical writing, this may simply be a way to make shorthand claims to authority without having to explain how these claims came about. Sometimes, selfing constructs a more marginalized, vulnerable Self, who divulges how they have been buffeted by the ebbs and flows of conducting the research. While this can be a way to remind readers that the author is only one actor among many involved in producing the research account, it can also direct attention away from the phenomena and individuals under study to focus on the author. Such 'naval gazing' and 'narcissism' has been criticized (see Cutcher, 2020) for saying more about how 'the process played out for the researcher than theoretical issues emerging from the study itself' (Langley and Klag, 2019: 529).

A third discursive practice concerns 'othering' – how the text 'hails' identities other than the author. Research in OMT has long been criticized for silencing the Other, especially women, people of colour, and other marginalized groups. If large numbers of society are excluded from study, research that is presented as relevant or even universal is not relevant or universal at all (Girei, 2017). To address this issue, some research accounts are written with the aim of exposing identities that would otherwise remain hidden, such as women, people of colour, members of the LGBTQI community, indigenous peoples, lower socio-economic classes, those for whom English is not a first language, and even critical theorists (see Cutcher et al., 2020). However, it is important to remember that including some voices will still mean that others are left out. For example, Prasad (2014) reflects on how his attempts to engage with the complexity of Palestinian identities in his research was accompanied by far less attention on the Israeli border guards who also featured in his study. It is impossible to ensure that all voices are expressed in the text on equal terms, and as the author of the account, the researcher ultimately speaks for (and often over) some voices, while remaining ignorant or dismissive of others.

Finally, contextualizing is a discursive practice that relates the research account to the wider institutional and political context. Many articles ignore context altogether to focus on the immediate concerns of the article or, if they do mention it, describe it in neutral terms that ignore power/knowledge relations (see Cutcher et al., 2020). Some articles include an explicit consideration of the complex web of power relations in which academics are positioned, which both constrains and enables them. For example, a reflexive study of refugee identities (Hardy et al., 2001) showed how the identity of the refugee research subject constructed in a paper published in *Human Relations* was shaped by the norms and conventions of the OMT research domain and the requirements of the specific journal. As a result, the authors admitted that the refugee identity they portrayed was very different to the identity 'found' in articles published in other journals; let alone the identity experienced by refugees themselves. This contextualization showed clearly how the researchers were subject to and resistant against the controls embedded in professional networks but it was not without problems. While acknowledging the collective nature of knowledge production, it nonetheless portrayed the authors in highly individualistic terms – as sufficiently astute and skilled to negotiate and circumvent supposedly inescapable social forces (also see Alvesson et al., 2008).

Conducting Reflexive Research Practices

It does not matter how much care is taken in authoring a research account if reflexivity is not also factored into research practice (Jeanes, 2017; Benson and Reilly, 2020). This involves researchers being open about their position 'in relation to the study, their reception by participants, the process of analysis [and] choosing between forms of representation as the research is being conducted' (Gilmore and Kenny, 2015: 56). Box 11.3 summarizes these reflexive research practices, again with some notes of caution.

BOX 11.3 CONDUCTING REFLEXIVE RESEARCH PRACTICES

Research practices are sensitive to	Categories	Caution
Context	Data are collected and analysis is conducted with a view to learning about the wider context	Researcher's conception of context is derived from their subjectivity – they may consider some aspects of context irrelevant, even though they are important to research participants
Self	The researcher is aware of how they are positioned in relation to research participants during the study	Researchers may adopt different positions, which can change over time; these positions may differ in relation to different groups in the study

Research practices are sensitive to	Categories	Caution
Other	The research subject's disadvantaged position in relation to the researcher is mitigated during the study	The research subject may remain powerless in relation to the researcher, regardless of various participative techniques; in other cases, research subjects can be quite powerful in relation to the researcher
Emotions	The researcher is transparent about the emotional impact of conducting the research	Researchers may be drawn towards greater emotional attachment for personal reasons; in some cases, there may be a need for greater emotional distance
Ethics	The orientation of the researcher in relation to their research should be embodied and affective	The subject position of a reflexive researcher has been constructed within the context of prevailing discourses of reflexivity in our field – it can render the researcher highly vulnerable

In the first instance, researchers are encouraged to contextualize their empirical study by collecting data on the wider temporal, political, cultural, and social fabric in which the particular study is located, rather than considering it as an abstract setting with a universal status (see Girei, 2017; Manning, 2018). In doing so, it becomes easier to understand the complex, ambiguous, and shifting nature of the power relations between researcher and those being researched, as well as their precarious positions, particularly of the latter (Gilmore and Kenny, 2015). However, what the researcher considers to be significant contextual dynamics may not be the same as what the research subject considers to be important.

Selfing in the context of research practice refers to the ways in which researchers acknowledge how they are influenced by their interactions with those whom they study (Gilmore and Kenny, 2015). The researcher can adopt different positions in relation to the study (Cunliffe and Karunanayakebe, 2013; Cutcher, 2020). The researcher can be an insider, seeing themselves at one with participants and working hard to identify with them (e.g., Prasad, 2014). In other situations, they may be an outsider – unable to fully understand or empathize, and even feeling awkward or unsafe (e.g., Levy, 2016; Girei, 2017). The researcher's position may change over the course of the study. Researchers who enter as outsiders may become insiders because they engage in identity work to make themselves more acceptable (e.g., Prasad, 2014), perhaps because of guilt at witnessing exploitation, a personal need for emotional attachment, or simply for pragmatic reasons, such as the belief that better data will be obtained.

Othering in reflexive research practice usually occurs when the researcher actively takes steps to include marginalized research subjects in conducting the study and redress any power imbalance. It involves recognizing the Other's 'capacity for intellectual autonomy and their own seeing, doing and thinking, thereby constructing a different knowledge' (Manning, 2018: 313; also see Riach, 2009). This may be achieved by providing research participants with opportunities to voice their understanding of issues, collect data, decide on research themes, and challenge findings. However, when marginalized Others are enrolled into a study – even when the research is conducted 'with' rather than 'on' them – the researcher is still in control of analyzing the data and presenting the findings and, ultimately, still in a position of power (Manning, 2018).

The various problematics around selfing and othering have led to demands for reflexive researchers to be more honest about the emotional component of conducting research. Gilmore and Kenny (2015) note the importance of emotional attachment, particularly when researchers desire to become closer to, and identify with, the Other. Such positive attachment can enhance the researcher's understanding and aid in developing multi-voicing techniques, but it may also compromise the analysis, particularly if the aim is to be critical (Gilmore and Kenny, 2015). It can also become manipulative if the goodwill and approval of research participants is exploited simply because it makes the researcher feel better. Moreover, situations may arise where researchers need to create distance, perhaps because they do not agree with values or actions of research participants (e.g., Girei, 2017). Levy (2016) recounts a situation where she experienced her research setting as unsafe because of its geograph- ical isolation and emotional manipulation by some research participants. She therefore needed to distance herself from it – physically and emotionally.

Levy's experience draws attention not only to the need to create distance from one's research subjects, but also the fact that, in some circumstances, research subjects *do* have power in relation to the researcher. While few of us have been in such an extreme position as her, there are many situations when we are highly dependent on research subjects – what researcher has not crossed their fingers that a senior manager or some other gatekeeper will not reject the project or restrict access; or sat through an interview feeling they are receiving the 'party line' and not much else? When a PhD or research grant is at stake, the researcher is very much dependent upon the goodwill of those whom they study.

Creating distance and protecting oneself vis-à-vis the research are issues that are rarely discussed. The reflexivity literature tends to be far more preoccupied with emotional attachment and acknowledging the researcher's privileged position. It is therefore important to remember that reflexivity always involves an ethical component (Jeanes, 2017; Rhodes and Carlsen, 2018). There may be risks to the research subject, but there are also risks to the researcher in conducting research. Requiring researchers to turn the analytical gaze on themselves and to expose their feelings may render them even more vulnerable. Exhortations of engaging in relationships that are 'embodied, responsive and affective, rather than just rational and knowing' (Rhodes and Carlsen, 2018: 1305) may lead researchers to place themselves in research settings that are potentially dangerous, as well as disclose personal information that leaves them professionally exposed.

CONCLUSION

This chapter sets the scene for how discourse scholars can conduct and write up reflexive research. A discursive approach is well suited to achieve the first form of reflexivity discussed in this chapter – problematizing the phenomenon under investigation. In many respects, this is the raison d'être of discursive studies – to unsettle established versions of reality and generate alternative ways of thinking. Self-reflexivity is more demanding. It requires researchers to show how they are complicit in the meaning-making processes that produce 'knowledge.' The theoretical assumptions associated with a discursive approach are entirely consistent with being self-reflexive, although it often requires separate, self-contained articles that interrogate the research process such that it becomes the subject of research (e.g., Thomas et al., 2009; Cunliffe and Karunanayakebe, 2013; Prasad, 2014; Gilmore and Kenny, 2015; Manning, 2018).

Finally, it is important to remember that reflexivity is a product of our academic community, influenced by institutional conventions and put into play through various rhetorical and linguistic manoeuvres (Alvesson et al., 2008). Reflexivity is, itself, a discourse – one with considerable currency in some parts of our field – where certain practices are privileged, while others are denigrated or ignored. It often dismisses the value of maintaining professional, distant relationships between researcher and researched and it underplays the negative implications of emotional attachments. As with any other discourse, researchers need to be critical of their claims to be reflexive, as well as cautious in how they practice it.

12. Materiality and discourse

This chapter takes a step away from my work and, instead, concentrates on what future research on discourse might look like. It seems likely that it will place a greater – and somewhat different – emphasis on materiality owing to ideas emerging in domains known as 'new materialism' and 'posthumanism' (e.g., Barad, 2003, 2007, 2013; Haraway, 2008; Bennett, 2010; Coole and Frost, 2010; Braidotti, 2013). This body of work is informed by disciplines ranging from science and technology studies, actor network theory, and feminist and political theory (Coole, 2013; Lemke, 2015; Gamble et al., 2019). While theoretical assumptions vary (Cohn and Lynch, 2017), it suggests a world that is inextricably material. 'The physical and the social both have material effects in an ever-changing world ... and a capacity for "agency" – the actions that produce the social world – extends beyond human actors to the non-human and inanimate' (Fox and Alldred, 2016: 4). Discourse theorists (among others) are accused of failing to address materiality satisfactorily by confining agency to human actors and positing a false binary relationship between language and materiality (see Lundborg and Vaughan-Williams, 2015; Gamble et al., 2019). In this chapter, I reflect on these criticisms, as well as consider some of the challenges facing discourse scholars wishing to engage with new ways of thinking about materiality.

THE CRITIQUE

Scholars in posthumanism and new materialism question the idea that the material world is comprised of fixed, stable entities. Instead, they assert that materiality is in constant flux.

> Regardless of how much a given piece of matter appears to be stable, its stability is always the result of a particular configuration of things; meaning that if this configuration is not maintained, the stability disappears ... there is nothing in this world that inherently possesses its properties. Every being, entity, or phenomenon acquires its properties by relating to other beings, entities, or phenomena. (Martine and Cooren, 2016: 146)

Agency arises from the coming together of multiple human and non-human elements, each of which contains their 'own energies and forces of transformation,' thereby giving rise to possibilities for agency (Lundborg and

Vaughan-Williams, 2015: 12). Neither humans nor non-humans 'possess' agency in the sense of a fixed property, instead 'agentic capacities' (Coole, 2013) arise as multiple elements of an assemblage coalesce 'in the performative and relational generation of action' (Kuhn and Burk, 2014: 6). This relationality emerges and manifests itself in various ways with the result that the capacity to act is indeterminate, tenuous, and partial. It is grounded in the *process* of assembling rather than in any fixed configuration of elements, regardless of how permanent the assemblage may appear to be.

Such thinking goes beyond the philosophical posthumanism associated with poststructuralists to include a form of post-anthropocentrism (Braidotti, 2006). Accordingly, many of these scholars have criticized Foucault's work for remaining within the 'traditional humanist orbit' and restricting agency to human subjects (Barad, 2007: 235). In privileging discourse, his work fails to account for the complex, dynamic relationality of materiality and discourse (Gamble et al., 2019; Fox and Alldred, 2016), where neither discursive practice nor material phenomena are 'ontologically or epistemologically prior' (Barad, 2003: 822). The 'representationalism' of the linguistic turn is problematic in that it renders 'material realities inaccessible behind the linguistic or discourse systems that purportedly construct or "represent" them – even when the express intention has been to deconstruct that material-discursive binary' (MacLure, 2013: 659).

Some discourse scholars reject this critique and defend Foucault's work as a basis for radical understandings of materiality. Hook (2007: 179) maintains that, while many researchers drawing on Foucauldian ideas may have emphasized the linguistic, Foucault himself emphasized that discourses are not only realized in 'the textuality of representation and knowledge, but in the regulating principles and actions of institutions, in forms of everyday practice, in actual material arrangements such as that of architectural structure.' Lemke (2015: 5) argues that elements of a posthumanist approach may be found in Foucault's idea of a 'government of things,' which 'takes into account the interrelatedness and entanglements of men [*sic*] and things, the natural and the artificial, the physical and the moral.' Lundborg and Vaughan-Williams (2015: 7) maintain that Foucault's work does, in fact, 'negotiate, problematise, and ultimately deconstruct the language/materiality binary while maintaining both as part of a complex and radical intertextuality.'

There is, then, an ongoing debate about the ability of research based on a discursive approach to address issues of materiality and posthuman agency. Some scholars question whether Foucault's work is an appropriate basis for exploring these new ontological understandings. Others reject the idea that Foucauldian conceptions of discourse are incompatible with the assumptions of new materialism and posthumanism, suggesting that 'an expanded conceptualization of discourse' can provide an enhanced understanding of materiality (Lundborg and Vaughan-Williams, 2015: 21). Either way, the debate poses a series of challenges for those using a discursive approach to study organizations.

THE CHALLENGES

One challenge is that the entanglement of the material and discursive is often taken to be empirical by discourse scholars, rather than ontological. Humans are assumed to be 'the actors who ultimately elect, more or less explicitly, how they respond to the material actors that engage them' (Hultin and Introna, 2019: 1364). Discourse is assigned primacy (Putnam, 2015). Materiality is not absent but is considered as 'surrounding human action, and its influence is not independent of the ends toward which, and the conditions under which, people act' (Gherardi, 2016: 685). Discourse scholars, therefore, need to consider how best to incorporate the idea that 'discourses are themselves also – and only – particular configurations or performances of matter' (Gamble et al., 2019: 112).

A second challenge concerns the language used to express these complex relationships, which can inadvertently reinforce the tendency to separate the discursive and the material. A range of terms have been used to convey this relational ontology, including mutual entailment, entanglement, imbrication, assemblage, and agencement, but they have been criticized for not doing enough to convey the inseparability involved in the 'constitutive (or ontological) entanglement of meaning and matter' (Martine and Cooren, 2016: 147). Even referring to material and discursive practices for analytical purposes 'invites the idea that there might be "material practices" on one side and "discursive ones" on the other and that they sometimes come together' (Martine and Cooren, 2016: 147). Removing hyphens – such as in sociomateriality – or introducing new terms such as 'more-than-humans' instead of 'non-humans' – does not appear to have solved this problem. Similarly, the use of 'assemblage' to translate Deleuze and Guattari's (1998) term 'agencement' has also been criticized for 'rigidifying the concept into the thingness of final or stable states' (Gherardi, 2016: 687). It conveys a static configuration, rather than 'the coming together of things that is a necessary and prior condition for any action to occur, including the actions of humans' (Braun, 2008: 671). Discourse scholars need, then, not only to understand the assumptions associated with new understandings of materiality, but to pick the words they use to convey them carefully.

A third challenge involves designing empirical studies so they engage more deeply with materiality, rather than only relying on textual data. If discourse scholars want to contribute to debates about materiality, then they will need to design their empirical studies accordingly. This is not to deny that the production, distribution, and consumption of texts have significant material and practical components. But texts are typically created by humans and are assumed to 'represent the abstracted intentions of the interactants whose conversations created them' (Kuhn and Burk, 2014: 155). As such, while offering interesting ways to interrogate the ways in which meanings travel and change through consumption, translation, and resistance, an exclusive focus on texts does not necessarily go very far towards escaping a humanist focus.

A fourth challenge concerns methodology. The traditional dependency on interviews, observations, and texts centres on the human as the key instrument for research, which is problematic in an era of 'postqualitative' research (MacLure, 2013). Initially, qualitative methods amounted to 'conventional interpretive inquiry ... a humanist subject who has an authentic voice, transparent descriptions of lived experiences, and the generally untroubled belief that better methods and richer descriptions can get closer to the truth' (Lather, 2013: 635). While qualitative methods in the postmodern era involved an interrogation of key concepts, such as validity, voice, authenticity, and reflexivity, they failed to launch a more fundamental critique of ontology. Postqualitative methodology emphasizes that methodologies do not just describe, they also perform (St Pierre, 2013). Researchers are themselves entangled in the human and non-human relations of the assemblages they seek to study (St Pierre and Adams, 2011; Coleman and Ringrose, 2013). These concerns shift the focus of methodology from 'epistemology (where what is known depends upon perspective) to ontology (what is known is also being made differently)' (Law and Urry, 2004: 397). They also raise a series of personal questions. How do we conceive of a research problem that is 'the imbrication of an agentic assemblage of diverse elements that are constantly intra-acting, never stable, never the same?' (Lather and St Pierre, 2013: 630). Where do the typical face-to-face methods of data collection, such as interviewing and observation, stand? How do we carry out our work if we are not 'responsibly autonomous human subjects?' (MacLure, 2013: 660). 'If we give up "human" as separate from non-human, how do we exist?' (Lather and St Pierre, 2013: 631).

CONCLUSION

New ways of thinking about materiality and agency pose challenges for researchers using a discursive approach. However, they also present opportunities: the ground is fertile for both theoretical discussion and empirical study. It is also important to note that a large body of research in OMT has already interrogated conventional understandings of materiality (e.g., D'Adderio and Pollack, 2014; Fotaki et al., 2014; Kenny and Fotaki, 2015; Monteiro and Nicolini, 2015; Pullen and Rhodes, 2015; Gherardi, 2016, 2017a, 2017b, 2019a, 2019b; Prasad, 2016; Duff and Sumartojo, 2017; Boxenbaum et al.,

2018; Ashcraft, 2020; Cooren, 2020). There are also many empirical studies that show how to incorporate materiality and discourse into empirical studies (see Box 12.1 for examples).

BOX 12.1 EMPIRICAL ARTICLES ENGAGING WITH POSTHUMANIST/POSTQUALITATIVE IDEAS

Carton, 2020	A study of the historical development of the management theory known as 'Blue Ocean Strategy' that shows how theory changes the assemblage which, in turn, changes reality
Coupland, 2015	A study of rugby league that illuminates a discursive space in which the production of organized, docile, masculine bodies, engaged in emotional labour, are crafted and mobilized through disciplinary practices
Dale and Latham, 2015	A study of embodiment that makes visible the entanglements between human and non-human bodies which co-constitute all human embodiment
Davies and Riach, 2019	A study that argues that enduring binaries among species fail to reflect the incremental and contingent practices as observed in 'bee-work.' The study also shows the productive relations that emerge when we depart from masculinist modes of sustainable thinking
Fotaki and Daskalaki, 2021	A study of women activists opposing extractivist mining in Greece to explore the role of affective embodiment as a foundation for activist feminist practices and to develop a theory of the protesting body altering spatial relations as a form of resistance
Harris et al., 2020	A study that draws upon feminist new materialism to analyze two critical events of sexual violence in the US – one in the military and another at a university
Hultin and Introna, 2019	A study that examines relationality in ongoing subject positioning as it is enacted in and through the ongoing flow of situated material-discursive practices in a study of refugees and case workers in reception centres
Hultin et al., 2021	A study of the mundane everyday organizing practices of Syrian refugees living in tented settlements in Lebanon that shows how material-discursive boundary making and invitational practices (organizing a home, cooking, eating, etc.) enact relational host/guest subject positions
Monteiro and Nicolini, 2015	A study that uses a posthumanist practice theory orientation to foreground the neglected role of material elements in institutional work by examining two prizes in the Italian public sector for best practices in public administration and healthcare
Paring et al., 2017	A study that examines how identity regulation is exercised through a sociomaterial process, mainly through consultants' bodily performances in an in-depth ethnography of a program aimed at constructing a new social identity among project managers
Skoglund and Redmalm, 2017	A study that extends biopolitics, traditionally understood as management of the human population, to include non-human animal life and posthuman life through a study of the dog of the US presidential family

Stowell and Warren, 2018	A study that explores the concept of 'embodied inhabitation' to bring a bodily and material perspective to bear on institutional maintenance using autoethnographic, visual data in the case of e-waste recycling workers
Wilhoit and Kisselburgh, 2015	A study that examines how materiality organizes through human passions which have the unintentional result of animating the material to constitute a collective in the case of US bike commuting
Wilhoit and Kisselburgh, 2019	A study that examines how non-humans are part of the actor network that resists in a study of bike community in the US

The depth and breadth of work challenging traditional conceptions of materiality indicate that discourse studies have already started to take a materialist turn (Hardy and Thomas, 2015; Quattrone et al., 2021). Arguably, one of Foucault's greatest contributions 'is his insistence on the mutual imbrication of ontology and epistemology' (Lundborg and Vaughan-Williams, 2015: 20). Consequently, discourse scholars are well practised in wrestling with such theoretical concerns and there is no reason to think they will not continue to do so. Discourse scholars will also likely continue to combine the discursive and the material in various forms of relationality in their empirical studies (regardless of the term they use to describe it). The future for researchers interested in using a discursive approach to study organizations is, accordingly, full of opportunities and – potentially – insights.

FINAL WORDS

I conclude this book on an optimistic note concerning the use of a discursive approach to study organizations. It helps us learn more about the challenges that organizations face and the challenges they pose, and there is plenty of scope to contribute to contemporary theoretical debates. The discursive approach – or approaches – future researchers will take will look different to the one that I took when I started out over 30 years ago and that is how it should be. Nonetheless, in revisiting the empirical studies that I have conducted over my career, I was struck by how topical they remain.

Refugees continue to leave an indelible imprint on society. They were exploited during Brexit. They continue to be labelled as illegal in Australia. And, as I write this, they are starting to arrive from Afghanistan. Will the same language be used? Will new understandings of refugees emerge? Will individuals be treated any differently in the future? During the 1990s, the world was wrestling with HIV/AIDS. Today, it wrestles with another disease – Covid-19. HIV/AIDS led to new kinds of treatments, identities, and organizations. What new meanings will Covid-19 bring about? It is certainly discursively reconfiguring risk, which is now firmly embedded in our every-day language and practice. And yet, paradoxically, at a time when there is such strong agreement about measuring risks using scientific techniques, there is also considerable disagreement about what a particular risk means – whether it be wearing masks, socially isolating, getting vaccinated, or demonstrating against lockdowns. Age continues to be a 'problem' for Western societies. By 2050, the proportion of the world's population over 60 years will be nearly double what it was in 2015 – at 22 percent (World Health Organization, 2018). Age-based stereotypes have proven hard to shake, reducing opportunities for older workers and creating disadvantage for the elderly. Organizations con-tinue to conduct their daily business – activities that, as always, need to be held up to the light, given talk of toxic cultures, increasing casualization, #MeToo, and big tech dominance. Finally, the need for sustainable practices intensifies, whether in the form of safer chemicals, fewer plastics, or greater responsibility in using finite resources. With the latest depressing report on climate change (IPCC, 2020), many citizens are lamenting that both sound science and pre-caution seem to have been ignored by so many for so long. If anything needs more meaning, it is surely the risks associated with climate change. While the theoretical ideas that underpin a discursive approach change and evolve over time, many of the concerns and problems – questions of value – with which we have to contend remain. So, there is considerable scope – not to mention, a need – to continue using a discursive approach to study organizations.

Appendix: the empirical studies

References to the specific articles featured in this book are provided below (Box A.1). They cover a range of different studies – from an investigation of the discourse of an individual workshop through to a comparison of discourse in different countries and over time. The original studies from which these articles are drawn are summarized in Table A.1. These summaries show the original 'hook' – why we became interested in conducting the study and the questions that we felt we could answer. I have then explained the way in which we collected and analyzed the data in each case to show how a discursive approach was used in different ways – to drill down into the micro dynamics of a particular situation, to illuminate the different ways in which meanings changed or endured over time, and to capture the complex way in which discourse circulates through and among organizations.

BOX A.1   THE ORIGINAL ARTICLES

Reference	Chapter
Ainsworth, S. and Hardy, C. 2007. The Construction of the Older Worker: Privilege, Paradox and Policy. *Discourse and Communication*, 1(3): 295–313.	5
Ainsworth, S. and Hardy, C. 2008. The Enterprising Self: An Unsuitable Job for an Older Worker. *Organization*, 15(3): 389–405.	5
Ainsworth, S. and Hardy, C. 2009. Mind over Body: Physical and Psychotherapeutic Discourses and the Regulation of the Older Worker. *Human Relations*, 62(8): 1199–1229.	5
Ainsworth, S. and Hardy, C. 2012. Subjects of Inquiry: Statistics, Stories, and the Production of Knowledge. *Organization Studies*, 33(12): 1693–1714.	5
Cutcher, L., Hardy, C, Riach, K., and Thomas, R. 2020. Reflections on Reflexive Theorizing: The Need for a Little More Conversation. *Organization Theory*, 1: 1–28.	11
Hardy, C. 2003. Refugee Determination: Power and Resistance in Systems of Foucauldian Power. *Administration and Society*, 34(4): 462–488.	10
Hardy, C., Bhakoo, V., and Maguire, S. 2020. A New Methodology for Supply Chain Management: Discourse Analysis and Its Potential for Theoretical Advancement. *Journal of Supply Chain Management*, 56(2): 19–35.	2, 8

Reference	Chapter
Hardy, C., Lawrence, T., and Phillips, N. 1998. Talk and Action: Conversations, Narrative and Action in Interorganizational Collaboration, in D. Grant, T. Keenoy, and C. Oswick (eds), *Discourse and Organization*, London: SAGE, pp. 65–83.	7
Hardy, C. and Maguire, S. 2010. Discourse, Field-Configuring Events and Change in Organizations and Institutional Fields: Narratives of DDT and the Stockholm Convention. *Academy of Management Journal*, 53(6): 1365–1392.	4, 8, 9
Hardy, C. and Maguire, S. 2020. Organizations, Risk Translation and the Ecology of Risks: The Discursive Construction of a Novel Risk. *Academy of Management Journal*, 63(3): 685–716.	2, 8
Hardy, C., Palmer, I., and Phillips, N. 2000. Discourse as a Strategic Resource. *Human Relations*, 53(9), 7–28.	7
Hardy, C. and Phillips, N. 1998. Strategies of Engagement: Lessons from the Critical Examination of Collaboration and Conflict in an Interorganizational Domain. *Organization Science*, 9(2): 217–230.	6
Hardy, C. and Phillips, N. 1999. No Joking Matter: Discursive Struggle in the Canadian Refugee System. *Organization Studies*, 20(1): 1–24.	6
Hardy, C. and Thomas, R. 2014. Strategy, Discourse and Practice: The Intensification of Power. *Journal of Management Studies*, 51(2): 320–348.	2, 10
Maguire, S. and Hardy, C. 2005. Identity and Collaborative Strategy in the Case of Canadian HIV/AIDS Treatment. *Strategic Organization*, 3(1): 11–45.	6, 8
Maguire, S. and Hardy, C. 2006. The Emergence of New Global Institutions: A Discursive Perspective. *Organization Studies*, 27(1): 7–29.	3, 4, 8
Maguire, S. and Hardy, C. 2009. Discourse and Deinstitutionalization: The Decline of DDT. *Academy of Management Journal*, 52(1): 148–178.	4, 8, 9
Maguire, S. and Hardy, C. 2013. Organizing Processes and the Construction of Risk: A Discursive Approach. *Academy of Management Journal*, 56(1): 231–255.	3
Maguire, S. and Hardy, C. 2019. The Discourse of Risk and Processes of Institutional Change: The Case of Green Chemistry, in T. Reay, T. Zilber, A. Langley, and H. Tsoukas (eds), *Institutions and Organizations: A Process View*, Oxford: Oxford University Press, pp. 154–173.	2, 8
Maguire, S., Hardy, C., and Lawrence, T. 2004. Institutional Entrepreneurship in Emerging Fields: HIV/AIDS Treatment Advocacy in Canada. *Academy of Management Journal*, 47(5): 657–679.	6, 8
Maguire, S., Phillips, N., and Hardy, C. 2001. When 'Silence = Death,' Keep Talking: Trust, Control and the Discursive Construction of Identity in the Canadian HIV/AIDS Treatment Domain. *Organization Studies*, 22(2): 285–310.	6, 8
Phillips, N. and Hardy, C. 1997. Managing Multiple Identities: Discourse, Legitimacy and Resources in the UK Refugee System. *Organization*, 4(2): 159–185.	6
Thomas, R., Sargent, L., and Hardy, C. 2011. Managing Organizational Change: Negotiating Meaning and Power-Resistance Relations. *Organization Science*, 22(1): 22–41.	7

Table A.1   *The original studies*

Study	Study design	Why it was interesting	Data collected	Data analysis
BPA	Part of a larger study comparing chemicals management in Canada and Australia	The Canadian government concluded BPA to be toxic and restricted baby bottles; the Australian government found it to be safe and did not restrict it – what accounted for this discrepancy? BPA was first mentioned as a potential endocrine-disrupting chemical in 1993 but, 20 years later, only Canada had restricted it – did BPA constitute a novel risk and, if so, how?	Texts: government websites in both countries provided texts on BPA Texts authored by key actors on BPA over the 20-year period from various websites, scientific articles, and media reports of national newspapers/broadcasters in each country. Interviews with key actors in both countries	We analyzed how key actors talked about BPA in relation to risk, noting differences in texts by endocrinologists, toxicologists, manufacturers, regulators, retailers, and NGOs We distilled this talk into a translated risk by each group; we identified the actions taken to manage the translated risk We analyzed whether the various risk management actions weakened or strengthened the meaning of BPA in relation to risk and whether they heightened the translated risks of other actors We assessed the cumulative effects on BPA over time *From this analysis, we were able to theorize the process of constructing a novel risk*

Study	Study design	Why it was interesting	Data collected	Data analysis
Canadian HIV/AIDS domain	A study of collaboration between the community and industry in the Canadian HIV/AIDS domain	CTAC was formed as a collaboration between industry and the community against a backdrop of adversarial relations between these two groups – how did this happen?	Interviews with key actors in the domain. Texts were used mainly for background purposes	From background materials, we identified new subject positions in the HIV/AIDS discourse (PWA, activist, treatment activist). From the interviews, we identified two subject positions related to CTAC (treatment advocate and compassionate pharmaceutical companies). We identified 'champions' of CTAC from supportive talk backed up by accounts of action and examined how community and industry champions were able to take up the relevant subject positions, as well as how they engaged with each other and their core constituency. We followed up on those who professed support for CTAC but who did not take action and identified aspects of identity that prevented them being champions. *From this analysis we were able to theorize the basis of trust and the nature of identity work that allowed the formation of CTAC*

Study	Study design	Why it was interesting	Data collected	Data analysis
Chemicals management in Canada	A comparison of how two chemicals – BPA and VAM – were assessed as part of a new chemicals management program in Canada (part of the larger study that included Australia)	VAM became 'risky' during the process but then became 'safe' again, while BPA became and remained 'risky' – how did these changes in meaning come about? Despite a standardized assessment process, the discursive work regarding the two chemicals was very different – why was this the case?	Texts: the government website provided background materials explaining how chemicals management was carried out, as well as the same suite of standardized texts for both chemicals Interviews with key actors in chemicals management	We examined the different practices used to assess chemicals, and distilled them into a list of eight practices which clustered into two 'bundles': normalizing and problematizing We compared the assessment of VAM and BPA and identified more normalizing with the former and more problematizing with the latter We identified how industry contested the conclusions of the draft assessments, as well as two forms of government response *From this analysis, we were able to show differences in scientific practice involved in assessing risk, as well as theorize the nature of the discursive work required to legitimate these practices*
CityWorks	A study of a workshop to facilitate a collaboration among organizations	An opportunity to observe the micro dynamics of discourse through direct observation – how was a new, collaborative organizational identity achieved?	Interviews were conducted with participants prior to the workshop Reflections of the workshop were provided by the co-author (running the workshop) Observations were provided by a student	We examined the interviews and workshop notes for evidence of patterns in what the workshop conversations discursively constructed We distilled these patterns into three components – identity, skills, and emotions *From this analysis, we were able to propose a model for how a new organization is discursively constructed*

Study	Study design	Why it was interesting	Data collected	Data analysis
DDT (1939–1972)	A study of the deinstitutionalization of DDT following the publication of *Silent Spring*	DDT use declined rapidly following *Silent Spring* – how did this happen and what role did *Silent Spring* play?	Texts on DDT (including some secondary data) from 1939 when its insect-killing properties were discovered until 1972 when the ban was announced Texts were identified from systematic searches (e.g., PhD dissertations, editorials) and our background knowledge (e.g., congressional reports) A sample of counter-texts was selected	*Silent Spring* was analyzed to identify three problematizations of the existing discourse on DDT – it was not safe, effective, or necessary We examined texts (relating to the three institutional pillars) from 1939 to 1972 to establish changes in the pattern of text authorship after *Silent Spring* We compared texts from 1962 and 1972 to see whether DDT was constructed as safe, effective, and necessary at the two points in time *This analysis allowed us to explain the deinstitutionalization of DDT from a discursive perspective – Silent Spring led to changes in patterns of authorship which, in turn, created new subject positions and bodies of knowledge, although not all of the problematizations were reproduced*

Study	Study design	Why it was interesting	Data collected	Data analysis
DDT (1998–2001)	Part of the study of the Stockholm Convention and a continuation of the study of DDT over time	DDT was expected to be eliminated by the Convention, but was only restricted – how did this happen?	Texts on the Convention and DDT by different actors were available on the UN website, which also posted materials during the meetings The co-author attended and observed some meetings Interviews with key actors at the meetings	Observations of the meetings indicated three different discursive spaces with different rules concerning text production, distribution, and consumption; we then collected the texts associated with each space We identified a narrative for DDT (evil threat) from texts across all discursive spaces during the first two meetings; we identified a counter-narrative (hero) during the third and fourth meetings and tracked how it traveled from texts in the media space to the corridor and plenary texts; we identified a final narrative (necessary evil) in the final legal text We traced how the counter- and final narratives changed the position of certain organizations in relation to the Convention *This analysis allowed us to elaborate the concept of discursive space; show the role of narratives in institutional work and how they can be consumed differently; and explain the actions of low-power organizations in influencing the Convention*

Study	Study design	Why it was interesting	Data collected	Data analysis
GlobalTel	A study of a telecommunications company that had undergone a major change in strategy	The company announced a new strategy of technological leadership and cost-cutting. Over three years, it appeared to jettison the former (which had accounted for its success) in favour of a greater emphasis on (counter-cultural) job cuts – how did this come about? There was resistance to the cuts but it had little impact – why did it fail and was there resistance to the other component of the strategy?	Company texts on the strategy, including press announcements and internal documents such as newsletters, training documents, etc. Media reports on the strategy during the three-year implementation period Interviews with managers and employees	We analyzed texts announcing the new strategy and identified two components – *be first and best* and *be cost effective* We examined how these two components were talked/ written about in subsequent texts and saw how the former was linked to a professional discourse and the latter was linked to a market discourse We examined the talk/text for descriptions of practices associated with the two components of the strategy, which we distilled into six analytical categories. We found that in the case of be cost effective, practices were more diverse, more pervasive, and lasted longer To examine resistance, we noted instances of struggles over the two components of the strategy which involved the introduction of alternative discourses; we then examined subsequent texts to see if they survived *This analysis allowed us to show how power was exercised through discourse in ways that intensified the market discourse and reinforced cost-cutting, but weakened the professional discourse and technological leadership; we showed how organized resistance to cost-cutting did not endure but unintentional resistance to technological leadership did*

Study	Study design	Why it was interesting	Data collected	Data analysis
Green chemistry	A study of a growing sub-branch of chemistry	Green chemistry has enjoyed quite rapid growth in the last 30 years – how did this happen? Green chemistry changes the traditional meaning of risk to focus elimination, rather than management – how was this achieved and what was the outcome?	Texts on green chemistry; some secondary data on the growth of green chemistry	We examined the growing institutionalization of green chemistry from a discursive perspective – patterns of text production, distribution, and consumption We compared how the object of knowledge – the molecule – was constructed in green chemistry compared to mainstream chemistry *This analysis allowed us to explain differences in the discourse of sustainability in chemistry and supply chain management, as well as show how the discourse of green chemistry created new conditions of possibility*
Mère et Enfant	Part of a study of collaboration between this NGO and other organizations in Palestine following the Oslo Agreement; this study focused on the crisis when the security forces tried to intervene	The challenges facing this organization are very different to those in Western countries – how did the delegate deal with the threat from the security forces?	Interviews with key actors Texts related to internationalization and localization Internal texts authored by the delegate	We identified two discourses associated with the crisis – localization and internationalization We identified the discursive work undertaken by the delegate to prepare the NGO for localization We then identified the discursive work he undertook to reinternationalize the NGO *This analysis allowed us to theorize a model of discourse as a strategic resource, where new symbols, narratives, etc. are embedded in the larger discursive context, and where concepts are successfully attached to relations and/ or material referents to create new objects and subject positions*

Study	Study design	Why it was interesting	Data collected	Data analysis
Older workers	A study of a 1999 Australian parliamentary inquiry into the challenges facing unemployed workers over 45 years of age	An opportunity to trace how older workers were portrayed in the inquiry by different actors – how did they construct the older worker?	Texts: the government website held all the documents related to the inquiry – submissions (dated and by actor), transcripts of hearings (dated and by location), and the final report	We identified four older worker identities from initial submissions; we then examined the final report to see if they survived; in the case of the two female versions that disappeared, we went back to the hearings and looked for talk and interactions that explained the disappearance. We identified instances where older workers commenced their appearance at a hearing with a story; we noted the way in which the chair 'invited' them to tell stories compared to other groups; we analyzed what happened when an older worker did not start with a story; and we traced one particular story by an older worker with numbers in it through the hearing to the final report, noting how the numbers and meaning changed. We noted instances in the inquiry text where the discourse of enterprise intersected with the discourse of age; we analyzed how these intersections served to regulate the older worker identity. *This analysis allowed us to show the micro dynamics of identity work and identity regulation, as well as how stereotypes are deeply embedded in talk and text without individuals necessarily being aware of it*

Study	Study design	Why it was interesting	Data collected	Data analysis
Refugee domain	Part of a larger study comparing refugee systems in the UK, Canada, and Denmark	Refugees appeared more empowered in the UK compared to the other two countries where there was more emphasis on integration – what could we learn about refugee identities by comparing the countries?	Texts: cartoons on refugees Interviews with key actors from each country	We examined how key actors talked about refugees and identified the identities they constructed for the refugee and the different discourses they drew on during this process We noted how languages and practices in different UK organizations created particular refugee identities We examined the ways in which organizations resisted the refugee determination system *This analysis allowed us to show how refugee identity is regulated; how refugee identity is linked to organizational identity; and how resistance is enacted*
Stockholm Convention	A study of the negotiations leading up to the Convention and the agreement of a legal text to regulate toxic chemicals (also includes the study of DDT during this time)	The existence of two competing discourses (sound science and precaution) could be tracked over time – how did different actors engage with the two discourses and how did the two discourses influence the legal text?	Texts on the Convention by different actors were available on the UN website, which also posted materials during the meetings The co-author attended and observed some meetings Interviews with key actors at the meetings	We identified four key actors who were most supportive of sound science (US, ICCA) and precaution (EU, IPEN) We examined how they engaged with both discourses in the texts they authored and in how they referred to other texts *This analysis allowed us to identify the nuances of the different actors' strategies, which involved reconciling the two discourses as well as promoting the preferred discourse; the legal text subordinated sound science to precaution, showing how a dominant, legacy discourse can be displaced*

Study	Study design	Why it was interesting	Data collected	Data analysis
Utel	A study of a culture change program in a newly formed 'spin-off' where a division of the larger company became a separate company (part of the larger GlobalTel study)	Our observations indicated senior management were receptive to some changes in the culture change program, but not others – why were there such different outcomes and what were the micro dynamics of the conversations around them?	Text: the transcription of the recording of the workshop Observations by the co-author who attended the workshop Follow-up interviews with participants	We identified two themes whose meaning was negotiated for comparison (based on observations of the workshop) We extracted all text pertaining to the two themes and iteratively distilled it into a summary of how the two sets of negotiations played out during the workshop We identified patterns in how senior and middle managers intervene in the negotiations, which we distilled into a set of discursive practices; we then compared which practices had been used in each set of negotiations *This analysis allowed us to identify the dynamics of negotiating and sharing a new meaning regarding organizational change among senior and middle managers versus a 'stand-off' between them*

References

ACS (American Chemical Society). 2017. Green Chemistry Academic Programs. ACS .org/content/acs/en/greenchemistry/students-educators/academicprograms.html (accessed December 1, 2017).

Ainsworth, S. and Hardy, C. 2004. Critical Discourse Analysis and Identity: Why Bother. *Critical Discourse Studies*, 1(2): 225–259.

Ainsworth, S. and Hardy, C. 2009. Mind over Body: Physical and Psychotherapeutic Discourses and the Regulation of the Older Worker. *Human Relations*, 62(8): 1199–1229.

Ainsworth, S. and Hardy, C. 2007. The Construction of the Older Worker: Privilege, Paradox and Policy. *Discourse and Communication*, 1(3): 295–313.

Ainsworth, S. and Hardy, C. 2008. The Enterprising Self: An Unsuitable Job for an Older Worker. *Organization*, 15(3): 389–405.

Ainsworth, S. and Hardy, C. 2012. Subjects of Inquiry: Statistics, Stories, and the Production of Knowledge. *Organization Studies*, 33(12): 1693–1714.

Albert, S. and Whetten, D.A. 1985. Organizational Identity. *Research in Organizational Behavior*, 7: 263–295.

Alcoff, L. 1988. Cultural Feminism versus Post-Structuralism: The Identity Crisis in Feminist Theory. *Signs: Journal of Women in Culture and Society*, 13(31): 405–436.

Alvesson, M. and Kärreman, D. 2000. Varieties of Discourse: On the Study of Organizations through Discourse Analysis. *Human Relations*, 53(9): 1125–1149.

Alvesson, M. and Kärreman, D. 2011. Decolonializing Discourse: Critical Reflections on Organizational Discourse Analysis. *Human Relations*, 64(9): 1121–1146.

Alvesson, M. and Willmott, H. 1992. On the Idea of Emancipation in Management and Organization Studies. *Academy of Management Review*, 17(3), 432–464.

Alvesson, M. and Willmott, H. 2002. Identity Regulation as Organizational Control: Producing the Appropriate Individual. *Journal of Management Studies*, 39(5): 619–644.

Alvesson, M., Hardy, C., and Harley, B. 2008. Reflecting on Reflexivity: Reflexive Textual Practices in Organization and Management Theory. *Journal of Management Studies*, 45(3): 480–501.

Alvesson, M., Bridgman, T., and Willmott, H. 2011. *The Oxford Handbook of Critical Management Studies*, Oxford: Oxford University Press.

Anastas, P.T. and Warner, J.C. 1998. *Green Chemistry: Theory and Practice*, Oxford: Oxford University Press.

Andrews, K. 1971. *The Concept of Corporate Strategy*, Homewood, IL: Dow Jones-Irwin.

Andrews, M. 1999. The Seductiveness of Agelessness. *Ageing and Society*, 19(3): 301–318.

Arnoldi, J. 2009. *Risk: An Introduction*, Cambridge: Polity Press.

Ashcraft, K.L. 2020. Communication as Constitutive Transmission? An Encounter with Affect. *Communication Theory*, 10.1093/Ct/Qtz027.

Ashley, D. 1990. Habermas and the Completion of the 'Project of Modernity,' in B.S. Turner (ed.), *Theories of Modernity and Post Modernity*, London: SAGE, pp. 88–107.

Attaran, A. and Maharaj, R. 2000. DDT for Malaria Control Should Not Be Banned. *British Medical Journal*, 321: 1403–1405.

Bamberg, M., De Fina, A., and Schiffrin, D. 2011. Discourse and Identity Construction, in S.J. Schwartz, K. Luyckx, and V. Vignoles (eds), *Handbook of Identity Theory and Research*, Berlin: Springer Verlag, pp. 177–199.

Barad, K. 2003. Posthumanist Performativity: Toward an Understanding of How Matter Comes to Matter, *Signs: Journal of Women in Culture and Society*, 28(3): 801–831.

Barad, K. 2007. *Meeting The Universe Halfway: Quantum Physics and the Entanglement of Matter and Meaning*, Durham, NC: Duke University Press.

Barad, K. 2013. Ma(r)king Time: Material Entanglements and Re-Memberings: Cutting Together-Apart, in P.R. Carlile, D. Nicolini, A. Langley, and H. Tsoukas (eds), *How Matter Matters: Objects, Artifacts, and Materiality in Organization Studies*, Oxford: Oxford University Press, pp. 16–30.

Barry, D., Carroll, B., and Hansen, H. 2006. To Text or Context? Endotextual, Exotextual, or Multi-Textual Approaches to Narrative and Discursive Organizational Studies. *Organization Studies*, 27(8): 1091–1110.

Beck, U. 1992. *Risk Society: Towards a New Modernity*, New Delhi: SAGE.

Beckert, J. 1999. Agency, Entrepreneurs, and Institutional Change: The Roles of Strategic Choice and Institutionalized Practices in Organizations. *Organization Studies*, 20(5): 777–799.

Bennett, J. 2010. *Vibrant Matter: A Political Ecology of Things*, Durham, NC: Duke University Press.

Benson, M. and O'Reilly, K. 2020. Reflexive Practice in Live Sociology: Lessons from Researching Brexit in the Lives of British Citizens Living in the EU-27. *Qualitative Research*, 1–17. Doi.Org/10.1177/1468794120977795.

Black, Y. 2020. The Play's the Thing: A Creative Collaboration to Investigate Lived Experiences in an Urban Community Garden. *Management Learning*, 51(2): 168–186.

Boivin, G., Brummans, B.H.J.M., and Barker, J.R. 2017. The Institutionalization of CCO Scholarship: Trends from 2000 to 2015. *Management Communication Quarterly*, 31(3): 331–355.

Boxenbaum, E., Jones, C., Meyer, R.E., and Svejenova, S. 2018. Towards an Articulation of the Material and Visual Turn in Organization Studies. *Organization Studies*, 39(5–6): 597–616.

Bracker, J. 1980. The Historical Development of the Strategic Management Concept. *Academy of Management Review*, 5(2): 219–224.

Braidotti, R. 2006. Posthuman, All Too Human: Towards a New Process Ontology. *Theory, Culture and Society*, 23(7–8): 197–208.

Braidotti, R. 2013. *The Posthuman*, Cambridge: Polity Press.

Braun, B. 2008. Environmental Issues: Inventive Life. *Progress in Human Geography*, 32(5): 667–679.

Bridge, G., Mccarthy, J., and Perreault, T. 2015. Editor's Introduction, in T. Perreault, G. Bridge, and J. Mccarthy (eds), *The Routledge Handbook of Political Ecology*, Abingdon: Routledge, pp. 3–18.

Brown, A.D. and Humphreys, M. 2006. Organizational Identity and Place: A Discursive Exploration of Hegemony and Resistance. *Journal of Management Studies*, 43(2): 231–257.

Brown, S.D. 2002. Michel Serres: Science, Translation and the Logic of the Parasite. *Theory Culture and Society*, 19(3): 1–27.

Brummans, B.H., Cooren, F., Robichaud, D., and Taylor, J.R. 2014. Approaches to the Communicative Constitution of Organizations, in L.L. Putnam and D.K Mumby (eds), *The SAGE Handbook of Organizational Communication*, Los Angeles, CA: SAGE, pp. 173–194.

Buchanan, D. and Dawson, P. 2007. Discourse and Audience: Organizational Change as Multi-Story Process. *Journal of Management Studies*, 44(5): 669–685.

Burman, E. and Parker, I. 1993. Against Discursive Imperialism, Empiricism and Constructionism: Thirty-Two Problems with Discourse Analysis, in E. Burman and I. Parker (eds), *Discourse Analytic Research: Repertoires and Readings of Texts in Action*, London: Routledge, pp. 155–172.

Burrell, G. 1988. Modernism, Postmodernism and Organizational Analysis: The Contribution of Michel Foucault. *Organization Studies*, 9(2): 221–235.

Callon, M. 1984. Some Elements of a Sociology of Translation: Domestication of the Scallops and the Fisherman of St. Brieuc Bay, in J. Law (ed.), *Power, Action and Belief: A Sociology of Knowledge*. Special issue of *Sociological Review*, 32(51): 196–233.

Carabine, J. 2001. Unmarried Motherhood 1830–1990: A Genealogical Analysis, in M. Wetherell, S. Taylor, and S. Yates (eds), *Discourse as Data: A Guide for Analysts*, London: SAGE, pp. 267–310.

Carlsen, A. 2006. Organizational Becoming a Dialogic Imagination of Practice: The Case of the Indomitable Gauls. *Organization Science*, 17(1): 132–149.

Carson, R. 1962. *Silent Spring*, New York: Houghton Mifflin.

Carter, C.R. and Rogers, D.S. 2008. A Framework of Sustainable Supply Chain Management: Moving toward New Theory. *International Journal of Physical Distribution and Logistics Management*, 38(5): 360–387.

Carton, G. 2020. How Assemblages Change When Theories Become Performative: The Case of the Blue Ocean Strategy. *Organization Studies*, 41(10): 1417–1439.

CBS. 1963. *The Silent Spring of Rachel Carson*, Video. New York: CBS News Archives.

Chalaby, J.K. 1996. Beyond the Prison-House of Language: Discourse as a Sociological Concept. *British Journal of Sociology*, 47(4): 684–698.

Chandler, A. 1962. *Strategy and Structure*, Cambridge, MA: MIT Press.

Chang, H., Ngunjiri, F., and Hernandez, K.C. 2013. *Collaborative Autoethnography*, London: Routledge.

Chia, R. 2000. Discourse Analysis as Organizational Analysis. *Organization*, 7(3): 513–518.

Cobb, S. and Rifkin, J. 1991. Practice and Paradox: Deconstructing Neutrality in Mediation. *Law and Social Inquiry*, 16(1): 35–62.

Cohn, S. and Lynch, R. 2017. Posthuman Perspectives: Relevance for a Global Public Health. *Critical Public Health*, 27(3): 285–292.

Coit Murphy, P. 2005. *What a Book Can Do: The Publication and Reception of Silent Spring*, Amherst, MA: University of Massachusetts Press.

Coleman, R. and Ringrose, J. 2013. *Deleuze and Research Methodologies*, Edinburgh: Edinburgh University Press.

Colomy, P. 1998. Neofunctionalism and Neoinstitutionalism: Human Agency and Interest in Institutional Change. *Sociological Forum*, 13(2): 265–300.

Contu, S., Palpacuer, F., and Balas, N. 2013. Multinational Corporations' Politics and Resistance to Plant Shutdowns: A Comparative Case Study in the South of France. *Human Relations*, 66(3): 363–384.

Coole, D. 2013. Agentic Capacities and Capacious Historical Materialism: Thinking with New Materialisms in the Political Sciences. *Millennium: Journal of International Studies*, 41(3): 451–469.

Coole, D. and Frost, S. 2010. Introducing the New Materialisms, in D. Coole and S. Frost (eds), *New Materialisms: Ontology, Agency, and Politics*, Durham, NC: Duke University Press, pp. 1–46.

Cooper, D.J., Ezzamel, M., and Willmott, H. 2008. Examining Institutionalization: A Critical Theoretic Perspective, in R. Greenwood, C. Oliver, K. Sahlin-Andersson, and R. Suddaby (eds), *The SAGE Handbook of Organizational Institutionalism*, London: SAGE, pp. 673–701.

Cooper, R. and Burrell, G. 1988. Modernism, Postmodernism and Organizational Analysis: An Introduction. *Organization Studies*, 9(1): 91–112.

Cooren, F. 2015. *Organizational Discourse*, Cambridge: Polity Press.

Cooren, F. 2020. Beyond Entanglement: (Socio-)Materiality and Organization Studies, *Organization Theory*, 1(3): 1–24.

Cooren, F. and Taylor, J.R. 1997. Organization as an Effect of Mediation: Redefining the Link between Organization and Communication. *Communication Theory*, 7(3): 219–259.

Cornelissen, J., Durand, R., Fiss, P.C., Lammers, J.C., and Vaara, E. 2018. Putting Communication Front and Center in Institutional Theory and Analysis. *Academy of Management Review*, 40(1): 10 27.

Coupland, C. 2015. Organizing Masculine Bodies in Rugby League Football: Groomed to Fail. *Organization Studies*, 22(6): 793–809.

Cuganesan, S., Boedker, C., and Guthrie, J. 2007. Enrolling Discourse Consumers to Affect Material Intellectual Capital Practice. *Accounting, Auditing and Accountability Journal*, 20(6): 883–911.

Cunliffe, A.L. 2003. Reflexive Inquiry in Organizational Research: Questions and Possibilities. *Human Relations*, 56(8): 983–103.

Cunliffe, A.L. and Karunanayakebe, G. 2013. Working within Hyphen-Spaces in Ethnographic Research: Implications for Research Identities and Practice. *Organizational Research Methods*, 16(3): 364–392.

Curran, D. 2016. *Risk, Power, and Inequality in the 21st Century*, New York: Palgrave Macmillan.

Cutcher, L. 2020. Conversations with the Self and Others: Practising Reflexive Researcher Identity Work, in A.D. Brown (ed.), *The Oxford Handbook of Identities in Organizations*, Oxford: Oxford University Press, pp. 311–325.

Cutcher, L., Hardy, C., Riach, K., and Thomas, R. 2020. Reflections on Reflexive Theorizing: The Need for a Little More Conversation. *Organization Theory*, 1(3): 1–28.

Czarniawska, B. 1997. *Narrating the Organization: Dramas of institutional Identity*, Chicago, IL: University of Chicago Press.

Czarniawska, B. and Sevón, G. (eds). 1996. *Translating Organizational Change*, Berlin: De Gruyter, pp. 13–48.

D'Adderio, L. and Pollock, N. 2014. Performing Modularity: Competing Rules, Performative Struggles and the Effect of Organizational Theories on the Organization. *Organization Studies*, 35(12): 1813–1843.

Dale, K. and Latham, Y. 2015. Ethics and Entangled Embodiment: Bodies-Materialities-Organization. *Organization*, 22(2): 166–182.

Davies, B. and Harré, R. 1990. Positioning: The Discursive Production of Selves. *Journal for the Theory of Social Behavior*, 20(1): 43–65.

Davies, O. and Riach, K. 2019. From Manstream Measuring to Multispecies Sustainability? A Gendered Reading of Bee-ing Sustainable. *Gender, Work & Organization*, 26(3): 246–266.

Deetz, S. 1992. Disciplinary Power in the Modern Corporation, in M. Alvesson and H. Willmott (eds), *Critical Management Studies*, London: SAGE, pp. 21–45.

Deleuze, G. and Guattari, F. 1998. *A Thousand Plateaus: Capitalism and Schizophrenia*, London: Athlone.

DiMaggio, P.J. and Powell, W.W. 1991. *The New Institutionalism in Organizational Analysis*, Chicago, IL: University of Chicago Press.

Du Gay, P. 1996. *Consumption and Identity at Work*, London: SAGE.

Duff, C. and Sumartojo, S. 2017. Assemblages of Creativity: Material Practices in the Creative Economy. *Organization*, 24(3): 418–432.

EC. 2000. *Communication from the Commission on the Precautionary Principle*, Brussels: European Commission.

Elliott, A. 2002. Beck's Sociology of Risk: A Critical Assessment. *Sociology*, 36(2): 293–315.

Epstein, S. 1996. *Impure Science: Aids, Activism, and the Politics of Science*, Berkeley, CA: University of California Press.

EU. 2000. *The European Union and The Precautionary Principle: EU Presidency Speech*, Pamphlet distributed at INC-5, Johannesburg.

Fairclough, N. 1992. *Discourse and Social Change*, Cambridge: Polity Press.

Fairclough, N. 1995. *Critical Discourse Analysis: The Critical Study of Language*, London: Longman.

Fairclough, N. 2003. *Analysing Discourse Textual Analysis for Social Research*, London: Routledge.

Fairclough, N. 2010. *Critical Discourse Analysis: The Critical Study of Language*, London: Routledge.

Fairclough, N. and Wodak R. 1997. Critical Discourse Analysis, in T.A. van Dijk (ed.), *Discourse as Social Interaction*, London: SAGE, pp. 258–284.

Fairhurst, G.T. and Putnam, L.L. 2019. An Integrative Methodology for Organizational Oppositions: Aligning Grounded Theory and Discourse Analysis. *Organizational Research Methods*, 22(4): 917–940.

Firang, D.Y. 2011. *Transnational Activities and their Impact on Achieving a Successful Housing Career in Canada: The Case of Ghanaian Immigrants in Toronto*, PhD, University of Toronto.

Fischer, F. 2003. *Reframing Public Policy: Discursive Politics and Deliberative Practices*, Oxford: Oxford University Press.

Fletcher, J.K., Bailyn, L., and Blake-Beard, S. 2009. Practical Pushing: Creating Discursive Space in Organizational Narratives, in J.W. Cox, T.G. LeTrent-Jones, M. Voronov, and D. Weir (eds), *Critical Management Studies at Work: Multidisciplinary Approaches to Negotiating Tensions between Theory and Practice*, Cheltenham, UK and Northampton, MA, USA: Edward Elgar Publishing.

Fotaki, M. and Daskalaki, M. 2021. Politicizing the Body in the Anti-Mining Protest in Greece. *Organization Studies*, 42(8) 1265–1290.

Fotaki, M., Metcalfe, B.D., and Harding, N. 2014. Writing Materiality into Management and Organization Studies through and with Luce Irigaray. *Human Relations*, 67(10): 1239–1263.

Foucault, M. 1972. *The Archeology of Knowledge*, London: Routledge.

Foucault, M. 1978. The *History of Sexuality*, Volume 1, Harmondsworth: Penguin.

Foucault, M. 1979. *Discipline and Punish: The Birth of the Prison*, Harmondsworth: Penguin.

Foucault, M. 1980. *Power/Knowledge: Selected Interviews and Other Writings 1972–1977*, Brighton: Harvester Press.

Foucault, M. 1981. The Order of Discourse, in R. Young (ed.), *Untying the Text: A Post-Structural Anthology*, London: Routledge, pp. 48–78.

Foucault, M. 1982. The Subject and Power, in H.L. Dreyfus and P. Rabinow (eds), *Michel Foucault: Beyond Structuralism and Hermeneutics*, Brighton: Harvester, pp. 208–226.

Foucault, M. 1985. *The Use of Pleasure: The History of Sexuality*, Volume 2, New York: Random House.

Fowler, R. 1991. *Language in the News: Discourse and Ideology in the Press*, London: Routledge.

Fowler, R. 1996. On Critical Linguistics, in C.R. Caldas-Coulthard and M. Coulthard (eds), *Texts and Practices: Readings in Critical Discourse Analysis*, London: Routledge, pp. 3–14.

Fox, N.J. and Alldred, P. 2016. *Sociology and the New Materialism*, London: SAGE.

Gabriel, Y. 2004. Narratives, Stories and Texts, in D. Grant, C. Hardy, C. Oswick, and L. Putnam (eds), *The SAGE Handbook of Organizational Discourse*, London: SAGE, pp. 61–78.

Gamble, C.N., Hanan, J.S., and Nail, T. 2019. What Is New Materialism? *Angelaki*, 24(6): 111–134.

Garcia, P. and Hardy, C. 2007. Positioning, Similarity, and Difference: Narratives of Individual and Organizational Identities in an Australian University. *Scandinavian Journal of Management*, 23(4): 363–383.

Gee, J.P. 1999. *An Introduction to Discourse Analysis: Theory and Method*, London: Routledge.

Gephart, R.P. 2002. Introduction to the Brave New Workplace: Organizational Behavior in the Electronic Age. *Journal of Organizational Behavior*, 23: 327–344.

Gergen, K.J. 1994. *Realities and Relationships: Soundings in Social Construction*, Cambridge, MA: Harvard University Press.

Gherardi, S. 2016. To Start Practice Theorizing Anew: The Contribution of the Concepts of Agencement and Formativeness. *Organization*, 23(5): 680–698.

Gherardi, S. 2017a. Sociomateriality in Posthuman Practice Theory, in S. Hui, E. Shove, and T. Schatzki (eds), *The Nexus of Practices: Connections, Constellations, and Practitioners*, London: Routledge, pp. 38–51.

Gherardi, S. 2017b. One Turn … and Now Another One: Do the Turn to Practice and the Turn to Affect Have Something in Common? *Management Learning*, 48(3): 345–358.

Gherardi, S. 2019a. If We Practice Posthumanist Research, Do We Need 'Gender' Any Longer? *Gender, Work and Organization*, 26: 40–53.

Gherardi, S. 2019b. Theorizing Affective Ethnography for Organization Studies, *Organization*, 26(6): 741–760.

Giddens, A. 1999. Risk and Responsibility. *Modern Law Review*, 62(1): 1–10.

Gilmore, S. and Kenny, K. 2015. Work-Worlds Colliding: Self-Reflexivity, Power and Emotion in Organizational Ethnography. *Human Relations*, 68(1): 55–78.

Girei, E. 2017. Decolonising Management Knowledge: A Reflexive Journey as Practitioner and Researcher in Uganda. *Management Learning*, 48(4): 453–470.

Grandy, G. and Mills, A.J. 2004. Strategy as Simulacra? A Radical Reflexive Look at the Discipline and Practice of Strategy. *Journal of Management Studies*, 41(7): 1153–1170.

Grant, D., Hardy, C., Oswick, C., and Putnam, L. (eds). 2004. *The SAGE Handbook of Organizational Discourse*, London: SAGE.

Greckhamer, T. 2010. The Stretch of Strategic Management Discourse: A Critical Analysis. *Organization Studies*, 31(7): 841–871.

Grossman, L.A. 2016. Aids Activists, FDA Regulation, and the Amendment of America's Drug Constitution. *American Journal of Law and Medicine*, 42(4): 687–742.

Gullette, M.M. 1997. *Declining to Decline: Cultural Combat and the Politics of the Midlife*, Charlottesville, VA: University Press of Virginia.

Hacker, J. 2006. *The Great Risk Shift: The Assault on American Jobs, Families, Health Care, and Retirement and How You Can Fight Back*, New York: Oxford University Press.

Hacker, P.M.S. 2013. The Linguistic Turn in Analytic Philosophy, in M. Beaney (ed.), *The Oxford Handbook of The History of Analytic Philosophy*, Oxford: Oxford University Press, pp. 927–947.

Hacking, I. 1986. Making Up People, in T.C. Heller, M. Sosna, and D.E. Wellbery (eds), *Reconstructing Individualism: Autonomy, Individuality, and the Self in Western Thought*, Stanford, CA: Stanford University Press, pp. 222–236.

Hacking, I. 2000. *The Social Construction of What?*, Cambridge, MA: Harvard University Press.

Hajer, M.A. 1995. *The Politics of Environmental Discourse*, Oxford: Oxford University Press.

Hall, S. 2001. Foucault: Power, Knowledge and Discourse, in M. Wetherell, S. Taylor, and S. Yates (eds), *Discourse, Theory and Practice: A Reader*, London: SAGE/Open University, pp. 72–81.

Halliday, M.A.K. and Matthiessen, C.M.I.M. 2004. *An Introduction to Functional Grammar*, London: Arnold.

Haraway, D. 2008. *When Species Meet*, Minneapolis, MN: University of Minnesota Press.

Hardy, C. 2001. Researching Organizational Discourse. *International Studies in Management and Organization*, 31(3): 25–47.

Hardy, C. 2003. Refugee Determination: Power and Resistance in Systems of Foucauldian Power. *Administration and Society*, 34(4): 462–488.

Hardy, C. 2004. Scaling Up and Bearing Down in Discourse Analysis: Questions Regarding Textual Agencies and Their Context. *Organization*, 11(3): 415–425.

Hardy, C. and Clegg, S.R. 1996. Some Dare Call It Power, in S.R. Clegg, C. Hardy, and W.R. Nord (eds), *The SAGE Handbook of Organization Studies*, London: SAGE, pp. 622–641.

Hardy, C. and Clegg, S.R. 1997. Relativity without Relativism: Reflexivity in Post-Paradigm Organization Studies. *British Journal of Management*, 8: S5–S17.

Hardy, C. and Maguire, S. 2010. Discourse, Field-Configuring Events and Change in Organizations and institutional Fields: Narratives of DDT and the Stockholm Convention. *Academy of Management Journal*, 53(6): 1365–1392.

Hardy, C. and Maguire, S. 2016. Organizing Risk: Discourse, Power and Riskification. *Academy of Management Review*, 41(1): 80–108.

Hardy, C. and Maguire, S. 2017. Institutional Entrepreneurship and Change, in R. Greenwood, C. Oliver, T. Lawrence, and R.E. Meyer (eds), *The SAGE Handbook of Organizational Institutionalism*, London: SAGE, pp. 261–280.

Hardy, C. and Maguire, S. 2020. Organizations, Risk Translation and the Ecology of Risks: The Discursive Construction of a Novel Risk. *Academy of Management Journal*, 63(3): 685–716.

Hardy, C. and Phillips, N. 1998. Strategies of Engagement: Lessons from the Critical Examination of Collaboration and Conflict in an Interorganizational Domain. *Organization Science*, 9(2): 217–230.

Hardy, C. and Phillips, N. 1999. No Joking Matter: Discursive Struggle in the Canadian Refugee System. *Organization Studies*, 20(1): 1–24.

Hardy, C. and Phillips, N. 2004. Discourse and Power, in D. Grant, C. Hardy, C. Oswick, and L. Putnam (eds), *The SAGE Handbook of Organizational Discourse*, London: SAGE, pp. 299–316.

Hardy, C. and Thomas, R. 2014. Strategy, Discourse and Practice: The Intensification of Power. *Journal of Management Studies*, 51(2): 320–348.

Hardy, C. and Thomas, R. 2015. Discourse in a Material World. *Journal of Management Studies*, 52(5): 680–696.

Hardy, C., Lawrence, T., and Phillips, N. 1998. Talk and Action: Conversations, Narrative and Action in Interorganizational Collaboration, in D., Grant, T. Keenoy, and C. Oswick (eds), *Discourse and Organization*, London: SAGE, pp. 65–83.

Hardy, C., Palmer, I., and Phillips, N. 2000. Discourse as a Strategic Resource. *Human Relations*, 53(9): 7–28.

Hardy, C., Phillips, N., and Clegg, S. 2001. Reflexivity in Social Studies: A Study of the Production of the Research Subject. *Human Relations*, 54(5): 3–32.

Hardy, C., Grant, D., Keenoy, T., Oswick, C., and Phillips, N. (eds). 2004. Special Issue on Organizational Discourse. *Organizational Studies*, 25(1).

Hardy, C., Lawrence, T., and Grant, D. 2005. Discourse and Collaboration: The Role of Conversations and Collective Identity. *Academy of Management Review*, 30(1): 1–20.

Hardy, C., Bhakoo, V., and Maguire S. 2020a. A New Methodology for Supply Chain Management: Discourse Analysis and Its Potential for Theoretical Advancement. *Journal of Supply Chain Management*, 56(2): 19–35.

Hardy, C., Maguire, S., Power, M., and Tsoukas, H. 2020b. Organizing Risk: Organization and Management Theory for the Risk Society. *Academy of Management Annals*, 14(2): 1032–1066.

Harris, K.L., Mcfarlane, M., and Wieskamp, V. 2020. The Promise and Peril of Agency as Motion: A Feminist New Materialist Approach to Sexual Violence and Sexual Harassment. *Organization*, 27(5): 660–679.

Henkin, H., Merta, M., and Staples, J. 1971. *The Environment, the Establishment, and the Law*, New York: Houghton Mifflin.

Heyes, C.J. 2014. Subjectivity and Power, in D. Taylor (ed.), *Michel Foucault: Key Concepts*, London: Routledge, pp. 159–172.

Hilgartner, S. 1992. The Social Construction of Risk Objects: Or, How to Pry Open Networks of Risk, in J.F. Short, Jr. and L. Clarke (eds), *Organizations, Uncertainties, and Risk*, Boulder, CO: Westview Press, pp. 39–51.

Hoffman, M. 2014. Disciplinary Power, in D. Taylor (ed.), *Michel Foucault: Key Concepts*, London: Routledge, pp. 27–40.

Holweg, M. 2007. The Genealogy of Lean Production. *Journal of Operations Management*, 25(2): 420–437.

Hook, D. 2007. *Foucault, Psychology and the Analytics of Power Discourse*, Houndmills: Palgrave Macmillan.

House of Representatives (Standing Committee on Employment, Education and Workplace Relations). 2000. *Age Counts: An inquiry into Issues Specific to Mature-Age Workers*, Canberra: Commonwealth of Australia.

Howard-Grenville, J., Nelson, A.J., Earle, A.G., Haack, J.A., and Young, D.M. 2017. If Chemists Don't Do It, Who Is Going To? Peer-Driven Occupational Change and the Emergence of Green Chemistry. *Administrative Science Quarterly*, 62(3): 524–560.

Hultin, L. and Introna, L. 2019. On Receiving Asylum Seekers: Identity Working as a Process of Material-Discursive Interpellation. *Organization Studies*, 40(9): 1361–1386.

Hultin, L., Introna, L., Göransson, M.B., and Mähring, M. 2021. Precarity, Hospitality and the Becoming of a Subject That Matters: A Study of Syrian Refugees in Lebanese Tented Settlements. *Organization Studies*: 1–29. Doi.Org/10.1177/01708406211026115.

ICCA. 2000a. *ICCA Comments on the Application of the Precautionary Principle in Regulatory Decision-Making*, August 15. Pamphlet distributed at INC-5, Johannesburg.

ICCA. 2000b. *UNEP Global POPs Treaty – INC-5: ICCA Statement on Key Issues*, Pamphlet distributed at INC-5, Johannesburg.

Iedema, R. and Wodak, R. 1999. Introduction: Organizational Discourses and Practices. *Discourse and Society*, 10(1): 4–19.

IPCC (Intergovernmental Panel on Climate Change). 2020. *Synthesis Report of the Sixth Assessment Report*, August 9. www.ipcc.ch/ar6-syr/ (accessed November 9, 2021).

IPEN (International Pollutants Elimination Network). 1998. *Background Statement and POPs Elimination Platform*, Pamphlet distributed at INC-1, Montreal.

Jacobs, K., Kemeny, J., and Manzi, T. 2003. Power, Discursive Space and Institutional Practices in the Construction of Housing Problems. *Housing Studies*, 18(4), 429–446.

Jarzabkowski, P. 2004. Strategy as Practice: Recursiveness, Adaptation, and Practices-in-Use. *Organization Studies*, 25(4): 529–560.

Jasanoff, S. 1998. The Political Science of Risk Perception. *Reliability Engineering and System Safety*, 59(1): 91–99.

Jeanes, E. 2017. Are We Ethical? Approaches to Ethics in Management and Organisation Research. *Organization*, 24(2): 174–197.

Kärreman, D. 2014. Understanding Organizational Realities through Discourse Analysis: The Case for Discursive Pragmatism. *Journal of Business Anthropology*, 3(2): 201–215.

Kenny, K. and Fotaki, M. 2015. From Gendered Organizations to Compassionate Borderspaces: Reading Corporeal Ethics with Bracha Ettinger. *Organization*, 22(2), 183–199.

Knights, D. 1992. Changing Spaces: The Disruptive Impact of a New Epistemological Location for the Study of Management. *Academy of Management Review*, 17(3): 514–536.

Knights, D. and Morgan, G. 1991. Strategic Discourse and Subjectivity: Towards a Critical Analysis of Corporate Strategy in Organisations. *Organisation Studies*, 12(3): 251–273.

Knights, D. and Willmott, H. 1989. Power and Subjectivity at Work: From Degradation to Subjugation in Social Relations. *Sociology*, 23(4), 535–558.

Kuhn, T. and Burk, N.R. 2014. Spatial Design as Sociomaterial Practice: A (Dis) Organizing Perspective on Communicative Constitution, in F. Cooren, E. Vaara, A. Langley, and H. Tsoukas (eds), *Language and Communication at Work: Discourse, Narrativity, and Organizing*, Oxford: Oxford University Press, pp. 147–172.

Kwon, W., Clarke, I., and Wodak, R. 2014. Micro-Level Discursive Strategies for Constructing Shared Views around Strategic Issues in Team Meetings. *Journal of Management Studies*, 51(2): 265–290.

Laclau, E. and Mouffe, C. 1987. Postmodernism without Apologies. *New Left Review*, 166: 79–106.

Langley, A. and Klag, M. 2019. Being Where? Navigating the Involvement Paradox in Qualitative Research Accounts. *Qualitative Research Methods*, 22(2): 515–538.

Lather, P. 2013. Methodology-21: What Do We Do in the Afterward? *International Journal of Qualitative Studies in Education*, 26(6): 634–645.

Lather, P. and St. Pierre, E.A. 2013. Post-Qualitative Research. *International Journal of Qualitative Studies in Education*, 26(6): 629–633.

Latour, B. 1986. The Powers of Association, in J. Law (ed.), *Power, Action and Belief*, London: Routledge and Kegan Paul, pp. 264–280.

Law, J. and Urry, J. 2004. Enacting the Social. *Economy and Society*, 33(3): 390–410.

Lawrence, T.B. 2017. High-Stakes Institutional Translation: Establishing North America's First Government-Sanctioned Supervised Injection Site. *Academy of Management Journal*, 60(5): 1771–1800.

Lear, L. 1997. *Rachel Carson: Witness for Nature*, New York: Henry Holt and Company.

Leclercq-Vandelannoitte, A. 2011. Organizations as Discursive Constructions: A Foucauldian Approach. *Organization Studies*, 32(9): 1247–1271.

Lefsrud, L.M. and Meyer, R.E. 2012. Science or Science Fiction? Professionals' Discursive Construction of Climate Change. *Organization Studies*, 33(11): 1477–1506.

Lemke, T. 2015. New Materialisms: Foucault and the Government of Things. *Theory, Culture and Society*, 32(4): 3–25.

Levy, N. 2016. Emotional Landscapes: Discomfort in the Field. *Qualitative Research Journal*, 16(1): 39–50.

Long, R.K., Jr. 1962. Letter to Editor, *Audubon Magazine*, 64(November–December): 299.

Lundborg, T. and Vaughan-Williams, N. 2015. New Materialisms, Discourse Analysis, and International Relations: A Radical Intertextual Approach. *Review of International Studies*, 41(1): 3–25.

Lupton, D. 2013. *Risk*, New York: Routledge.

MacLure, M. 2013. Researching without Representation? Language and Materiality in Post-Qualitative Methodology. *International Journal of Qualitative Studies in Education*, 26(6): 658–667.

Maguire, S. and Hardy, C. 2005. Identity and Collaborative Strategy in the Case of Canadian HIV/AIDS Treatment. *Strategic Organization*, 3(1): 11–45.

Maguire, S. and Hardy, C. 2006. The Emergence of New Global institutions: A Discursive Perspective. *Organization Studies*, 27(1): 7–29.

Maguire, S. and Hardy, C. 2009. Discourse and Deinstitutionalization: The Decline of DDT. *Academy of Management Journal*, 52(1): 148–178.

Maguire, S. and Hardy, C. 2013. Organizing Processes and the Construction of Risk: A Discursive Approach. *Academy of Management Journal*, 56(1): 231–255.

Maguire, S. and Hardy, C. 2016. Risk Work: Three Scenarios from a Study of Industrial Chemicals in Canada, in M. Power (ed.), *Riskwork: Essays on the Organizational Life of Risk Management*, Oxford: Oxford University Press, pp. 130–149.

Maguire, S. and Hardy, C. 2019. The Discourse of Risk and Processes of Institutional Change: The Case of Green Chemistry, in T. Reay, T.B. Zilber, A. Langley, and H. Tsoukas (eds), *Institutions and Organizations: A Process View*, Oxford: Oxford University Press, pp. 154–173.

Maguire, S., Phillips, N., and Hardy, C. 2001. When 'Silence = Death', Keep Talking: Trust, Control and the Discursive Construction of Identity in the Canadian HIV/AIDS Treatment Domain. *Organization Studies*, 22(2): 285–310.

Maguire, S., Hardy, C., and Lawrence, T.B. 2004. Institutional Entrepreneurship in Emerging Fields: HIV/AIDS Treatment Advocacy in Canada. *Academy of Management Journal*, 47(5): 657–679.

Manning, J. 2018. Becoming a Decolonial Feminist Ethnographer: Addressing the Complexities of Positionality and Representation. *Journal of Management Learning*, 49(3): 311–326.

Martens, M.L., Jennings, J.E., and Jennings, P.D. 2007. Do The Stories They Tell Get Them the Money They Need? The Role of Entrepreneurial Narratives in Resource Acquisition. *Academy of Management Journal*, 50(5): 1107–1132.

Martine, T. and Cooren, F. 2016. A Relational Approach to Materiality and Organization: The Case of a Creative Idea, in L. Introna, D. Kavanagh, S. Kelly, W. Orlikowski, and S. Scott (eds), *Beyond Interpretivism? New Encounters with Technology and Organization*, Cham: Springer, pp. 143–166.

Meriläinen, S., Tienari, J., Thomas, R., and Davies, A. 2004. Management Consultant Talk: A Cross-Cultural Comparison of Normalising Discourse and Resistance. *Organization*, 11(2): 539–564.

Miller, H.I. and Conko, G. 2001. The Perils of Precaution. *Policy Review*, 107(June): 25–39.

Mintzberg, H. 1987. Crafting Strategy. *Harvard Business Review*, 2(July–August): 66–74.

Molder, H.T. 2015. Discursive Psychology, in K. Tracey (ed.), *The International Encyclopedia of Language and Social Interaction*, Hoboken, NJ: John Wiley and Sons, pp. 1–11. onlinelibrary.wiley.com/doi/epdf/10.1002/9781118611463.wbielsi158.

Monsanto. 1962. The Desolate Year. *Monsanto Magazine*, October: 4–9.

Monteiro, P. and Nicolini, D. 2015. Recovering Materiality in Institutional Work: Prizes as an Assemblage of Human and Material Entities. *Journal of Management Inquiry*, 24(1): 61–81.

Mrak, E. 1969. *Report of the Secretary's Commission on Pesticides and Their Relationship to Environmental Health – Parts I and II*, Washington, DC: US Department of Health, Education and Welfare.

Mumby, D.K. 2001. Power and Politics, in F. Jablin and L.L. Putnam (eds), *The New Handbook of Organizational Communication: Advances in Theory, Research and Methods*, Thousand Oaks, CA: SAGE, pp. 585–623.

Mumby, D.K. 2011. What's Cooking in Organizational Discourse Studies? A Response to Alvesson and Kärreman. *Human Relations*, 64(9): 1147–1161.

Mumby, D.K. and Stohl, C. 1991. Power and Discourse in Organization Studies: Absence and the Dialectic of Control. *Discourse and Society*, 3: 313–332.

Mumby, D.K., Thomas, R., Martí, I., and Seidl, D. 2017. Resistance Redux. *Organization Studies*, 38(9): 1157–1183.

Murphy, A.G. 1998. Hidden Transcripts of Flight Attendant Resistance. *Management Communication Quarterly*, 11: 499–535.

NACA (National Agricultural Chemicals Association). 1962. *Fact and Fancy*, Washington, DC: National Agricultural Chemicals Association.

Neff, G. 2012. *Venture Labor: Work and the Burden of Risk in Innovative Industries*, Cambridge, MA: MIT Press.

Nickerson, V. and Goby, V.P. 2018. Convergence and Collaboration: Co-Creating Meaning within Culturally Diverse Workforces. *International Journal of Organizational Analysis*, 26(5): 941–952.

O'Riordan, T. and Jordan, A. 1995. The Precautionary Principle in Contemporary Environmental Politics. *Environmental Values*, 4(3): 191–212.

Odum, P. 1959. *Fundamentals of Ecology*, 2nd edition, Philadelphia, PA: Saunders.

Odum, P. 1971. *Fundamentals of Ecology*, 3rd edition, Philadelphia, PA: Saunders.

Oliver, N. and Hunter, G. 1998. The Financial Impact of 'Japanese' Manufacturing Methods, in R. Delbridge and J. Lowe (eds), *Manufacturing in Transition*, London: Routledge, chapter 5.

Owusu, T.Y. 1996. *The Adaptation of Black African Immigrants in Canada: A Case Study of Residential Behaviour and Ethnic Community Unity Formation among Ghanaians in Toronto*, PhD, University of Toronto.

Pagell, M. and Shevchenko, A. 2014. Why Research in Sustainable Supply Chain Management Should Have No Future. *Journal of Supply Chain Management*, 50(1): 44–55.

Paltridge, B. 2000. *Making Sense of Discourse Analysis*, Cammeray, NSW: Antipodean Educational Enterprises.

Paring, G., Pezé, S., and Huault, I. 2017. Welcome to the Whiteboard, the New Member of the Team: Identity Regulation as a Sociomaterial Process. *Organization*, 24(6): 844–865.

Parker, I. 1992. *Discourse Dynamics*, London: Routledge.

Pascale, R.T. 1984. Perspectives on Strategy: The Real Story behind Honda's Success. *California Management Review*, 26(3): 47–72.

Phillips, N. and Hardy, C. 1997. Managing Multiple Identities: Discourse, Legitimacy and Resources in the UK Refugee System. *Organization*, 4(2): 159–185.

Phillips, N. and Hardy, C. 2002. *Discourse Analysis: Investigating Processes of Social Construction*, Thousand Oaks, CA: SAGE.

Phillips, N., Lawrence, T., and Hardy, C. 2004. Discourse and Institutions. *Academy of Management Review*, 29(4): 1–18.

Polkinghorne, D. 1988. *Narrative Knowing and the Human Sciences*, Albany, NY: State University of New York Press.

Pollan, M. 2001. Precautionary Principle. *New York Times Magazine*, December 9: 92–93.

Pomerantz, A. and Fehr, B.J. 1997. Conversation Analysis: An Approach to the Study of Social Action as Sense Making Practices, in T.A. van Dijk (ed.), *Discourse as Social Interaction*, London: SAGE, pp. 64–91.

Porter, M.E. 1985. *Competitive Advantage: Creating and Sustaining Superior Performance*, New York: Free Press.

Potter, J. and Wetherell, M. 1987. *Discourse and Social Psychology: Beyond Attitudes and Behaviour*, London: SAGE.

Prasad, A. 2014. You Can't Go Home Again: And Other Psychoanalytic Lessons from Crossing a Neo-Colonial Border. *Human Relations*, 67(2): 233–257.

Prasad, A. 2016. Cyborg Writing as a Political Act: Reading Donna Haraway in Organization Studies. *Gender, Work and Organization*, 23(4): 431–446.

Prichard, C. 2006. The Organization of Organizational Discourse. *Management Communication Quarterly*, 20: 213–226.

Prichard, C., Jones, D., and Stablein, R. 2004. Doing Research in Organizational Discourse: The Importance of Researcher Context, in D. Grant, C. Hardy, C. Oswick, and L. Putnam (eds), *The SAGE Handbook of Organizational Discourse*, London: SAGE, pp. 213–236.

PSAC (President's Scientific Advisory Committee). 1963. *The Use of Pesticides: President's Science Advisory Committee Report*, Washington, DC: US Government Printing Office.

Pullen, A. and Rhodes, C. 2015. Ethics, Embodiment and Organizations. *Organization*, 22(2): 159–165.

Pullen, A., Helin J., and Harding, N. 2000. *Writing Differently*, Bingley: Emerald Publishing.

Putnam, L.L. 2015. Unpacking the Dialectic: Alternative Views on the Discourse–Materiality Relationship. *Journal of Management Studies*, 52(5): 706–716.

Putnam, L.L. and Fairhurst, G. 2001. Discourse Analysis in Organizations: Issues and Concerns, in F.M. Jablin and L.L. Putnam (eds), *The New Handbook of Organizational Communication: Advances in Theory, Research and Methods*, Newbury Park, CA: SAGE, pp. 235–268.

Quattrone, P., Ronzani, M., Jancsary, D., and Höllerer, M.A. 2021. Beyond the Visible, the Material and the Performative: Shifting Perspectives on the Visual in Organization Studies. *Organization Studies*, 42(8): 1197–1218.

Ramsey, J.L. 2015. On Not Defining Sustainability. *Journal of Agricultural and Environmental Ethics*, 28(6): 1075–1087.

Reed, M. 2004. Getting Real about Organizational Discourse, in D. Grant, C. Hardy, C. Oswick, and L. Putnam (eds), *The SAGE Handbook of Organizational Discourse*, London: SAGE, pp. 413–420.

Reinharz, S. 1997. Who Am I? The Need for a Variety of Selves in Fieldwork, in R. Hertz (ed.), *Reflexivity and Voice*, Thousand Oaks, CA: SAGE, pp. 3–20.

Reisigl, M. 2018. The Discourse-Historical Approach, in J. Flowerdew and J.E. Richardson (eds), *The Routledge Handbook of Critical Discourse Studies*, London: Routledge, pp. 44–59.

Rhodes, C. 2019. Sense-ational Organization Theory! Practices of Democratic Scriptology. *Management Learning*, 50(1): 24–37.

Rhodes, C. and Carlsen, A. 2018. The Teaching of the Other: Ethical Vulnerability and Generous Reciprocity in the Research Process. *Human Relations*, 71(10): 1295–1318.

Riach, K. 2009. Exploring Participant-Centred Reflexivity in the Research Interview. *Sociology*, 43(2): 356–370.

Ribicoff, A. 1966. *Pesticides and Public Policy: The Report of the Committee on Government Operations* (US Senate, 89th Congress, 2nd Session, Report 1379), Washington, DC: US Government Printing Office.

Robichaud, D. 2015. Organizational Discourse Studies, in K. Tracey (ed.), *The International Encyclopedia of Language and Social Interaction*, Hoboken, NJ: John Wiley and Sons, pp. 1–7. onlinelibrary.wiley.com/doi/epdf/10.1002/9781118611463.wbielsi162.

Rose, N. 1989. *Governing the Soul: The Shaping of the Private Self*, London: Routledge.

Roy, C.M. 1995. *Living and Serving: Persons with HIV in the Canadian AIDS Movement*, Ottawa: Canadian AIDS Society.

Russell, S. and McCabe, D. 2015. Regulators, Conformers and Cowboys: The Enterprise Discourse, Power and Resistance in the UK Passive Fire Protection Industry. *Organization Studies*, 6(12): 1693–1714.

Samuel, D., Found, P., and Williams, S.J. 2015. How Did the Publication of the Book *The Machine That Changed the World* Change Management Thinking? Exploring 25 Years of Lean Literature. *International Journal of Operations and Production Management*, 35(10): 1386–1407.

Sandin, P., Peterson M., Hansson, S.O., Rudén, C., and Juthe, A. 2002. Five Charges against the Precautionary Principle. *Journal of Risk Research*, 5(4): 287–299.

Sawicki, J. 1991. *Disciplining Foucault*, London: Routledge.

Schoeneborn, D., Kuhn, T., and Kärreman, D. 2019. The Communicative Constitution of Organization, Organizing, and Organizationality. *Organization Studies*, 40(4): 475–496.

Schüssler, E., Rüling, C., and Wittneben, B.B.F. 2014. On Melting Summits: The Limitations of Field-Configuring Events as Catalysts of Change in Transnational Climate Policy. *Academy of Management Journal*, 57(1): 140–171.

Scott, W.R. 1995. *Institutions and Organizations*, Thousand Oaks, CA: SAGE.

Scott, W.R. 2008. *Institutions and Organizations: Ideas and Interests*, Thousand Oaks, CA: SAGE.

Skoglund, A. and Redmalm, D. 2017. 'Doggy-Biopolitics': Governing Via the First Dog. *Organization*, 24(2): 240–266.

Smith, D.E. 1990. *Texts, Facts, and Femininity: Exploring the Relations of Ruling*, New York: Routledge.

St Pierre, E.A. 2013. The Posts Continue: Becoming. *International Journal of Qualitative Studies in Education*, 26(6): 646–657.

St Pierre, E.A. and Adams, E. 2011. Post Qualitative Research: The Critique and The Coming After, in N.K. Denzin and Y.S. Lincoln (eds), *Handbook of Qualitative Research*, Thousand Oaks, CA: SAGE, pp. 611–626.

Stirling, A. 1999. *On Science and Precaution in the Management of Technological Risk*, Brussels: European Commission Joint Research Centre.

Stirling, A. and Gee, D. 2002. Science, Precaution and Practice. *Public Health Reports*, 117: 521–533.

Stowell, A.F. and Warren, S. 2018. The Institutionalization of Suffering: Embodied Inhabitation and the Maintenance of Health and Safety in E-Waste Recycling. *Organization Studies*, 39(5–6): 785–809.

Swidler, A. 1986. Culture in Action: Symbols and Strategies. *American Sociological Review*, 51(2): 273–286.

Taylor, J.R. 2011. Organization as an (Imbricated) Configuring of Transactions. *Organization Studies*, 32(9): 1273–1294.

Taylor, J.R. and Van Every, E.J. 1993. *The Vulnerable Fortress: Bureaucratic Organization and Management in the Information Age*, Toronto: University of Toronto Press.

Taylor, J.R. and Van Every, E.J. 2000. *The Emergent Organization: Communication as Its Site and Surface*, Mahwah, NJ: Lawrence Erlbaum and Associates.

Taylor, J.R., Cooren, F., Giroux, N., and Robichaud, D. 1996. The Communicational Basis of Organization: Between the Conversation and the Text. *Communication Theory*, 6(1): 1–39.

Thomas, R. and Davies, A. 2005. Theorising the Micro-Politics of Resistance: New Public Management and Managerial Identities in the UK Public Services. *Organization Studies*, 26(5): 683–706.

Thomas, R. Tienari, J., Davies, A., and Meriläinen, S. 2009. Let's Talk about Us: A Reflexive Account of a Cross-Cultural Research Collaboration. *Journal of Management Inquiry*, 184(4): 313–324.

Thomas, R., Sargent, L., and Hardy, C. 2011. Managing Organizational Change: Negotiating Meaning and Power–Resistance Relations. *Organization Science*, 22(1): 22–41.

Townley, B. 1993. Foucault, Power/Knowledge, and Its Relevance for Human Resource Management. *Academy of Management Review*, 18(3): 518–545.

Tregidga, H., Milne, M., and Kearins, K. 2014. (Re)Presenting 'Sustainable Organizations'. *Accounting, Organizations and Society*, 39(6): 477–494.

Tretheway, A. 2001. Reproducing and Resisting the Master Narrative of Decline. *Management Communication Quarterly*, 15(2): 183–226.

Trucost. 2015. *Making the Business and Economic Case for Safer Chemistry: Report for the American Sustainable Business Council and Green Chemistry and Commerce Council*, Trucost.Com/Publication/Making-Business-Economic-Case-Safer-Chemistry (accessed January 13, 2018).

Tsoukas, H. 2005. Afterword: Why Language Matters in the Analysis of Organizational Change. *Journal of Change Management*, 18(1): 96–104.

Tsoukas, H. 2009. A Dialogical Approach to the Creation of New Knowledge in Organizations. *Organization Science*, 20(6): 941–957.

Tsoukas, H. and Chia, R. 2002. On Organizational Becoming: Rethinking Organizational Change. *Organization Science*, 13(5): 567–582.

UNCED (United Nations Commission on Environment and Development). 1992. *Rio Declaration on Environment and Development*, New York: United Nations.

UNEP (United Nations Environment Programme). 2002. *Ridding the World of POPs: A Guide to the Stockholm Convention on Persistent Organization Pollutants*, Geneva: UNEP.

US. 2000a. *US Objectives for a Global Treaty on Persistent Organic Pollutants*, Fact sheet released by the Bureau of Oceans and International Environmental and Scientific Affairs, US Department of State.

US. 2000b. *United States Position on Precaution*, Press release, December 4.

US. 2000c. *Opening Statement of the United States*, Address to INC-5, Johannesburg, South Africa.

van Dijk, T.A. 1997a. *Discourse as Structure and Process*, London: SAGE.

van Dijk, T.A. 1997b. *Discourse as Social Interaction*, London: SAGE.

Van Maanen, J. 1988. *Tales of the Field: On Writing Ethnography*, Chicago, IL: University of Chicago Press.

Vaz, P. and Bruno, F. 2003. Types of Self-Surveillance: From Abnormality to Individuals 'at Risk'. *Surveillance and Society*, 1(3): 272–291.

Wachter, R.M. 1991. *The Fragile Coalition: Scientists, Activists and AIDS*, New York: St-Martin's Press.

Walton, S. and Boone, B. 2014. Engaging with a Laclau and Mouffe Informed Discourse Analysis: A Proposed Framework. *Qualitative Research in Organizations and Management*, 9(4): 351–370.

Watts, M.J. 2015. Now and Then: The Origins of Political Ecology and the Rebirth of Adaptation as a Form of Thought, in T. Perreault, G. Bridge, and J. Mccarthy (eds), *The Routledge Handbook of Political Ecology*, London: Routledge, pp. 19–50.

WCED (World Commission on Environment and Development). 1987. *Our Common Future*, Oxford: Oxford University Press.

Westley, F. 1990. Middle Managers and Strategy: The Microdynamics of Inclusion. *Strategic Management Journal*, 11(5): 337–351.

Whittington, R. 1996. Strategy as Practice. *Long Range Planning*, 29(5): 731–735.

Whittle, A., Mueller, F., and Mangan, A. 2009. Storytelling and Character: Victims, Villains and Heroes in a Case of Technological Change. *Organization*, 16(3): 425–442.

Wiener, J.B. and Rogers, M.D. 2002. Comparing Precaution in the United States and Europe. *Journal of Risk Research*, 5(4): 317–349.

Wiggins, S. 2018. *Discursive Psychology: Theory, Method and Applications*, London: SAGE.

Wilhoit, E.D. and Kisselburgh, L.G. 2015. Collective Action without Organization: The Material Constitution of Bike Commuters as Collective. *Organization Studies*, 36(5): 573–592.

Wilhoit, E.D. and Kisselburgh, L.G. 2019. The Relational Ontology of Resistance: Hybridity, Ventriloquism, and Materiality in the Production of Bike Commuting as Resistance. *Organization*, 26(6): 873–893.

Willmott, H. 2011. Institutional Work: For What? Problems and Prospects of Institutional Theory. *Journal of Management Inquiry*, 20(1): 67–72.

Wodak, R. 1996. The Genesis of Racist Discourse in Austria since 1989, in R. Caldas-Coulthard and M. Coulthard (eds), *Texts and Practices: Readings in Critical Discourse Analysis*, London: Routledge, pp. 107–128.

Wodak, R. 2015. Critical Discourse Analysis: Discourse-Historical Approach, in K. Tracey (ed.), *The International Encyclopedia of Language and Social Interaction*, Hoboken, NJ: John Wiley and Sons, pp. 1–14. onlinelibrary.wiley.com/doi/epdf/10.1002/9781118611463.wbielsi116.

Womack, J.P., Jones, D.T., and Roos, D. 1990. *The Machine That Changed the World*, New York: Free Press.

Wood, L.A. and Kroger, R.O. 2000. *Doing Discourse Analysis: Methods for Studying Action in Talk and Text*, Thousand Oaks, CA: SAGE.

Wooten, M. and Hoffman, A.J. 2017. Organizational Fields: Past, Present and Future, in R. Greenwood, C. Oliver, T. Lawrence, and R.E. Meyer (eds), *The SAGE Handbook of Organizational Institutionalism*, London: SAGE, pp. 130–148.

World Health Organization. 2018. *Ageing and Health: Key Facts*, who.int/news-room/fact-sheets/detail/ageing-and-health, February 5.

WWF (World Wildlife Fund). 2000. UNEP Global POPs Treaty (INC5/Johannesburg), Incorporating Precautionary Measure. Pamphlet distributed at INC-5, Johannesburg, August.

Ybema, S., Oswick, C., Beverungen, A., Ellis, N., and Sabelis, I. 2009. Articulating Identities. *Human Relations*, 62(3): 299–322.

Zietsma, C., Groenewegen, P., Logue, D.M., and Hinings, C.R. 2017. Field or Fields? Building the Scaffolding for Cumulation of Research on Institutional Fields. *Academy of Management Annals*, 11(1): 391–450.

Zilber, T.B. 2006. The Work of the Symbolic in Institutional Processes: Translations of Rational Myths in Israeli Hi-Tech. *Academy Management Journal*, 49(2): 281–303.

Zilber, T.B. 2007. Stories and the Discursive Dynamics of Institutional Entrepreneurship: The Case of Israeli High-Tech after the Bubble. *Organization Studies*, 28(7): 1035–1054.

Zucker, L.G. 1977. The Role of Institutionalization in Cultural Persistence. *American Sociological Review*, 42: 726–743.

Index

Printed and bound by CPI Group (UK) Ltd, Croydon, CR0 4YY

16/04/2025